D1544877

Bureaucratic Ambition

Johns Hopkins Studies in Governance and Public Management
Kenneth J. Meier and Laurence J. O'Toole Jr., Series Editors

Bureaucratic Ambition

Careers, Motives, and the Innovative Administrator

Manuel P. Teodoro

The Johns Hopkins University Press
Baltimore

© 2011 The Johns Hopkins University Press
All rights reserved. Published 2011
Printed in the United States of America on acid-free paper
9 8 7 6 5 4 3 2 1

The Johns Hopkins University Press
2715 North Charles Street
Baltimore, Maryland 21218-4363
www.press.jhu.edu

Library of Congress Cataloging-in-Publication Data

Teodoro, Manuel P., 1972–
Bureaucratic ambition : careers, motives, and the innovative administrator /
Manuel P. Teodoro.
    p. cm. — (Johns Hopkins studies in governance and public management)
Includes bibliographical references and index.
ISBN-13: 978-1-4214-0245-1 (hardcover : alk. paper)
ISBN-10: 1-4214-0245-9 (hardcover : alk. paper)
1. Bureaucracy—United States. 2. Public administration—United States.
3. Local government—United States. 4. Ambition—Political aspects—United
States. 5. Administrative agencies—United States—Management. I. Title.
JS331.T46 2011
351.73—dc22   2011009849

A catalog record for this book is available from the British Library.

*Special discounts are available for bulk purchases of this book. For more
information, please contact Special Sales at 410-516-6936 or
specialsales@press.jhu.edu.*

The Johns Hopkins University Press uses environmentally friendly book
materials, including recycled text paper that is composed of at least 30
percent post-consumer waste, whenever possible.

For Kathleen

Contents

Preface

I used to work at a consulting firm that specialized in municipal finance, governance, and economics. On that job I learned that professionals—bureaucrats and consultants—usually craft policy alternatives and wield a great deal of control over the government policy agenda on most issues. A consultant myself, I observed very different approaches to policymaking by different administrators, even when they faced very similar financial, institutional, and environmental conditions. Some bureaucrats engaged their elected officials proactively and sought the media spotlight, while others almost seemed to hide from their elected officials and shunned media attention. A pattern seemed to emerge: the administrators who were most active in their professional communities appeared to be the most likely to pursue innovative policies. They also seemed to move from one employer to another with greater frequency than did their peers. These experiences led me to wonder: how do job mobility and policy innovation relate to one another? Where does bureaucratic career ambition come from? How does career ambition drive bureaucrats' political decisions?

This book is the result of my efforts to answer those questions. Along the way I ran into some much bigger, more fundamental questions. We toss the term *professional* around quite casually, but what does it really mean to be a professional public administrator? What causes individuals to take entrepreneurial risks in public administration? What are the implications of bureaucratic ambition for democratic governance? This book raises and addresses all of these questions. Although certainly it doesn't answer all of them definitively, I hope that the reader will find new ways to think about and analyze these questions empirically.

The process of thinking rigorously and scientifically about bureaucratic ambition, professionalism, innovation, and democracy forced me to confront some normative biases that I brought to the project. As I developed a theory and research strategy for this study, my own prejudice in favor of professions and against populism became clear. I identify as a professional, especially with respect to public utilities. I am a member of the American Water Works Association (AWWA); I serve on one of its national committees and enjoy close collegial relationships with other AWWA professionals. In general, I tend to believe in expertise and the benevolence of public policy professions. Conducting this study made me acutely aware of my normative bias in this area, which emerged especially clearly as I studied "San Alonso" (a case study related in chapter 2). The drawbacks and trade-offs that accompany bureaucratic professionalism became more apparent as this study unfolded. Professions and professionals are not always as benevolent as we might wish that they were. Professionalism sometimes sits in uncomfortable tension with pluralistic, democratic governance. The process of theorizing about and empirically exploring this tension has muddied, not clarified, the normative waters. I believe that I am wiser, if less confident, for the mud.

Another personal bias I confronted through this project merits brief mention here. In retrospect, I embarked on this study carrying the general unease with the police that I imagine is probably common among academics. Many hours of talking with police officers and law-enforcement administrators gave me a new perspective on the challenges that these individuals take on in their everyday work. The stories that police officers tell about their work are inspiring, uproariously funny, and devastatingly sad. I have a newfound respect for police officers, especially for the individuals who choose to make a career in law enforcement and police administration. I hope that this research might be of some value to public administrators in general and to police administrators in particular.

Plan of the Book

Chapter 1 introduces the argument that is developed and supported in the rest of the book. Chapter 2 offers case studies of bureaucratic political action in three governments—qualitative investigations that bring stories of bureaucratic entrepreneurs, successful and failed alike, to the fore. The pseudonymous narratives in this chapter help to motivate the study and give texture to the quantitative analyses presented in later chapters. Each case demonstrates the tensions and trade-offs in the principal-agent and client-professional relationships between elected officials and mezzo-level bureaucrats.

Chapter 3 is the theoretical heart of the book, identifying the political behaviors of interest and the important independent variables that cause them. The chapter culminates in a set of hypotheses for empirical investigation and a brief discussion of the survey design used to evaluate the theory.

Chapters 4, 5, and 6 are the book's central empirical chapters. Chapter 4 shows how career paths shape the relationship between bureaucrat and elected official, leading to more professional innovation or less. Quantitative analyses demonstrate that agencies' hiring practices and individual bureaucrats' career paths affect policy outcomes. Chapter 5 investigates the motivational roots of bureaucratic ambition, applying personality psychology to demonstrate that differences in human motivation cause some bureaucrats to be more politically active than others. Chapter 6 marries career path to motivation and shows how career opportunity structures create processes by which administrators with different qualifications and motive profiles advance or fail to advance in their careers.

The book concludes with a consideration of the study's normative implications for democratic governance in an age of professionalized public agencies. The final chapter also relates the study's findings to ongoing research on bureaucratic politics and professionalism in public administration and identifies avenues for further research.

Acknowledgments

When I was a child, I imagined that writing a book must be a profoundly, almost romantically solitary exploit. In reality, of course, producing a scholarly book is an inexorably social act. To the extent that this book succeeds, its success is due to the financial, intellectual, and personal support of many individuals and organizations. This project was possible thanks to the generous financial support of several institutions. Most critically, the book is based upon research supported under a National Science Foundation Graduate Research Fellowship. Research awards from the Nonprofit and Public Management Center and the Interdisciplinary Committee on Organizational Studies at the University of Michigan provided funding for various expenses. A dissertation completion grant from the Rackham School of Graduate Studies and a Gerald R. Ford Fellowship provided additional research funding and support for my final year of studies at Michigan. Discretionary grants from the Colgate University Research Council have supported research assistantships and various other efforts to refine the book. I owe special thanks to Mary Corcoran, director of the Ford School's joint PhD programs in Public Policy, who helped me negotiate the considerable practical obstacles to graduate studies for students with young children.

Dozens of scholars have helped me with their attention to this project. Foremost are my dissertation advisor Rick Hall and committee members Nancy Burns, Barry Rabe, and David Winter. Each brought infectious enthusiasm to the project and offered guidance on matters methodological, theoretical, and stylistic. My undergraduate mentor and friend Jim Hogan read and commented on major portions of the text in its early stages. Adam Burnett graciously taught me about geographic analysis of climatic moisture and helped me apply the water scarcity metric that I use in chapter 4. Michael Cohen, Martha Feldman, Rick Feiock, Liz Gerber, Michael Hayes, Debra Holzhauer, Jennifer Jensen, Michael Johnston, David Konisky, Casey LaFrance, Robert Maranto, Ken Meier, Rob Mickey, Michael Mintrom, Leanne Powner, Rebecca Shiner, Charles Shipan, Chad Sparber, George Teodoro, Joe Wagner, Steve Wasby, and Patrick Wolf each read, discussed, and/or remarked on all or part of the book at various stages of its development. Each offered advice that substantially improved the project. I also thank anonymous reviewers from the Johns Hopkins University Press, the *American Journal of Political Science*, *Public Administration Review*, and the *Journal of Public Administration Research and Theory* for valuable feedback on several parts of the manuscript. I thank Jessica Bauer, Charlotte Burns, Katrina Engelsted, Adam Hughes, Peter Mao, and Brooke Sweet for their excellent research assistance. Thanks to JHU Press editors Henry Tom and Suzanne Flinchbaugh for shepherding me through the publication process. Very sadly, Henry passed away shortly after his retirement and before *Bureaucratic Ambition* made it into print; I remain indebted to him for his guidance and support. *Requiescat in pace.*

In conversations and correspondence, Kees Corssmit, Louis Dekmar, Brian Georgia, David LaFrance, and Paul Matthews offered me their important perspectives as active professionals in law enforcement and water utilities. Scores of other public administrators and public policy professionals contributed to this book by participating in interviews. Although though they must remain anonymous, I am profoundly grateful for their dedication to their jobs and their contributions to this research.

The conventions of academic etiquette demand that I absolve all of the aforementioned people and organizations of responsibility for the many errors and shortcomings that likely plague this book, despite their efforts to steer me right. I do so partly because they really are blameless and partly because, as an ambitious professional, it is strategically rational for me to conform to the norms of my profession (as I explain in chapter 3).

My most heartfelt acknowledgments are to my family, who encouraged me throughout the process of researching and writing despite the considerable costs to them. I thank my mother, Dee Teodoro, for terrific copyediting of several chapters and for her maternal pride and affection. I thank my father, Reynaldo Teodoro, for his confidence in me throughout my academic career and for the ambition that I seem to have inherited from him. My Foley in-laws in Grand Rapids—John, Terry, Ed, Kandi, Patrick, and Paula—have been materially and emotionally generous in support of this project. My daughter Tess was just five years old and my son Tony was just three when I started to work on this book; as I complete it, they are twelve and ten, respectively. True to the old saying, these days have been long, but the years have been short. Caring for young children while studying, teaching, researching, and writing full-time is mentally and physically draining. But Tess and Tony have been indefatigable cheerleaders throughout the process, providing the rejuvenation that only a child's love can.

Finally, I thank my beloved wife, Kathleen. Her sacrifices and contributions have made this book possible. She has been a patient and sharp-witted sounding board for my ideas as they have evolved. She has served the project as protocol officer, pilot test subject, and occasional copyeditor. As a smart, hard-working professional she has provided creative material for my study of organizations, along with bread for our table. She has been a marvelous mother, a loving companion, and a loyal fan. I dedicate this book to her.

Thank you, Katie Rose.

Bureaucratic Ambition

CHAPTER ONE

Principles, Principals, and Ambition

The Politics of Bureaucratic Entrepreneurship

> Innovations are so heavily dependent on executive interests and beliefs as to make the appearance of a change-oriented personality enormously important in explaining change. It is not easy to build a useful social science theory out of "chance appearances."
>
> JAMES Q. WILSON, *BUREAUCRACY*

This book advances a theory of bureaucratic ambition, its effects on innovation in public agencies, and its impact on democratic governance in an era of professional public administration.

The names of America's most prominent, transformational public administrators are easily familiar to scholars of American politics or public administration. William Bratton, William Mulholland, Gifford Pinchot, Alice Rivlin, and James Lee Witt are icons of agency leadership who—for better or worse—defined their professions, transformed their agencies, and changed the broader political landscape. These administrators' triumphs and tragedies are chronicled by the media, and scholars of the policy process have branded them *policy entrepreneurs*. Policy entrepreneurs have become a theoretical staple of public policy studies, and bureaucratic executives are among the political actors most often identified as policy entrepreneurs. Like their counterparts in the business world, policy entrepreneurs recognize latent demand for policy changes and then expend resources and take risks to drive innovation in government. Policy entrepreneurship is an evocative concept because it captures the role that individual leadership so clearly plays in policy innovation.[1]

But for all the excellent accounts of bureaucratic politics and policy entrepreneurship that scholars have produced, the sources of bureaucratic policy entrepreneurship have been elusive: we know very little about where these entrepreneurial bureaucrats come from (Mintrom and Norman 2009). What makes some bureaucrats pursue innovations more than others do? Why are some bureaucrats more politically assertive than others? In case studies and anecdotal accounts, entrepreneurial bureaucrats seem to exhibit uncommon energy, resourcefulness, creativity, and toughness. But these exceptional qualities have limited bureaucratic policy entrepreneurship as a model of politics, as James Q. Wilson observed in his seminal *Bureaucracy* (1989). If entrepreneurial administrators have exceptional personalities, do they appear merely by chance, ex nihilo? Moreover, the implications of bureaucratic policy entrepreneurship for democratic governance have been unclear. Where do professional administrators' loyalties lie? Who wins and loses when entrepreneurial administrators drive policy change?

Consider the career of Robert C. White. As a precinct police commander in Washington, DC, White equipped officers with confiscated bicycles when the city council was slow to fund a bike patrol that it had earlier approved. He created and was the first leader of the District of Columbia's public housing police force. Later, as the chief of police in Greensboro, North Carolina, White attended a different church each week to spread "a vision of a police force that was truly part of the community."[2] In Greensboro, Chief White also defused racial tensions over a police shooting of a nineteen-year-old black suspect. He advanced innovative reforms in community policing and persuaded Greensboro's reluctant city council to spend $9 million on new police substations. In January 2003, White was hired by Louisville, Kentucky, to head a police department twice as large as Greensboro's. A track record of innovation led to his move; Louisville's mayor indicated that he hired White because he "has experience with a large urban police force, once created another police agency from scratch and, in his most recent job, dismantled . . . 'a good ol' boy's organization' and began appointing more women and minorities to top posts." White's new position was the latest in an ongoing path of career advancement that led him from one city to another.

In this book, I argue that ambition and opportunity for career advancement in the professional labor market cause some administrators to pursue innovative policies according to the norms of their professions, just as Chief White did. Where opportunities for career advancement are only within single organizations, administrators are less likely to innovate and more likely to follow elected officials' directives. Not all bureaucrats are alike, of course; Chief White may have been ambitious, but surely not all administrators are. Bureaucratic ambition is a matter of personality psychology, as well as of economic opportunity. Different administrators have different motives, and these differences affect bureaucrats' willingness to assume risks and expend resources in pursuit of their professions' preferred policies. Innovation emerges from the bureaucracy when ambition—the intersection of career opportunity and motivation—creates a policy entrepreneur.

Any would-be bureaucratic policy entrepreneur must make two related decisions: which policies to pursue and how hard (if at all) he or she should try to change policy. Explaining policy entrepreneurship requires explaining both of these decisions. Hence, the first phenomenon that this book seeks to explain is *professional innovation*: the extent to which an administrator introduces policies that reflect prevailing professional norms and values. The term *innovation* describes a specific phenomenon: the introduction of a policy that is new to the government adopting it. Any policy that is new to a government is an innovation, but policies are more or less *professionally* innovative. I add the adjective *professional*, recognizing that some innovations reflect professional fashion more than others. I do not mean to connote any normative dimension to professional innovation; policy innovation and professionalism are neither inherently good nor bad. Other scholars who have studied policy innovation have used the term this value-neutral way, capturing only the introduction of a policy that is new to the government adopting it (Walker 1969). *Innovation* in its popular use is perhaps unintentionally laden with positive normative baggage, suggesting that innovations are always progressive improvements. But "innovation is not necessarily good," as James Q. Wilson observed; "there are at least as many bad changes as good" (1989, 227).

Bureaucrats' *political advocacy* is the second phenomenon my theory seeks to explain. Administrators may exert varying degrees of effort in securing an innovation: they may introduce policy alternatives, place items on the legislative agenda, participate in official proceedings, organize legislative coalitions, build support with appeals to the public and interest groups, communicate through the media, lobby legislators directly through informal contact, or do nothing at all. Bureaucrats' lobbying efforts in these legislative phases of the policy process are the central interest in this study.

The bureaucrats of interest in this book are, like Chief White, professionals who direct operational divisions of local government in the United States. These individuals occupy the "mezzo-level" of administration, below elected executives and above the line personnel who run programs. Uniquely situated to influence both policy design and execution, mezzo-level administrators are key policymakers at the federal (Carpenter 2001), state (Rabe 2004), and local (Schneider, Teske, and Mintrom 1995) levels. At the local level, these mezzo-level administrators are the professional executive officers whose careers are largely devoted to specific public administration professions, such as city engineers, school superintendents, police chiefs, and fire chiefs.

The policies of interest in this study transcend ordinary day-to-day management of an agency. Following Aberbach, Putnam, and Rockman (1981), my interest is in political action that falls either in the legislative phases of the policy process or might reasonably be of interest to elected legislatures and political executives. An administrator's decision to develop new enforcement guidelines for environmental rules is a policymaking act; his choice to hold staff meetings on Tuesday mornings is not. A policy issue need not reach the formal agenda of the legislative body for legislators to be interested in it, or potentially interested in it.

Finally, this book argues that ambition bears on the crucial trade-off between professionalism and responsiveness, or innovation and accountability, in public administration. As long as governments have tried to fashion themselves as democracies, political theorists have recognized a tension between administrative efficiency and democratic responsiveness. Woodrow Wilson put that tension at the heart of his famous 1887 article "The Study of Administration," seeking an intellectual distinction that would make government efficiency the aim of public administration, democratic responsiveness the province of politics and political science.[3] In the 124 years since Wilson's article, volume upon volume of scholarship has cast elections and legislatures as the appropriate venues for political decision making and bureaucracies as neutral instruments for efficient policy implementation.[4] Nearly as voluminous, however, is the empirical research that shows bureaucrats to be deeply and pervasively engaged in politics and policymaking, blurring the distinction between politics and administration. The reality that administrators are involved in politics and policymaking is both a violation of many social scientists' models and a potential threat to the democratic responsiveness that elections and legislatures are meant to provide. Bureaucratic agencies have always presented accountability challenges, but in an era of professional public administration, bureaucrats are accountable to both elected officials and to their professional communities. This book aims to show how career ambition conditions bureaucrats' respective loyalties to each.

The central argument of this book, then, is that ambition—psychological motives manifested in a career opportunity structure—drives administrators' political behavior in predictable ways, with important consequences for innovation and democratic governance in a state administered by professional bureaucrats.

At the risk of stealing thunder from the rest of the text, the balance of this introductory chapter situates its arguments in the existing research on the topic and then reviews the book's main arguments and findings. A brief note on terminology is worthwhile at this point. Studies in the public administration tradition generally refer to individuals employed by bureaucratic agencies as *administrators*; political scientists and public policy scholars tend to use the term *bureaucrats*. Since it seeks to engage scholarship across all of these fields, this book uses the terms *administrator* and *bureaucrat* interchangeably and attaches no ameliorative or pejorative meaning to either word.

Bureaucracy, Professionals, and Ambition

This study perches on the shoulders of an eclectic band of giants, building on works in public administration, political science, economics, sociology, and psychology. My aim in crafting this review is not to catalogue other scholars' findings on these topics, for the literature is voluminous and the sidetracks many. Rather, I seek to engage existing research creatively, pouring works from across the social sciences into a synthetic stew that will feed a new theory of bureaucratic policy entrepreneurship.

Bureaucratic Politics

As noted earlier, bureaucrats often become policy entrepreneurs and so are important drivers of policy innovation. But we know very little about why some administrators emerge as policy entrepreneurs. Broadly stated, scholars have depicted bureaucratic political behavior in one of two ways: table 1.1 lists representative works in each category. Admittedly, I do considerable violence to the rich, elegant, and substantial literature on bureaucratic politics by summarizing it in this binary way, and the literature is worthy of a much more detailed and rigorous review. Nonetheless, the two broad categories shown in

Table 1.1   Selected research on bureaucratic politics

Principal-agent theories

Niskanen, *Bureaucracy and Representative Government* (1971)
Moe, "The New Economics of Organization" (1984)
Weingast, "The Congressional-Bureaucratic System: A Principal-Agent Perspective" (1984)
McCubbins and Schwartz, "Police Patrols vs. Fire Alarms" (1984)
Bendor, Taylor, and Van Gaalen, "Stacking the Deck: Bureaucratic Missions and Policy Design" (1987)
Wood and Waterman, "The Dynamics of Political Control of the Bureaucracy" (1991)
Brehm and Gates, *Working, Shirking, and Sabotage* (1997)
Huber and Shipan, *Deliberate Discretion? Institutional Foundations of Bureaucratic Autonomy* (2003)

Professionalism theories

Kaufman, *The Forest Ranger* (1960)
Mosher, *Democracy and the Public Service* (1968)
Lipsky, *Street-Level Bureaucrats* (1980)
Green, *The Profession of Local Government Management* (1989)
Brint, *In an Age of Experts* (1997)
Brehm and Gates, *Working, Shirking, and Sabotage* (1997)
Carpenter, *The Forging of Bureaucratic Autonomy* (2001)
O'Leary, *The Ethics of Dissent: Managing Guerilla Government* (2005)
Meier and O'Toole, *Bureaucracy in a Democratic State: A Governance Perspective* (2006)

table 1.1 quickly place this study within the broader body of research on bureaucratic politics and public administration.

In the first set of studies, bureaucrats are depicted as agents in a principal-agent relationship. Rooted in the economic theory of insurance and labor contracts, the main idea is that elected officials are principals who hire bureaucrats as agents to carry out public policy on their behalf. Bureaucratic agents respond to incentives and procedural constraints placed upon them by their elected principals. Under principal-agent models, agents are assumed to enjoy informational advantages over their principals. Administrators have expertise that their principals do not, and often they can make important decisions without the approval of their principals. For this reason, principals must monitor or procedurally constrain agents' behavior to be sure that the agents faithfully carry out their duties and do not shirk or otherwise behave in ways that contravene the principals' wishes. At their best, principal-agent models offer elegant and parsimonious, yet flexible, intuitive, and empirically falsifiable explanations of bureaucratic politics.[5]

But the principal-agent framework for analyzing administrative behavior fits awkwardly with a considerable body of empirical research. In reality, public policy is almost never a matter of legislative bodies or elected executives issuing laws to neutral (or recalcitrant or shiftless) civil servants for execution. Rather, the implementation and evaluative processes are inextricably linked to the legislative process, with professional administrators involved throughout (Eulau and Prewitt 1973; Waste 1989).

Moreover, most principal-agent theories of bureaucratic politics cast the bureaucratic agency as an anthropomorphic whole interacting with a similarly anthropomorphic legislative principal (Niskanen 1971; Moe 1982; McCubbins and Schwartz 1984; Wood and Waterman 1991; Huber and Shipan 2002). This "unitary actor" assumption is an analytical convenience that is useful in many studies of institutions. The trouble is that while elected executives and majoritarian legislatures may, in a limited sense, make decisions as anthropomorphic wholes, administrative agencies do not. The anthropomorphic depiction of administrative agencies leads many principal-agent theories to make unrealistic assumptions about bureaucratic preferences (most often a budget-maximizing goal) and to disregard bureaucrats' values. As Daniel Carpenter (2006) has remarked, bureaucrats stripped of their own values are merely "automatons or kleptocrats," mindlessly responding to organizational incentives put before them by elected officials or greedily maximizing their reward with minimal effort. Taken as a whole, it is perhaps sensible to assume that a bureaucracy would like to maximize its budget, ceteris paribus. But bureaucracies do not make political decisions—bureaucrats do. For any given bureaucrat in a given agency, a larger agency budget may or may not be desirable (Campbell and Naulls 1991; Young 1991). *Policy entrepreneurship* makes little sense within a unitary actor framework: policy entrepreneurs are by definition individuals, and in any given government, some bureaucrats may emerge as policy entrepreneurs while others do not. Organizational theorists and scholars of public administration have long recognized that the individuals who compose bureaucratic agencies make individual decisions based on unique goals and constraints (Lipsky 1980; Brehm and Gates 1997; Lin 2000; Simon 1997). A useful theory of bureaucratic policy entrepreneurship must therefore account for the behavior of *individual* administrators.

Finally, virtually all principal-agent theories ignore the possibility of voluntary exit by the bureaucrat. For administrators in the United States, exit from employment in an agency is a very real and often quite attractive alternative to working, shirking, or sabotage. As Albert Hirschman has famously demonstrated, the presence or absence of an exit alternative affects fundamentally the behavior of individuals in economic or political situations (1970). Most principal-agent theories of politics preclude the possibility of administrators voluntarily leaving their agencies for other organizations; they thus miss the possibility that bureaucrats might make decisions with intentional exit in mind. The possibility of voluntary exit for the agent necessarily blunts both the incentive for an administrator to maximize her budget and the coercive power that a principal can exert over the administrator through sanction or procedural constraints.

The line of research on bureaucratic politics in the lower part of table 1.1 is more diverse, both substantively and methodologically. What these works hold in common is a finding that, for various reasons, elected officials have little control over their bureaucratic agents. Indeed, several highlight the ways in which administrators operate proactively in politics, driving policy changes, influencing public opinion, and shifting the policy preferences of their putative principals.[6] Recognizing that American government bureaucracies are now largely professionalized, studies in the lower portion of table 1.1 find that administrators' professional norms and values determine their behavior, though these works differ on the ways in which professionalism is created and manifested politically. Significantly, *Working, Shirking, and Sabotage* by John Brehm and Scott Gates (1997) is listed in both the top and bottom portions of table 1.1. Brehm and Gates develop a principal-agent model, but find empirically that bureaucrats' professional identities and professional values—not principals' monitoring, procedural constraints, incentives, and sanctions—determine bureaucrats' behavior. With a play on words, Brehm and Gates call their bureaucrats "principled agents."

Among the many merits of these works on administrative professionalism are their attention to individual administrators as units of political analysis and a recognition that administrators' policy preferences can vary from a simple, stylized budget-maximizing stance. But the social processes that generate administrators' preferences remain exogenous to most of these studies, and variation among professional administrators remains unexplained.[7] Studies of bureaucratic professionalism indicate that administrators' preferences trump principals' coercive mechanisms, but by leaving administrators' preferences out of the model, they beg the question. In effect, these studies conclude that professional bureaucrats act professionally because they are professionals. If bureaucrats act according to their own preferences, why do they prefer the policies that they do? How do we explain behavioral differences among administrators within an agency or profession?

The classic *Inside Bureaucracy* (1967) by Anthony Downs is one of very few theoretically rigorous studies that recognizes heterogeneity among administrators and theorizes about how differences in bureaucrats' preferences affect bureaucratic politics. Downs assumes that administrators rationally pursue their self-interest, but his theory allows them to pursue ends like "personal loyalty," "pride in proficient performance of work," and "serving the public interest" in addition to income, security, and perquisites. To this end, Downs lays out a taxonomy of five bureaucrat types (*climbers, conservers, zealots, advocates, and statesmen*) and derives hypotheses predicting each type's behavior in various institutional settings within agencies.[8] Downs argues that each of these types responds differently to different organizational incentives. Exit from an agency by "jumping" to another is one of the alternatives Downs's theory makes available to its bureaucrats. The availability of alternative employment may lead bureaucrats—especially Downs's climbers—to modify their political decisions (95–96). Downs thus adds an important ingredient to a compelling theory of bureaucratic behavior: individual goal diversity.

Nevertheless, while Downs (1967) alludes to individuals' psychological predispositions in establishing his categories of bureaucrats, his typology is grounded in no psychological theory. Downs's bureaucratic types are thus not so much psychological as they are behavioral: "zealots" are recognizable in their zealous behavior, "climbers" in their career maximizing, and so on. Downs's taxonomy is important because it allows for goal diversity in an organization, but its lack of psychological grounding points to a need for a more fundamental theory of bureaucratic motivation.

In sum, the body of scholarship on bureaucratic politics says that administrators' political decisions are determined by both their elected *principals* and their professional *principles*. This subtle difference in spelling marks a fundamental tension that arises when professional bureaucrats serve a democratic state. On the one hand, we expect bureaucrats to be responsive agents for their elected officials. On the other hand, we want administrators to apply their specialized expertise in setting and executing policy. Indeed, expertise is the very reason that governments hire professionals (as opposed to unskilled, undifferentiated labor—through patronage, for instance). But when making political decisions, where do administrators' loyalties lie? With their elected principals? Or with their professional principles? Frederick Mosher called this "*the* moral question of the public service in American democracy" (1968, 210; italics in original).

Professional Public Administrators

Professionals are persons with specialized scientific, technical, or other formal education, whose labor value is reducible to their expertise in providing some knowledge-based service. Professionals form organizations, or professional societies, to facilitate information exchange and to self-regulate or seek government regulation. Professions establish the ethical principles and guidelines for practice that professionals are supposed to observe. Professions also define professionals' paths to career advancement to a greater or lesser extent.[9]

If a common theme emerges from the many excellent studies of professions and professionalism across disciplines, it is that professions are labor-market phenomena. Professions serve the economic interests of their members. Professions initially arise as safeguards against unscrupulous practitioners, but also as a means of building legitimacy and cultivating demand for services (Polanyi 1957; Larson 1977; Brint 1997). Professional credentialing and licensing regimes provide signals of quality and consistency to buyers in a market for expert labor (Abbott 1988). Professions also create and sustain oligopolies that restrict access to the market for expert labor (Olson 1965; Larson 1977). I do not mean to say that professions and professional norms are reducible to sheer economic self-interest, for public-spiritedness and benevolence are important features of professions, too. A large and growing body of research on "public service motivation" consistently finds that many public administrators have a strong sense civic duty connected to their work (Staats 1988; Perry and Wise 1990; Crewson 1997; Wright 2001). Recent findings have connected this kind of altruism to administrators' self-reported professional identity (Perry 1997; Moynihan and Pandey 2007). One need not be a cynic, however, to notice that the way that a profession defines "the public good" typically involves identifying needs for expert services, cultivating a clientele, and creating job opportunities for professionals.

For eighty years or so, U.S. government administration has been organized as a profession, or, more accurately, as several professions: military officers administer military organizations, engineers administer public utilities, educators administer school districts, social workers administer human service organizations, and so on. As Mosher observed, "For better or worse—or better *and* worse—much of our government is now in the hands of professionals" (1968, 132). Understanding the role that bureaucratic professionalism plays in politics requires recognizing that, whatever else they are, professions are economic constructs that include paths to career advancement for the ambitious. The administrators who head local agencies behave according to these constructs, with important consequences for governance.

Studies in political science that identify professionalism as a key to bureaucratic political behavior typically suggest that the socializing effects of professions explain the political choices that administrators make (see the lower half of table 1.1). The process of professional accreditation, through formal education, apprenticeship, and so forth, imbues individuals with the ethics of their professions. Steeped in the cultures of their professions, administrators come to understand good and bad policy according to the conventions of their professional peers—so goes the argument. Professionals also may gain purposive and solidary benefits from the prestige and fellowship that professional identity brings. This socialization process causes administrative professionals to seek good standing among their peers and thus to be, as Brehm and Gates put it, "principled" (1997).

But professional socialization is a problematic explanation for bureaucratic behavior. Professional identity and the prestige associated with a profession are collective goods that offer free-riding opportunities for bureaucrats. A school superintendent may enjoy good standing in his profession and the prestige and perquisites of office without incurring the costs of championing his peers' favored causes. It is not clear why administrators would take significant political risks because of professional identity alone. Moreover, appeal to professional norms as drivers of administrative action cannot explain variation in administrators' pursuit of professionally sanctioned goals. Why do some cling doggedly to their professional norms, even launch crusades for professionally sanctioned policies, while others give up or stand silent? How do we understand which political battles professional administrators fight and which they avoid?

Ambition

Canonical political thinkers from Machiavelli to Madison have begun with the assumption that ambition is the root cause of political behavior. Joseph

Schlesinger's 1967 book *Ambition and Politics* is the defining work of empirical political science built on ambition. Schlesinger demonstrates that elected officials' career goals influence important political decisions, including with which party to affiliate, when to seek elected office, and which offices to seek. Understanding a politician's behavior therefore requires looking beyond his immediate institutional incentives and considering the effects of immediate choices on long-term career advancement. Schlesinger's theory also recognizes that individual strength of commitment to career advancement goals varies. Some politicians are "progressively ambitious," hoping to climb from office to progressively more powerful office. Others are content to maintain their current offices indefinitely ("static ambition"), or simply retain their offices for a limited period of time ("discrete ambition"). Unfortunately, Schlesinger's study and most subsequent works on ambition theory are limited to elected politicians, and few studies of policy entrepreneurship address ambition (Mintrom and Norman 2009). While some notable studies suggest ambition as a possible cause of public administrators' behavior (Downs 1967; Kingdon 1984; Schneider, Teske, and Mintrom 1995), none investigate bureaucratic ambition systematically. Moreover, despite the concept's centrality to their theories, Machiavelli, Madison, Schlesinger, Downs, and other ambition theorists do not attempt to study ambition itself.[10] Rather, existing works on ambition in politics assume their subjects' ambition, and then theorize about ambition's consequences given social and institutional constraints.

As is obvious, however, bureaucrats are not uniformly and monotonically motivated, scholars' stylized assumptions notwithstanding. Career ambition varies among individuals and can manifest itself in different behaviors. Happily, personality psychologists have developed theories and empirical methods for understanding the motives of individuals situated in organizations. David McClelland (1975, 1998) and David Winter (1991, 2003) identify three dimensions to the motives that drive behavior in organizations: the achievement motive, a concern for excellence and unique accomplishment; the power motive, a concern for prestige and impact on others; and the affiliation motive, a concern for establishing and maintaining close relationships with others. These three motives are stable elements of individual personality that manifest themselves in behavior within organizations. Motive theory offers a means of understanding the psychological wellsprings of ambition. Ambition for career advancement is associated with the achievement and power motives, though each for different reasons. The achievement motive drives ambition in pursuit of excellence in a chosen endeavor and is associated with entrepreneurship in business. The power motive drives ambition in pursuit of clout over others and is associated with success in hierarchical organizations. Put another way, ambition for career advancement is a means to an end under the achievement motive, and as an end in itself under the power motive.

The links between public administrators' psychological motivations and their political behavior remain largely unexplored. Meanwhile, psychological research on motivational theory in organizations is mostly noninstitutional; in most theories of human motivation, individuals are not constrained by structural conditions like constitutions, finances, markets, and so on. In this sense, personality psychologists' research on political behavior has developed as a theoretical mirror image of political scientists': psychologists have theorized about motivation, taking social conditions as given; political scientists have theorized about institutions and social conditions, taking motivation as a given. A more satisfactory theory of bureaucratic ambition must situate human motivation in the institutional context of public administration.

A Theory of Bureaucratic Ambition

To theorize about bureaucratic ambition and policy entrepreneurship is to make claims about both government structures and individual behavior. In disciplinary parlance, a theory of bureaucratic ambition is at once institutional and behavioral.[11] Government agencies, professions, and public-sector job markets are *institutions* in Douglass North's broad sense of the term: "[the] humanly devised constraints that shape human action" (1990, 3). Institutional theories of politics are about how government institutions channel people's political actions in predictable ways, for institutions don't make political decisions—people do. At the same time, understanding how bureaucrats behave politically, as opposed to bureaucracies, requires thinking about individual motives and rationality, as well as the institutional conditions and constraints under which individuals make political choices. In this way, a theory of bureaucratic ambition must also be a *behavioral* theory. This book makes three claims about the political behavior of professional public administrators:

1. The relationship between an elected official and a public agency chief administrator is at once a principal-agent relationship and a client-professional relationship. Job mobility in professional admin-

istrative labor markets determines which of the two relationships is dominant in driving political decisions.

2. Individual administrators have different motives and so have different degrees of ambition that drive more or less political activity.

3. Bureaucrats' political decisions cause them to advance with varying success in different governments, so that bureaucratic policy entrepreneurs are more likely to emerge in some governments than in others.

The first of these claims is institutional, the second behavioral, the third both institutional and behavioral. In this introduction I briefly summarize my theory of bureaucratic ambition; chapter 3 lays out the theory more thoroughly.

A Market for Policy Entrepreneurs: Mobility and Innovation

Jobs are temporary matches of individuals with employers; for public administrators, the employers are governments. But individuals and agencies do not latch on to one another at random, like so many atoms in Brownian motion. Rather, bureaucratic jobs exist within an opportunity structure. *Opportunity structure* describes a profession's educational and/or apprenticeship requirements, as well as jobs and paths to advancement within a profession. Opportunity structures present individuals with both possibilities and constraints, for while multiple paths are available for advancement in a profession, the number and types of paths that are available vary considerably across professions in ways beyond the control of most individuals. Bureaucratic jobs vary in status. Many low-status jobs exist in a profession; high-status jobs are few. A professional occupies a status position within an opportunity structure at any given point in his or her career. For purposes of this study, the size of an agency is the indicator of the agency head's job status.

Opportunity structures are observable in the predominant patterns of career advancement within professions. Paths to advancement vary across career opportunity structures. Professions with vertical advancement within a single organization may be thought of as featuring career "ladders" for administrators, as in the U.S. armed services. Professions in which advancement to high positions typically entails changing employers feature diagonal career "ramps" for administrators. Figure 1.1 depicts two prominent professional careers that demonstrate typical "ladder" and "ramp" advancement patterns.

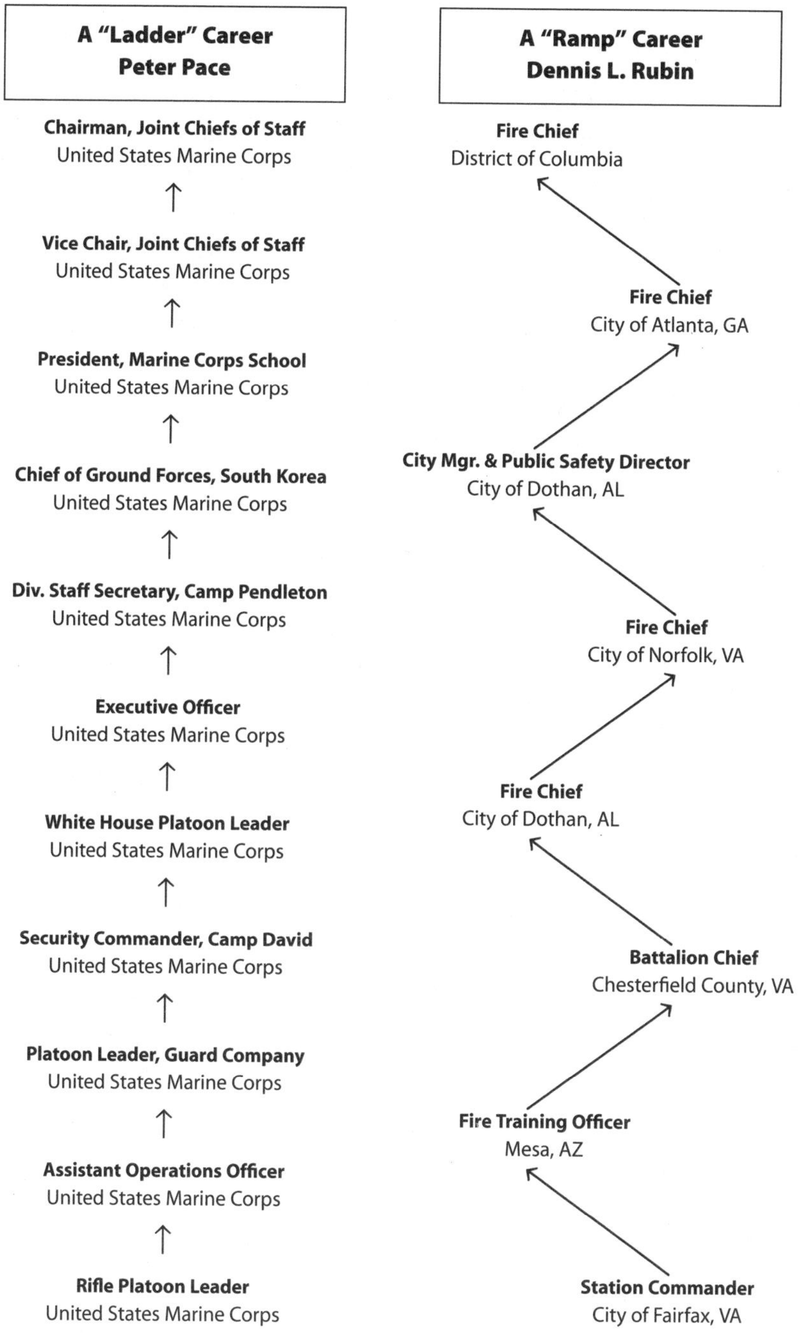

A "Ladder" Career Peter Pace	A "Ramp" Career Dennis L. Rubin

Chairman, Joint Chiefs of Staff
United States Marine Corps

↑

Vice Chair, Joint Chiefs of Staff
United States Marine Corps

↑

President, Marine Corps School
United States Marine Corps

↑

Chief of Ground Forces, South Korea
United States Marine Corps

↑

Div. Staff Secretary, Camp Pendleton
United States Marine Corps

↑

Executive Officer
United States Marine Corps

↑

White House Platoon Leader
United States Marine Corps

↑

Security Commander, Camp David
United States Marine Corps

↑

Platoon Leader, Guard Company
United States Marine Corps

↑

Assistant Operations Officer
United States Marine Corps

↑

Rifle Platoon Leader
United States Marine Corps

Fire Chief
District of Columbia

Fire Chief
City of Atlanta, GA

City Mgr. & Public Safety Director
City of Dothan, AL

Fire Chief
City of Norfolk, VA

Fire Chief
City of Dothan, AL

Battalion Chief
Chesterfield County, VA

Fire Training Officer
Mesa, AZ

Station Commander
City of Fairfax, VA

Figure 1.1 Administrative career advancement patterns—ladder and ramp

On the left is Peter Pace's ascent from rifle platoon leader to chairman of the Joint Chiefs of Staff, which progressed entirely within the U.S. Marine Corps. On the right, the path that took Dennis Rubin from station commander in Fairfax to fire chief in Washington, DC, included changes in employer with each change in title. Robert C. White, the Louisville police chief mentioned at the beginning of this chapter, is also a ramp climber whose path to progressively higher-status administrative positions jobs took him from Washington, DC, to Greensboro, North Carolina, to Louisville, Kentucky.

Opportunity structures and the career paths that they create affect the relationships between bureaucrats and elected officials in important ways. The potential for a bureaucratic agent to advance in his or her career via voluntary exit to another organization dampens the coercive mechanisms and weakens the procedural constraints that an elected principal can exert over the agent. Voluntary exit for the bureaucrat also can strengthen her ties to her professional community and create an incentive for her to cultivate a professional reputation pursuant to advancement via movement to other organizations.

As noted earlier in this chapter, professions exist in large part to provide signals of quality to buyers in the market for expert labor. The fluidity and competitiveness of the professional labor market has profound implications for professional behavior. Consider the archetypal profession of medicine: a patient's relationship with a doctor is a principal-agent relationship on one level, for the patient (principal) hires the doctor (agent) to provide a service. Insofar as the patient-doctor relationship is a principal-agent relationship, the patient expects the doctor to follow his instructions and prescribe the treatments he prefers. On another level, a patient's relationship with a doctor is client-professional relationship, for the doctor's professionalism limits her willingness to do the patient's bidding. For physicians, there sometimes is a tension between the wishes of the patient (principal) and the strictures of profession (principle). Since she must consider her need to treat other patients in the future, she must maintain licensure and standing in her profession. A doctor's career concerns may cause her to put her professional *principles* before the wishes of her patient-*principal*. It is easy to imagine that a doctor's decision calculus might be different if her patient is the one and only patient she treats or ever will treat.[12]

Public administration professions operate similarly, I argue. Like a patient who hires a doctor, a school board expects its professional agent, a superintendent, to follow its orders, but also to offer advice and direction and to apply his professional judgment over many policy matters. Just so, presidents pick military chiefs of staff, governors pick state police commanders, and mayors pick fire chiefs to follow orders in a principal-agent sense, but also to apply their knowledge and judgment in a client-professional sense.

When selecting an agency head, elected officials apply different criteria to candidates, depending on whether the organization promotes its top professional administrators from within or hires them from outside. The influence of professions and professional norms on the hiring process is strong when an organization hires an executive from outside. Elected officials usually are lay people hiring professionals, and so they use professional credentials and reputation as signals of candidates' quality. Because elected officials do not know external candidates personally, they also rely heavily on the judgment of search consultants, who are usually former members of the profession themselves, and external reviews by other professionals. For this reason a professional reputation is especially important for external candidates. These processes and standards of professionalism are either less significant or absent when governments promote top administrators from within. A search consultant is not necessary to identify or vet internal candidates. An internal candidate is a known commodity and so elected officials need not rely on outsiders' assessments of his or her quality. For agencies promoting administrators from within, a reputation for predictability and adherence to local norms is more important than a professional reputation.

A simultaneous adaptation process occurs among administrators. Bureaucrats ambitious for career advancement observe the behavior of those who successfully "get ahead" in a profession or organization and then mimic this winning behavior (March and March 1977). For an administrator who is "diagonally" ambitious for a job outside his current agency, adaptation means building a professional reputation, since credentials and a reputation for innovation are important selection criteria for higher-status agency heads (DiMaggio and Powell 1983). On a diagonal career path, then, a bureaucrat seeks to introduce professionally fashionable policy innovations to his agency. For administrators seeking advancement within their current agencies, successful adaptation means building a reputation for adhering to organizational norms and maintaining the status quo. Sitting atop an agency with vertical advancement, the bureaucrat is not so interested in professional innovations.

I argue that, due to these selection criteria and adaptive responses, the link between elected official and bureaucrat is more a client-professional relationship when the agency head is hired from outside and more a principal-agent relationship when he or she is promoted from within. Both the seller and buyer of professional administrative labor carry expectations about their relationship to the job and behave accordingly. A bureaucrat who thinks of himself as an agent who serves an elected principal values democratic responsiveness; one who sees herself as a professional who serves a government client values professional innovation. Elected officials who regard administrators as their agents in a principal-agent sense value bureaucratic *accountability*; elected officials who think of administrators as professionals in a client-professional sense value bureaucrats' *expertise*. Figure 1.2 illustrates the possible intersections of the role orientations that bureaucrats and elected officials carry into their relationships.

Where role orientations align (quadrants II and IV), the political relationship between bureaucrat and elected official is likely to be smooth and stable. The shared understanding of a principal-agent relationship in quadrant II fosters stability in the job and increases bureaucrats' accountability to elected officials. But for better or worse, jobs in quadrant II are unlikely to generate significant policy innovation, or at least are likely to innovate slowly. Bureaucratic jobs that align in quadrant IV will tend to exhibit a high degree of innovation and technical expertise, but elected officials' deference to professional administration, coupled with agency executives' penchant for pushing innovations, can lead to a bureaucracy that is insensitive to citizens and elected officials. When role conceptions misalign (quadrants I and III), bureaucrats and elected officials carry different values to their relationship. In quadrant III, bureaucrats and elected officials take up mutually deferential positions, with bureaucrats initiating little innovation, even as elected officials look to their administrators to provide it. Conflicts are likely to arise in quadrant I, where bureaucrats approach their jobs as professional innovators while their elected officials expect deference.

In a sense, quadrant II in figure 1.2 (mutual principal-agent relationship) is something of a default position for elected officials and bureaucrats. In the absence of some need for innovation, elected officials tend to prefer bureaucrats who will satisfy their preference for hierarchical accountability and the stability that accompanies it. For this reason, entrepreneurial bureaucrats are likely to be relatively uncommon across public administration professions. Bureaucratic policy entrepreneurship is most likely to emerge when and where bureaucrats approach their work as professionals serving government

Bureaucrat's Role Orientation

		Principal-Agent	Client-Professional
Elected Official's Role Orientation	*Principal-Agent*	II. Responsiveness *Accountability*	I. Innovation *Accountability*
	Client-Professional	III. Responsiveness *Expertise*	IV. Innovation *Expertise*

Figure 1.2 Bureaucratic role conceptions and values
Each quadrant contains the value corresponding to the role orientation that a bureaucrat or elected official holds. Plain text indicates the bureaucrat's evaluation of what the role entails; italics indicate the elected official's evaluation.

"clients." Bureaucrats will be most responsive to their professional communities and seek to bring professional innovations to their governments. Political stability will accompany this innovation when elected officials approach administrators as professionals, and so quadrant IV represents another potential (but probably less common) equilibrium position. Policy stagnation and slow change will accompany stability in quadrant III, where elected officials and bureaucrats assume mutually-deferential postures. Rapid professional innovation is likely to occur in quadrant I, perhaps accompanied by significant political conflict between bureaucrats and elected officials.

Of course, casting the relationship between elected official and bureaucrat as either *principal-agent* or *client-professional* forces continuous phenomena into binary categories. In reality, public agency heads may think of their elected officials sometimes more as "the boss," and at other times more as "the client." The categories shown in figure 1.2 simply provide a convenient and familiar 2×2 framework in which to think about bureaucratic politics. I discuss the dynamics of principal-agent and client-professional relationships further in chapter 2.

The main point here is that administrators and elected officials can carry different expectations into their relationships, and that job mobility and career path, not just professional socialization, causes differences in bureaucratic professionalism. In this way, public administration professions are not only labor markets, but markets for policy innovation: bureaucratic policy entrepreneurs emerge where government demand for innovation meets a supply of mobile, professional administrators. From a theoretical perspective, the critical difference between principal-agent and client-professional is that an agent responds to the incentives established by a principal, whereas a mobile professional responds to incentives for political behavior largely beyond the control of any one client.

Consequently, the extent to which governments adopt professional innovations depends upon their bureaucratic selection processes, and administrators' policy initiatives reflect their own career concerns. Hiring an administrator from outside involves an assessment of professional reputation, and so an external hire signals, explicitly or implicitly, a desire for the kind of innovation for which professions are known. But when governments hire a professional from outside, professionals are more likely to take entrepreneurial political risks, and so the priorities of profession are more likely to become manifest as policy. Policy innovation does not follow from the mere presence of professionals, but from *mobile* professionals. Professional sensibilities may abound among bureaucrats everywhere, but job mobility offers license to put professional principles into practice, and so opens the door for policy entrepreneurship.

Human Motivation and Bureaucratic Policy Entrepreneurs

Given a bureaucrat's preference for some policy innovation, an equally important decision remains: how much (or little) political effort to exert in pursuit of innovation? Beneath an individual's proximate interests in specific policy goals (say, budget maximizing or environmental protection), I argue that administrators' political actions are driven by motives embedded within their personalities. In this study I employ a theory of human motivation in an effort to answer Mintrom and Norman's (2009) call to unearth the motivational roots of policy entrepreneurship and Daniel Carpenter's call for "greater psychological realism" in theorizing about bureaucratic politics (2006, 42).

Several prominent studies of bureaucratic politics (including James Q. Wilson's *Bureaucracy*, quoted at the top of this chapter) recognize the importance of personality in explaining the emergence of policy leadership among administrators. In recent decades, political scientists and public administration scholars have been reluctant to theorize about psychological motives in studies of administrative behavior, however. For many, the reluctance to include motives in models of political behavior is not because motives are irrelevant but rather because theorizing about personalities in ways that generate falsifiable hypotheses is difficult to do with political scientists' usual array of theoretical and methodological tools. In their book *Public Entrepreneurs*, Schneider, Teske, and Mintrom (1995) explicitly sidestep the psychological dimension of policy entrepreneurship for this reason (74).

In theorizing about bureaucratic psychology I turn to the three-dimension motive scheme developed by McClelland (1975, 1998) and Winter (1978, 1996), described briefly earlier in this chapter. In public administration, individuals with strong achievement motivation may seek career advancement as a means to or consequence of accomplishing excellent performance. Individuals with a strong power motivation seek career advancement as a means of gaining fame and/or authority over others. Ambition for career advancement is a result of high levels of the achievement and/or power motives, though for different reasons. Chapters 3 and 5 discuss motivation much more thoroughly; for now it will suffice to say that achievement motivation fuels political advocacy.

Personality Filters

Even if bureaucrats' motives are measurable and linked to political behavior, the theoretical value of motivation is limited if the emergence of entrepreneurial personalities is simply a matter of "chance appearance," as Wilson (1989) suggested in this chapter's epigraph. However, the present study demonstrates that differences in opportunity structures and career paths lead to varying degrees of policy innovation, and that differences in motive lead to varying levels of political activity. I argue that, taken together, these two phenomena systematically favor some kinds of bureaucrats over others in different public administration professions. Wilson's "change-oriented personalities" emerge not by "chance appearance," but rather because patterns of professional advancement create patterns of policy entrepreneurship in public administration.

Individuals who have strong achievement motivation are more likely to advance along diagonal career paths than on vertical career paths. Achievement-motivated bureaucrats also more actively advocate for their policy proposals. Given diagonal opportunities for advancement, these administrators promote the kinds of innovations that diagonal organizations reward through selection. Vertical opportunity structures may frustrate achievement-motivated individuals inasmuch as these opportunity structures reward longevity, shrewdness, and "playing by the rules" over professional innovation. Meanwhile, the power motive reflects a concern for influence or impact on others, and so high-status jobs may satisfy the power motive whether the administrator arrives at his post vertically or diagonally. Governments that routinely promote from within, however, will select individuals who adhere to local preferences and thrive in hierarchical organizations. In the absence of strong achievement motivation, power-motivated individuals will seek out and remain in vertical career opportunity structures because they satisfy the power motive without a need for professional policy innovation.

Where many diagonal advancement opportunities exist, achievement-motivated bureaucrats are likely to advance by advocating for professionally innovative policies. Where advancement opportunities are few or primarily within the bureaucrat's current government, power-motivated bureaucrats are likely to advance by adhering to local organizational norms with relatively little regard for professional sensibilities. Thus, the emergence of bureaucratic policy entrepreneurs is not a matter of mere "chance appearance" but rather a predictable consequence of institutional arrangements.

Empirical Inquiry

For several reasons, local government in the United States provides an excellent context in which to study bureaucratic ambition. Coherent and diverse professions have evolved in American local government administration: law enforcement, teaching, firefighting, public health, social work, and so on are distinct and established professions. With thousands of governments available for comparative study, American local government provides ample variation on institutional variables while largely controlling for cultural and economic variables. A focus on local government carries limitations, to be sure, and these limitations are discussed at length in chapter 7. However, local government offers excellent traction on the theoretical issues at hand and so is a good place to begin a study of bureaucratic ambition (though certainly not a good place to end it).

The present inquiry employs case studies of professional administrators in three American local governments, as well as data from an original behavioral survey of two distinct populations of local agency heads: police chiefs and water utility managers. By studying these two very different professions, I seek to demonstrate the theory's validity across substantive policy areas. I chose to survey police chiefs and water utility managers because both professions are ubiquitous throughout the United States. The survey of chiefs of police included a psychological probe to gather data on motivation.

Implications for Governance

Leaving aside the politics-administration dichotomy, this book proceeds from what Kenneth Meier and Laurence O'Toole have called a "governance perspective" (2006), which recognizes that bureaucratic agencies are inextricably entwined with electoral, legislative, and judicial elements of the state, and so are essential to democratic governance. This perspective also recognizes that bureaucrats' own values inevitably play an important part in their political decisions. The finding that institutional structures channel bureaucratic ambition into political behavior casts new light on the perennial tension between professionalism and responsiveness that arises when professional administrators serve democratic governments.

Put simply, as a professional in a labor market, a bureaucrat ultimately serves two masters: the employer that pays her salary today, and the universe of employers who might potentially pay her salary in the future. From a normative perspective, the most important finding of *Bureaucratic Ambition* is that she will tend to value the latter over the former to the extent that she is ambitious. For administrators whose careers proceed entirely within a single agency, the present and future employers are one in the same. For professions with significant job mobility, responsiveness to the market means adherence to the norms and values of the profession. As an agent responding to his elected principal, an administrator is ethically bound to follow orders. At the same time, as a professional responding to his elected client, an administrator is bound by professional standards of practice. Both forces condition the bureaucrat's political behavior; ambition helps determine the strength of each force.

Inevitably, the innovations wrought by ambitious bureaucrats in any specific situation serve some political interests more than others. But if this theory is correct, then governments may use organizational design, hiring, and promotional policies to enable or inhibit the emergence of policy entrepreneurs from public agencies. Bureaucratic ambition creates political winners and losers; the institutions that channel ambition into political decisions determine who those winners and losers are.

In crafting a theory of bureaucratic ambition, this book weaves together theories of politics, professional labor markets, and personality psychology, analyzes data on agency executives' careers, political behavior, and personalities, and then weighs the normative dimensions of bureaucratic ambition in light of the philosophy of public administration. I hope that the reader will find the enterprise compelling, even convincing, and at least interesting. It is, admittedly, ambitious.

CHAPTER TWO

Glorious Heroes, Tragic Heroes, Antiheroes

How Bureaucratic Entrepreneurship Happens (or Doesn't)

> I'm an engineer with twenty years in the profession. I'm just stupid enough to keep pushing. That's the engineer in me. . . . My calculus was: "Damn it, this is the right thing to do."
>
> CHIEF ENGINEER, SAN ALONSO UTILITIES, RECENTLY FIRED

> I was willing to go with the flow. I wasn't going to jump out there and bash the mayor.
>
> THE SAN ALONSO UTILITIES DIRECTOR OF FINANCE, THE ONLY SENIOR UTILITIES EXECUTIVE NOT FIRED

Government bureaucrats are frequently lampooned as insensitive, incompetent, or even corrupt. Scholarly works on the bureaucracy, particularly in the political science literature, often echo these themes, depicting bureaucrats as risk-averse, mechanical, or budget-maximizing. Nearly as often, however, the media identify administrators as policymaking heroes: the school superintendent striving to close the achievement gap, the urban police chief reaching out to minority communities, the ecologist who campaigns to clean up a contaminated river. Bureaucratic policy entrepreneurs also abound in scholarly accounts of the policy process, and studies in the public administration tradition sometimes lionize professional bureaucrats as innovators and guardians of the public interest.

No simplistic depiction of public administrators is universally valid, of course. The phrase *bureaucratic ambition* is not an oxymoron, but neither is it a valid analytical assumption. Some administrators are shiftless satisficers,[1] some are entrepreneurial innovators, and some act each part at different times. Policy entrepreneurship is risky by definition, and innovative administrative heroes are as often tragic as they are glorious. Bureaucrats can also conform to stereotype, too, remaining antiheroes who eschew policy leadership and instead faithfully carry out their elected principals' orders. For students of public administration, as for students of literature, the interesting theoretical questions are: what makes some main characters glorious heroes? What makes others tragic heroes? What do we make of antiheroes? And whose political interests do bureaucratic policy entrepreneurs serve?[2]

This chapter relates accounts of professional public administrators and their entrepreneurial efforts (or lack thereof) toward policy innovation in three American local governments. Each narrative describes a government and the political decisions of its agency heads. Each case is also about policy innovation, showing how administrators introduce new policies to local governments, assertively or reluctantly. Investigating individual bureaucrats and their actions in context helps motivate the theory that follows in the next chapter and also adds depth and texture to the quantitative analyses in subsequent chapters.

Three Cases

The first case study focuses on the major metropolitan city of "Greenport" (as explained below, names of towns and people have been disguised) and the tumultuous tenure of its police chief, "Calvin Jensen." A classic diagonal climber, Chief Jensen served as a senior administrator or chief in several American cities over the course of his career, and as chief of police in Greenport he occupied one of the very highest status positions in the law-enforcement profession. The second case study describes the "Mount Brantley School District" and superintendent "Jude Alesky." A thirty-two-year employee of Mount Brantley schools, Alesky's vertical career path and long service as superintendent are unusual for the school administration profession, where mobility is the norm. The final study centers on the city of "San Alonso" and its director of utilities, "Carmen Osborne." The study of San Alonso looks at Osborne's handling of a controversy over a major infrastructure project.

The accounts offered here are not comparative case studies in the strict research design sense. That is, the cases were not selected with careful attention to important variables or comparability across cases. Neither are these "hard cases" in the sense that the governments studied do not feature institutional or social conditions especially conducive or unfriendly to bureaucratic policy entrepreneurship. Rather, these cases were selected for their illustrative qualities; they "make the unfamiliar familiar" and are chiefly useful in helping to understand other kinds of data (Datta 1990, 38). Specifically, these cases illustrate the promises and perils of bureaucratic policy entrepreneurship for administrator and elected official alike.

Method

Each investigation began with an interview with the agency head who is the main subject of the case. Media accounts, official archival review, and interviews with other administrators, elected officials, and community leaders contributed to narratives for the three governments that I studied. I employed a snowball sampling method to contact individuals for interviews who may have had significant political interactions with the administrator at the heart of the case study. All interviews were tape-recorded with the participant's permission. I also investigated how exit and hiring decisions were made when bureaucrats changed positions. In each case, I explored the ways that these individuals' motives and career opportunities affected their decisions to advance policy. In all interviews, I avoided identifying policymaking, careers, ambition, or opportunity structure as my variables of interest to avoid influencing interviewees' responses with theoretical cues.

A Note on Presentation

Under the research protocols required by the University of Michigan's Behavioral Sciences Institutional Review Board, people interviewed for this study were promised that their participation would remain confidential and that their identities would be masked with pseudonyms in any publications based on their participation. Consequently, the names and places given in this chapter are all pseudonyms, and some factual details have been changed to preserve confidentiality. Most of the direct quotations in this chapter are from interviews, though a few are from media accounts or official documents, such as meeting minutes, court documents, and hearing transcripts. Quotations from official documents and media accounts are not cited in order to protect participants' identities. Internet search engines present an additional challenge for preserving anonymity; where I have drawn quotations from media accounts or official documents, I have made minor changes in wording to make Internet searches of quoted material more difficult. I have done my best to retain the substance and meaning of participants' comments while guarding against accidental identification. That these cases must be masked by pseudonyms is frustrating from a scientific perspective since it makes replication of the study impossible. Essentially, the reader of this chapter simply must trust its author. However, the skeptical reader may take some comfort in knowing that the cases related here are simply illustrative, meant to complement and whet the appetite for the more rigorous and replicable empirical analysis offered in subsequent chapters.

Case A: Calvin Jensen and the Greenport Police Department

After four years of military service, a young Cal Jensen returned to his native Palmfield, a very large city in the U.S. West, intending to go to college. Palmfield was growing rapidly at the time, and its police department was expanding to match. Lured by the police department's generous educational benefits, Jensen decided to join. "I joined thinking I'd stick around for four or five years," Jensen recalled. "Of course it didn't happen that way—I fell in love with the job."

Ramp Climbing

The department apparently fell in love with Jensen, too. Three years after joining, Jensen earned the highest-ever score on the sergeant's exam and was quickly promoted. He continued to excel, and by age thirty Jensen, promoted to captain, was running the toughest precinct in Palmfield. Two years later he became the first African American promoted to major in Palmfield, supervising patrol and investigations over a quarter of the city. After twenty years in the Palmfield Police Department, Jensen was assistant chief and eligible to retire with benefits. He was on the short list to ascend to the chief's office, but after twenty years in Palmfield, his career path shifted from vertical to diagonal with a move to Potter's Mountain:

> The mayor of Potter's Mountain saw me on TV. I was representing the police department with a [drug-enforcement] program I helped create. Back in those days we were being very aggressive about drug enforcement. . . . I was on [national news show] talking about the issue. The mayor of Potter's Mountain saw me on the program, called me the very same day, and said: "Hey, listen—if you're available, I'd like to hire you to help us get this kind of program here."

So Jensen left Palmfield to head a new program in Potter's Mountain, a large city in the South. He stayed in Potter's Mountain for three years. The next opportunity materialized in Hollydown, a large western city, where Jensen took his first job as chief of police. Like law-enforcement agencies in many other large cities at the time, the Hollydown Police Department struggled with crack cocaine and its accompanying gang violence, but under Jensen's leadership it gradually began to win the support of the minority community and drive gangs out of the city.

After five years in Hollydown, Jensen was recruited to become chief of police in Ashfax, a very large southern city with a homicide rate that routinely ranked among the nation's highest. Ashfax's police facilities and equipment were antiquated. The police department was mostly white, though it served a majority black population, and racial tension between the police and the public was pronounced. Jensen was Ashfax's first African American chief and the first chief hired from outside in more than forty years. He won city council funding for facility replacements and equipment upgrades and he developed new training and operations protocols. He replaced several midlevel and senior administrators in the department and imposed a stricter disciplinary regime on his officers to prevent abuse. A year after arriving in Ashfax he launched Operation Purge, a multifaceted program to reduce violent crime. The program was enormously successful and became a national model. Operation Purge won accolades from the Department of Justice, and in 1999 Jensen shared a stage with President Clinton at an event honoring innovative local government leaders. Cal Jensen was becoming a law-enforcement celebrity.

It was no great surprise, then, when Jensen's telephone rang one afternoon with another mayor offering a job. Glen Atkins had just been elected mayor of Greenport, a very large city in the Northeast at the heart of a major metropolitan area. Like many other large cities, Greenport was once a prosperous center of industry with a thriving and diverse middle class, but had been in steady decline for decades due to suburbanization and an erosion of its industrial base. Crime was high and increasing. The Greenport Police Department (GPD) was in a similarly bad state, with failing facilities and a departmental culture that was widely perceived as troubled. The GPD had recently been involved in several high-profile incidents that involved use of force and civil rights violations. A U.S. Justice Department (DOJ) investigation of the GPD was under way. Mayor Atkins had been elected as a reformer and he set out to find a new chief from outside the city to reform Greenport's largest bureaucracy and address its violent crime problem. In many respects, Greenport's situation was a larger and more intense version of Ashfax's at the time of Jensen's arrival. The mayor indicated that he would look to Jensen to provide direction to the city's overall law-enforcement program. Besides the exceptional salary and benefits Jensen would enjoy in Greenport, the city was among the largest in the United States and so offered Jensen an opportunity to join the elite of the police profession at the apex of his career. When he took the job, he was the first chief hired from outside in nearly a century.

Arriving in Greenport

Jensen was no stranger to administrative challenges after his experience in Ashfax and he expected to face serious problems in Greenport. But the difficulties that Jensen encountered on his arrival astonished him. The department was financially strapped, with obligations to union contracts and lawsuits, leaving him little budgetary discretion. The department's headquarters were located in a building so dilapidated that one wing had to be sealed off due to rodent infestation shortly after Jensen arrived. Information technology was decades behind the times: e-mail was unknown, and records were kept on bound paper blotters, much as they had been a century ago. More than $3 million in cash and property was missing from the department's property-management facility. The Justice Department probe into GPD practices was uncovering a disturbing pattern of officer misconduct. Undaunted, Jensen jumped into his new job with enthusiasm. He appointed new senior executives whom he judged to be free from corruption. He hired an assistant chief to deploy new information technology, instituted new procedures for the handling of evidence, and made myriad other changes.

Jensen cut an unusually high profile for a municipal bureaucrat. Past police chiefs had maintained a cool and sometimes adversarial relationship with the press. Jensen lavishly shared information with local media. He sought out journalists directly and provided them with information on the GPD. He appeared on local and national television programs, sometimes facing hostile questions. He gained credibility with journalists by sharing good and bad news alike. A police beat reporter for the city's daily newspaper recalled incidents in which Jensen called him personally:

One time he suspended some cops for a high-speed chase in which I think a person was killed. The chase was supposed to be cut off at some point, but the cops kept going. [Jensen] put that out himself when he did it. He let me know personally, he called me when he did it. There were some cases with some officers who did things, abuses, so egregiously that he was upset about it and he would let us know.

Cultivating a relationship with the media was part of Jensen's effort to reform the GPD. "Jensen was very open. He gives you his cell [phone] number, he returns calls, he was accessible," said the reporter. "He was trying to make a lot of changes, and you got the sense he was almost trying to use the media to get the message out."

Bulldog

Some members of the city council welcomed Jensen as a change agent that the GPD needed; those whose loyalties were to Greenport's police union were suspicious of him for a similar reason. Jensen made frequent appearances in official city council sessions and actively promoted his reform agenda, though he rarely contacted council members personally outside of official meetings. Jensen's media presence sometimes made council members feel blindsided: he would sometimes announce significant policy initiatives or crime investigations without first briefing the council. He spent little time learning about the council members, their agendas, and their loyalties. One council member, whose general opinion of Jensen is positive, admitted that the chief could be a "bulldog":

He didn't come in and get the lay of the land first. He didn't come in and figure out who the constituencies were and try to do things to get them on board and get them comfortable. He didn't take the time to figure out what really needs to be changed and what doesn't. He just came in with a plan and hit it. . . . He changed the names of departments on the first day and made everybody wear tie clips. That just irritated everybody and didn't accomplish anything. He publicly took on the city council in his first month on the job before he figured out that maybe we weren't his worst enemy and it might be better to have a different relationship with us.

Jensen's hard-charging approach also rankled many of the GPD's rank-and-file officers and the union that represents them. Jensen's reforms within the department included the disciplining and/or removal of several officers for misconduct. Jensen suspended officers without pay when they were caught falsifying their timecards or when they were charged with misdemeanors. He angered several senior officers by passing them over for promotion—formerly a virtually automatic, seniority-based process—in favor of officers and supervisors whom Jensen deemed more accomplished and promising. Clashes between Jensen and the union reached a crescendo when he refused to promote and attempted to discipline an officer who had been involved in several fatal shooting incidents. Conflicts with the union over promotion and disciplinary decisions plagued Jensen's administration throughout his tenure.

Jensen attempted to turn the department's most glaring problem, the Justice Department's civil rights investigation of the GPD, into his most effective political tool. City officials and GPD administrators had resisted the Justice Department probe prior to Jensen's arrival. With his administrative discretion severely limited by the union contract, Jensen realized that the Justice Department might force the city to make some of the policy changes that he wanted. The Justice Department investigation was an embarrassment to the city, and the threat of a federal civil rights prosecution against the GPD had forced the city into negotiations for reforms. Before Jensen's arrival, Justice Department officials had been negotiating with GPD attorneys on a consent decree to change GPD policies and practices, but progress had been slow. Jensen soon made the Justice Department negotiation his top priority and began meeting with Justice Department officials personally, rather than through second- and third-tier administrators in his agency. Working through the Justice Department to accomplish his policy aims required that he maintain an adversarial public stance on the process while cooperating with the Justice Department in private. Jensen himself said:

> We had two conversations going on. At a political level, we were saying we didn't want the feds to come in because it made the city look like it couldn't handle its own business. On another level, I *wanted* the feds to come in because it was the only way I could break some of the chains that the union had around management prerogatives. . . . I thought the [federal consent decree] would give me leverage with the public, with the media, and within the department to bring light to these issues.

The consent decree would directly or indirectly touch on virtually every phase of the GPD's operations and facilities: training, supervision, and disciplinary policies would change, superceding the union contract; patrol, investigation, arrest, and detention procedures would be revised; and the city would be required to fund major improvements to police facilities. Jensen would be able to claim that the federal government was forcing the reforms and so perhaps win over recalcitrant officers who might otherwise simply resist and resent the outsider chief.[3]

Cancaljensen.com

Jensen did not get the chance to see this strategy through, however. Resistance to his aggressive reform agenda began grew almost at once, especially among the department's rank-and-file. Among Jensen's fiercest critics was Dan Weaver, a veteran GPD officer. Weaver had been an outspoken critic of Greenport's elected officials, especially Mayor Atkins, whom Weaver thought was corrupt and lazy. Like many of his fellow officers, Weaver resented many of Jensen's reforms and proposals, as well as the new chief's high-handed approach toward subordinates. Shortly after Jensen's arrival in Greenport, Weaver launched a Web site on which he posted information about Jensen's reforms and complaints about them, along with calls for Jensen's dismissal. While many of the remarks Weaver posted on cancaljensen.com were comments on Jensen's policies, some were reports about internal investigations and rumors of corruption.

At first, cancaljensen.com was simply an annoyance to Jensen. But as Weaver's attacks grew more vitriolic, the site began to attract more and more readers and the Web site became a distraction to Jensen. One night while Weaver was working, Jensen telephoned him and ordered him to take down the site. Weaver refused. An angry Jensen suspended Weaver without pay. Weaver filed a union grievance and a wrongful termination lawsuit against the GPD. He also ratcheted up the rhetoric on cancaljensen.com. Weaver soon had new grist for his Web site as rumors of scandal involving the mayor began to emerge.

An Internal Affair

Among the staff appointments Jensen made on his arrival was the placement of seventeen-year GPD veteran Captain Eddie Rodriguez as deputy chief for internal affairs. In this job, Rodriguez would head the division of GPD that was responsible for investigating crimes and misconduct by GPD officers. Rodriguez had been suspicious of Jensen as an outsider to GPD, but he grew to respect the new chief and his reform agenda. For his part, Jensen saw Rodriguez as an officer with a clean record and exceptional intelligence and initiative. Jensen passed over several other senior supervisors to appoint Rodriguez to the internal affairs post. Rodriguez was, said one observer of the GPD, "one of the guys who Jensen really felt bought into his theories and philosophies."

Rodriguez arrived at work one morning to find a voice message on his answering machine: an anonymous caller claimed to have witnessed officers assigned to the mayor's security unit escorting several guests in and out of the city marina clubhouse late at night. Inside the clubhouse, the caller claimed, the mayor was hosting a party at which illegal drugs were being used. The caller claimed to have witnessed one of the officers escort an intoxicated Mayor Atkins into a city vehicle with a prostitute.

Anonymous tips to the internal affairs office were common. Many of the calls were frivolous, but in this case the caller related details that gave Rodriguez reason to believe that the allegations might be legitimate. Internal affairs staff had already been investigating reports of officers on the mayor's security staff abusing expense accounts. Rodriguez expanded the investigation of the security unit to include a probe of the anonymous caller's allegations. Internal affairs staff began interviewing members of the mayor's security unit about various reports of their behavior, including the alleged party. Information gathered through these initial inquiries substantiated Rodriguez's suspicion that some members of the mayor's security unit had abused expense accounts. One member of the security staff provided information that largely corroborated the anonymous informant's account of the marina party.

Before Rodriguez delivered his report to Chief Jensen, Mayor Atkins telephoned the chief with questions about the internal affairs investigation. Jensen was aware that Rodriguez was investigating the mayor's security unit, but had not spoken with him about the investigation for nearly a month and did not know the status of the investigation. Mayor Atkins asked Jensen to meet with him personally the next day. At that meeting, Mayor Atkins told the chief that he had heard rumors about an alleged party at the marina and asked if internal affairs was investigating the situation. Jensen told the mayor that that internal affairs was looking into some reports, but that no official investigation was under way. Atkins told Jensen that the rumors were false and then abruptly ended the meeting.

The implications of the mayor's response sank in to Jensen as he made his way back to police headquarters. On his return, a furious Jensen summoned Rodriguez and his investigators to his office demanding answers. Whether or not the rumors of the marina party were true, Jensen realized that a probe of the mayor's office would distract from and possibly undermine his GPD reform efforts. "The chief was pissed off," recalled one of the internal affairs investigators. "He was saying: 'you guys are investigating the fucking Mayor? That's the stupidest shit I've ever heard.' I remember that specifically, because I'd never heard Chief Jensen use foul language before."

A Mayoral Message

Two days later, Jensen received a terse e-mail from the mayor ordering Rodriguez's removal as head of internal affairs. Jensen received no advanced warning, and neither the mayor nor his staff offered any explanation for Rodriguez's sacking. The mayor in Greenport appoints division heads, who serve at the pleasure of the mayor. These appointments are typically a formality, however; selection of division heads effectively are made by the chief of police and only nominally appointed by the mayor. Mayor Atkins's dismissal of one of chief's closest deputies was a signal of the mayor's authority. "[The mayor's actions] said that this is a department where the chief isn't going to have any real power," said one city council member. Another council member described the relationship between Atkins and Jensen this way:

> The mayor had campaigned on police reform, and he intentionally hired a guy from outside with a reputation as a reformer. At first the two of them were on the same page, and Jensen was willing to take the heat when the mayor wasn't. Jensen, for all his flaws, really was about reform. He didn't know anybody in this city. He has no friends or relatives here. He had no debts to pay in this city. So he was promoting people and placing people who he thought were the best to do the job. The mayor and his administration are much more old school. Cronyism, nepotism—those things are not only seen as OK, they're seen as part of the job.

An angry and demoralized Chief Jensen bore the media and city council spotlight following the firing of Rodriguez. Jensen's critics within the department did not observe the rift between the mayor and the chief, or at least did not acknowledge it. Cancaljensen.com heaped more criticism on the chief, whom it depicted as dumping GPD veteran Rodriguez when his investigation began to approach the mayor. In fact, "Jensen was pretty upset [with the mayor]," the police beat reporter said. "He felt he had been undermined. . . . Rodriguez was one of his guys."

Jensen resigned five weeks later. Cheers and applause erupted in precinct stations around the city when Jensen's resignation was announced. His tenure as chief of police in Greenport had lasted a little more than two years. After a short hiatus from law-enforcement work, Jensen accepted a job heading a law-enforcement agency in another state.

A New Chief

Mayor Atkins replaced Jensen quickly, forgoing a national search in favor of an internal promotion. Atkins appointed Assistant Chief Jerry Cook, a twenty-eight-year GPD veteran, as Greenport's new chief of police. Both the rank-and-file officers and activists in favor of reform respected Cook for his intellect and spotless service record. The consent decree that Jensen had negotiated with the Justice Department came into effect as Cook took over as chief. With the legitimacy of his long service with the GPD and armed with the consent decree (or perhaps forced by it), Cook carried on many of the reforms that Jensen had initiated.

But Cook's behavior diverged from Jensen's in significant ways. Whereas Jensen rarely passed up an opportunity to appear in the news media or before the city council, Chief Cook maintained a low public profile. In the words of the police-beat reporter:

> Cook is the complete opposite of Jensen. You have to go through a spokes-person to get to him. He doesn't like to answer questions or do interviews. When you do an interview with him, he wants to know exactly what you're going to ask and exactly what you're talking about. He cuts off press con-ferences early. He's definitely not comfortable in the media spotlight, whereas Jensen kind of thrived in it.

Cook rarely appeared at council meetings without being summoned. Cook also was more deferential in his dealings with the police union and in his handling of promotions and assignments. Jensen had refused to promote an officer because of a checkered service record, despite pressure from a pair of city council members. One of Cook's first acts as chief was promoting that officer. "That promotion was a signal to everyone in the department that it was truly back to business as usual," said a city council member.

The difference between the two chiefs' approaches to the job was most marked in Chief Cook's handling of another mayoral scandal that emerged a few months after Cook became chief. Trouble began when a newspaper reporter wrote a cultural article on a locally famous liquor store. During an interview, the store's proprietor mentioned several local celebrities that he served and boasted that he had recently delivered a large order for a campaign fundraiser for Mayor Atkins. The store's proprietor showed the reporter a copy of the items he delivered to the mayor, explaining how he customized a wine list to match his client's budget of $19,900. The article was published just as a reporter who covered city politics for the same newspaper was reviewing budget documents for a different story. The mayor's party budget figure struck her as strange; she had just read that the mayor's discretionary spending authority was limited to $20,000; expenditures greater than $20,000 required approval of the city council. Another visit to the shop and detailed review of city financial documents confirmed her suspicions: the entire $19,900 liquor bill had been paid by the city and charged to the police department.

The resulting investigation dominated local newspaper headlines, radio talk shows, and television news broadcasts for nearly two months. Mayor Atkins initially denied any knowledge of the purchase. But as more evidence emerged, the mayor admitted hosting the fundraiser but denied having anything to do with the wine. Eventually Chief Cook took responsibility for the purchase. Mayor Atkins and Chief Cook appeared together at a city hall press conference, where Atkins explained to the gathered reporters that Cook had asked a member of the mayor's staff to order the wine as gifts for retiring officers and visiting dignitaries, but that they had been delivered to the mayor's office by mistake. Atkins's staff then assumed that the wine was intended for the mayor's fundraiser and sent them on to the party's caterer. Atkins dismissed the similarity of the order's price and the discretionary spending limit as coincidence. A city council member described his incredulity at the press conference performance:

> This was a farce. . . . [Cook] came out and said that he ordered the booze, that the mayor was not aware of it, and that when he learned of it the mayor was surprised. Nobody believes that. *Nobody* believes that. But Chief Cook publicly took that position. Also, because he sort of wears his feelings on his sleeve a little bit, he very publicly, very uncomfortably took that position. I mean, everybody who saw that press conference knew what was going on.

Cook officially took responsibility for the scandal. "It was a terrible, terrible position he was put in, because he's a decent man who's trying to do the right thing," said another city council member. "But I think he's a political operative for the mayor."

Case B: Superintendent Jude Alesky and the Mount Brantley School District

By the time he entered college, Jude Alesky knew he wanted a career in schools. He graduated from college with a degree in education and began his first job teaching history and coaching basketball at nearby Mount Brantley High School. "I knew during my first month on the job [as a teacher] that I wanted to be a superintendent," Alesky told me.

Mount Brantley School District is a public school system serving about four thousand students in a semirural area in the Midwest. After three years as a teacher, Alesky began his first stint as an administrator when he became assistant principal at Mount Brantley High School. After four years, he was promoted to principal at the middle school and then to principal of the high school, where he worked for thirteen years. When he was appointed superintendent in 1992, it was the first time in more than fifty years that Mount Brantley School District had promoted its top administrator from within the district. With more than thirty-five years' service in a single school system and nearly fifteen years as superintendent, Alesky was an oddity in a profession where mobility and turnover were pronounced. Mount Brantley's school board, too, exhibited extraordinary stability. The board's president had held his post for nearly twenty years, and Mount Brantley school board incumbents rarely lose their seats when standing for reelection.

Members and observers of the Mount Brantley school system consistently cite Alesky's active communication with and sensitivity to the board and community as hallmarks of his tenure as superintendent. Alesky fills a two-inch binder with "everything I can think of" for his board in anticipation of each biweekly meeting. "I try to anticipate the issues that are likely to come up, the questions that they're going to have. I know most of them pretty well, so I can get them decisions and information that will satisfy them before they have to ask."

Alesky maintains frequent contact with board members outside official channels. Mount Brantley's board president describes Alesky's communication with the board this way:

> He's always in contact. There's always a phone call if something unusual comes up in the district. He doesn't want us to be caught off-guard, so there's always a heads-up. Last year we had a bus accident which was fairly serious [*sic*]. Jude was on the phone with me literally as soon as he was off the phone with the police. He gave me all the detail he had available, as soon as he had it—the injuries, the citation the driver received, and everything. Then he called an hour later with an update. . . . When there's a serious problem at one of the schools, we'll know about it before the kids get home.

In fact, Alesky and his board president enjoy an unusually cordial relationship. At the end of my interview with Alesky, I asked him for names of others in Mount Brantley whom I should speak with as part of the snowball sampling procedure. He suggested that I speak with the school board members. When I asked for contact information for board members, Alesky recited their telephone numbers and e-mail addresses from memory.

Alesky is a public champion for schools in the community. He is in frequent contact with the local newspaper reporters who cover his district. He prepares a package of information for journalists in anticipation of each board meeting and occasionally contacts them personally to alert them of potential good news stories about his district. The Mount Brantley school board members that I spoke with regard Alesky, not the board, as the head of the school system. Alesky sets the formal agenda for board meetings and develops all major policy proposals. "We see Jude and his staff as educational leaders," said the district's board president. "Jude is the leader on most of the issues that we face, and the board looks to him for direction."

Yet despite his high level of political engagement with the board, media, and community, Alesky has not been especially innovative. Mount Brantley schools do not lag behind national trends significantly, but neither is the district an educational policy pathbreaker. Alesky's approach to policy is cautious and conservative; he prefers to adopt policies with long-standing, proven records of performance elsewhere, rather than aggressively pursuing policy innovations. Some interviewees from the district had difficulty identifying policy innovations adopted in recent years. Asked about recent innovations, Alesky pointed to the district's new online student information system, implemented during the prior school year. The system allows parents to log in to the district's Web site to track their students' school records and other information. The information system is a valuable improvement to Mount Brantley's schools, but the district is hardly an "early adopter." Thousands of U.S. school districts and tens of thousands of schools were already using such systems when Mount Brantley adopted it.

No Child Left Behind

Mount Brantley's response to the 2001 No Child Left Behind Act (NCLB) is illustrative of Alesky's posture toward innovation. Enacted by the U.S. Congress and signed into law by President George W. Bush in January 2002, NCLB is a sweeping federal policy that mandated significant changes for local public school systems. Among the reforms required for local school districts are a stringent new testing regime, extensive reporting requirements, and provisions for families to opt out of poorly performing schools in favor of better-performing schools.

Mount Brantley school officials, faculty, and staff were initially wary of NCLB and the new burdens that it would place upon the district. A school board member recalled:

> We've always thought of our schools as very good schools, and we kind of resented having to do these things. Nobody likes mandates; we'd rather have made decisions on our own. . . . The staff was pretty apprehensive. But I think we realized that this thing was just happening, and there was nothing we could do about that. So the whole mindset was that we're going to attack [these requirements] and deal with them.

Alesky's response was characteristically thorough and consultative. He gathered curriculum directors, school principals, and several faculty from the district into planning sessions and developed a series of policies to address NCLB requirements. Despite initial apprehension, implementation of the new policies proceeded smoothly, especially if compared with a pair of nearby districts where NCLB generated open conflict between faculty and administrators. Three different individuals I interviewed attributed the relative ease of implementation to Alesky's familiarity with and credibility among the district's faculty and staff. Five years on, Alesky is overwhelmingly positive about the effect that NCLB has had on his district: "No Child Left Behind has been great," he said, adding: "The testing and evaluations we use now force us to be competitive—and that's a good thing."

While Alesky is effusive in his praise of NCLB and has been diligent in his implementation of NCLB-related reforms, it is unlikely that the reforms would have occurred without the federal mandates. A portion of my conversation with Alesky merits quotation here:

ALESKY: We now look very carefully at the curriculum that each grade takes on, and we use testing to show how well students are getting the material. So if the students aren't getting what they're supposed to get by the end of the year, we know we've got a problem.

Q: How did you do teacher evaluations before?

ALESKY: We did it sort of intuitively, which is how it had been done ever since I became a teacher. We just did it by parent perceptions, by classroom observation, sort of by feel. Now we have better ways of dealing with parents, since we can show them evidence for how teachers are doing with their students. It's helped make our teachers better. We now have a heavy focus on curriculum during our professional development time. Our teachers work with each other much better to make sure the curriculum meshes.

Q: Had Mount Brantley ever done these kinds of things before? Did you ever think about using these methods before No Child Left Behind?

ALESKY: No, never. It's really focused us. I think we'd still be happy going along as usual.

In short, Alesky's leadership of Mount Brantley has been active in the sense that he is engaged with elected officials and the community at large, but not aggressively innovative with respect to educational policy.

Career Path

As noted earlier in this section, Alesky's long service in Mount Brantley—he was in his sixteenth year of the superintendency at the time of this study—is unusual for a school superintendent. Earlier in his career Alesky had considered moving to another district a few times. But leaving Mount Brantley has not been a serious consideration for him. "I have such strong ties to this community—I bleed green and gold," Alesky said, referring to Mount Brantley High School's team colors. "I have children in this community, and now I have grandchildren. That's just too much to leave behind."

Case C: Carmen Osborne, the San Alonso Water Department, and the Los Rios Project

Clint Yob, the chief engineer of the San Alonso Water Department, switched on the radio as usual to listen to the news during his morning drive to work on September 11, 2001. Terrorists had hijacked and crashed jetliners into New York City's World Trade Center and the Pentagon. Moments later, the announcer described the collapse of the World Trade Center's South Tower. Yob felt sick to his stomach. Which city was next? San Alonso was one of the largest cities in the West, and Yob knew its most vulnerable point was the Los Rios dam and reservoir, part of the water system that he operated. Yob had long worried about the vulnerability of the aging facility, and now a nightmare scenario was developing. He switched off the radio and called his boss, Utilities Director Carmen Osborne. By noon that day, armed guards were posted at Los Rios.

Osborne and her staff had long believed that the century-old facility was obsolete and that it posed serious risks to public health and safety. The aging Los Rios works were expensive to maintain. Birds, animals, and refuse frequently fell or were dumped into the reservoirs. San Alonso avoided serious contamination because vast volume of water in the reservoir diluted these biological toxins. Utilities department executives had attempted to retire Los Rios in the late 1970s. That effort was scuttled due to high costs, but the city's recently completed master plan included replacement of the dam and reservoir within the coming decade.

September 11 added a frightening new dimension to the problems Osborne saw at Los Rios: one-half of the city's drinking water flowed through the facility, and destruction of the dam or contamination of the reservoir could cost hundreds or thousands of lives. Osborne described how the terrorist threat affected her assessment of Los Rios:

> September 11th lent urgency to that project, because frankly that facility is very vulnerable. It's right in the city. You can go nearly right up to the water's edge. Prior to 9/11, one of the deterrents [to terrorism] we had was that, to get a lethal dosage of stuff into the water supply, because of the volume of the water, you'd need truckloads of the stuff. But now you need only a few grams of the stuff— and it's not hard to get a few grams in there. Besides that, it was aging infrastructure that needed replacement anyway. So basically we accelerated that project.

Osborne and Yob were both licensed, experienced civil engineers with postgraduate degrees and several years of deep involvement in the American Water Works Association. Though she began her career as a consulting engineer with a private firm, Osborne had worked for San Alonso utilities for more than twenty years. Osborne's deputy director, Adam Alvarez, was part of an Environmental Protection Agency (EPA) advisory panel developing water quality rules for municipal systems. Their collective professional judgment was that the city should remove the antiquated Los Rios dam and reservoirs as soon as possible and replace them with several sealed reservoirs and pump stations in scattered locations to disperse risk and improve efficiency.

A Transformation Plan

Osborne understood that work in the political arena was an integral part of her role as leader of the city's utilities. "It's my job—as a translator, if you will, between the technical people in the utility, the council, and the public—to be nonpolitical" she said. "But I was also a steward of that water system. So you have to be as nonpolitical a politician as you can. Part of the job is to count votes." Osborne was methodical in her efforts to gain approval for her Los Rios plan. She laid out her concerns to Mayor Gordon Bellinger within two weeks of the September 11 attacks, quickly convincing him to go forward with the Los Rios replacement. With a green light from the mayor, Osborne began briefing city council members individually. Her budget proposal for fiscal year 2002/2003 put the Los Rios project atop the capital-development list. None of the council members objected to Osborne's plans, and in May 2002 the city council approved $92 million for the Los Rios retirement and replacement project; $3.5 million of that budget was earmarked for transforming the Los Rios site parkland. The department hired Holtzer-Sanborn, a multinational engineering firm that had experience in San Alonso, and began detailed planning for the Los Rios replacement.

 · Meanwhile, Deputy Director Alvarez continued his participation with the EPA's advisory committee on water quality standards. The committee's proposed rules for municipal water would require San Alonso either to replace Los Rios or add a pair of very expensive new treatment facilities in the city. The proposed rules represented a consensus of utility experts from around the country, and they would lend further support to the department's Los Rios plan. Utility executives sought to use compliance with federal regulation as a means of promoting their plan. "We thought [the EPA] could be the bad guy,"

Alvarez said in an interview. "It's hard to get anything done without a regulatory foot to your backside."[4]

Alvarez also launched the department's public information and involvement campaign. His efforts won editorial support from the city's major newspapers. He laid out a public outreach process with a series of four public meetings. Alvarez had led similar public processes successfully in another major city, and Osborne was confident that clearly explained, sound engineering principles would win public support. "We wanted a serious, serious public process to go along with the project," Osborne told me.

The first public meeting on the Los Rios project came almost exactly a year after the September 11 attacks.[5] For executives of the utilities department, the public meetings served three purposes. First, public meetings would establish a project's legitimacy and guard against second-guessing and charges of secrecy. Second, public meetings and their accompanying media coverage would provide a forum to educate the public on the health and safety risks that made the project necessary. Department executives and their engineering consultants were careful to depict the meetings as consultative and advisory, presented multiple alternatives, and used rhetoric that suggested a desire for public input on their plans. But the major policy decision—to remove and replace Los Rios—was obvious so far as utility executives were concerned; they had already won the elected officials' approval. Their language stressed that many options were under consideration during the public process, but department managers saw the meetings as opportunities to articulate the scientific reasoning that made their proposal imperative. The department's presentations and informational materials framed the issue in terms of safety, security, and health. Third, meetings would gather citizen input on the park transformation plan.

This aesthetic dimension of the project was the main point on which department administrators sought substantive contributions from citizens. Even if the public was ultimately not persuaded, the council had already approved the Los Rios removal. Osborne understood that aesthetics would be an important concern for the public, and she was providing ample opportunity for the community to shape the final park transformation. In short, Osborne and her senior engineering staff approached the public involvement process as a kind of consensus-building exercise, not with the intention of facilitating ordinary citizens' influence over the policy process (Dahl 1961).

Citizen Response

As utility installations go, Los Rios is extraordinarily beautiful. The Los Rios dam is something of a local tourist attraction and an excellent and accessible example of gilded era design. The dam captures water flowing from two rivers and channels part of it into a large, open-air reservoir that is used to regulate the flow of water into San Alonso. Los Rios sits at the confluence of two rivers in the foothills of nearby mountains, and on a clear day its reservoir becomes a reflecting pool for the snow-capped mountain peaks that rise in the distance. Los Rios was a remote location when it was built, but a century of growth has left it surrounded by residential development. Thanks to their proximity to Los Rios, neighbors of the dam enjoy some of the most valuable residential real estate in the state. The trails that weave through the Los Rios reservoir area are popular with joggers, bicyclists, and dog walkers.

Ogden Warner was a lifelong resident of San Alonso who enjoyed walking the Los Rios trails near his home. He followed with interest the considerable media attention that Los Rios received following the September 11 attacks. Media coverage of the Los Rios issue eventually faded. He was startled when an editorial supporting retirement of Los Rios appeared in one of the city's major daily newspapers, along with a notice of a public meeting on the project. Warner was an educated professional and followed local politics in the newspapers, but he was by no means a political activist. The meeting notice and apparent decision to destroy Los Rios alarmed him into action.

To Warner and many other San Alonsans, Los Rios was not merely a utility facility but a historical treasure and cultural asset. As with most significant public works projects, costs and potential cost overruns were a concern for many citizens. The threat to public health from contamination of the reservoir seemed far-fetched to Warner; the system was well over a century old, and no significant toxic outbreak had yet struck the city. Los Rios had served San Alonso well—why replace it with an unknown? If it ain't broke, why fix it? Moreover, the water department's Los Rios plans struck some long-time observers of San Alonso politics as opportunism. It was no secret that the water department's engineers wanted to replace Los Rios with new facilities, and September 11 provided a convenient pretext for doing so. Finally, some citizens were alarmed at what they perceived to be a too-cozy relationship between the water department executive staff and Holtzer-Sanborn's senior management. The lead Holtzer-Sanborn consultant on the Los Rios project was one of the firm's senior executives in San Alonso and the former chief engineer of the San Alonso water department. The deputy utilities director, Alvarez, served on the EPA advisory commission with Holtzer-Sanborn's regional vice president. The firm already enjoyed a majority of San Alonso's utility engineering contracts, and the firm stood to gain tens of millions of dollars in design and construction contracts through the Los Rios project. "The people making money from the project shouldn't be the ones making decisions," Warner complained.

Warner printed five hundred flyers and distributed them through the neighborhood surrounding Los Rios in hopes of getting people to attend the first public meeting on the proposal; more than two hundred showed up. Water department representatives were surprised by the turnout. Holtzer-Sanborn's lead project consultant was the primary presenter at the meeting. Sensing hostility, he emphasized that Los Rios removal was a council decision, and he narrowed the meeting's scope to focus on the park transformation design. Warner was incensed. "The water department did everything wrong at that meeting," he said. "They discouraged people from giving testimony. They disparaged people who commented."

Warner was not alone in his anger: in the parking lot after the meeting adjourned, a handful of other citizens signed up for an opposition e-mail list. The list's membership grew. A month later, several of the list's subscribers formed the Los Rios Alliance (LRA) and began an active campaign to fight the water department's Los Rios plan. Dozens of LRA members attended the water department's final scheduled public meeting and coordinated their participation in proceedings. The same week, LRA members had separate meetings with Mayor Bellinger and several city council members to discuss their concerns about Los Rios. Bellinger told LRA's representatives that his decision was made and that he remained comfortable with it. A majority of council members were similarly settled in their positions in favor of the water department's plan, though two were noncommittal.

Having made little progress lobbying their elected officials directly, LRA members sought alternative avenues. An LRA member consulted with the State Historic Landmark Commission and began developing an application to have Los Rios listed on the National Parks Service's National Registry of Historic Places. While neither the commission nor the registry could force the water department to spare Los Rios, both could require the department to consult with historians and to consider the facility's cultural and historical significance in their planning. The LRA's volunteer gathered documents and crafted an application. Her efforts were ultimately successful: eighteen months later, the Los Rios dam and two of its reservoirs were added to the National Registry. In the process, she generated interest from a number of historic preservation experts, who wrote letters to San Alonso officials opposing the water department's Los Rios plan.

The LRA launched a simultaneous public lobbying campaign. With money gathered from members, LRA printed thousands of flyers and postcards to generate greater membership and financial contributions. A Web site was set up to publicize the LRA's policy positions and events. Contacts with local newspapers led to the first front-page featured stories and television news coverage of opposition to the Los Rios plan. At one of LRA's first official meetings, alliance leaders scheduled a protest march at Los Rios. LRA members canvassed San Alonso neighborhoods door-to-door, distributing flyers, telling residents about the water department's plans, and inviting participation in the march. Warner contacted reporters from newspapers and television stations to alert them to LRA's plans, and he prepared press information packets for journalists who showed up. As the date of the march approached, LRA leaders began participating in radio call-in programs to complain about the water department's plans and to call for participation in the demonstration.

The February weather was cold but sunny and clear on the Saturday of the march, and more than one thousand people attended. Organizers handed out signs and leaflets and led a serpentine march along the trails that wound about Los Rios. Crews from two local television stations and reporters from both of the city's major daily newspapers were on hand. An iconic image was splashed across the front page of San Alonso's leading newspaper the next day: marchers walking along the calm blue waters of the Los Rios reservoir, framed by tall evergreens against a backdrop of the San Alonso skyline.

Buoyed by their success with the media, LRA leaders began writing letters and op-ed essays for local newspapers calling for the city to reopen the decision process. The general editorial endorsements that the major daily newspapers had given to the water department's plans began to shift to skepticism, or at least concern for the city's decision process: "Water Department Drowns Democracy behind Los Rios Dam," declared one columnist's headline. "Save Los Rios" t-shirts and bumper stickers began appearing on San Alonso's citizens and their cars. LRA members began their own alternative engineering and health-risk analyses of Los Rios and the San Alonso water system. More than two hundred LRA members packed the city council chambers during its first regular meeting following the march, and the LRA's enthusiasm did not wane with time. LRA attendance at council meetings remained strong as spring turned into summer. By the end of the summer, the LRA had a set of technical analyses to rival the city's.

But the water department's plans to retire the Los Rios facility received a grim and unexpected boost as summer ended. Late one night, a drunken man drove his motorcycle into the park and up a berm surrounding the Los Rios reservoir. Motorcycle and rider careened into the reservoir as a pair of guards watched from twenty yards away. The man had drowned by the time guards reached him, and his vehicle settled to the bottom of the reservoir. "It's two o'clock in the morning, and I get a phone call to shut down the reservoir," Yob recalled. "This happened within twenty yards of two police officers. Talk about vulnerability." The water supply suffered no serious contamination as a result of the incident, but the drowning attracted newspaper headlines and highlighted the facility's exposure. "Imagine if someone *really* wanted to contaminate the water," said Yob.

In light of the incident at the reservoir, the city's official policy remained unchanged: popular, long-serving Mayor Bellinger remained supportive of the water department's plans, as did a majority of the city council. The water department was completing its technical planning for the Los Rios replacement as autumn arrived.

Debate Reopened

In October 2003, Gordon Bellinger announced that he would not seek reelection the following year. LRA leaders recognized the opportunity that the mayoral election would provide—"We had gotten pretty smart by that time," Warner said—and they drafted candidate questionnaires on Los Rios and water department management, promising to mobilize support for or opposition to candidates depending on their stance on the Los Rios issue. Two council members were openly contemplating mayoral campaigns, and by November some city council members who had originally expressed support for the water department's Los Rios plans began to equivocate.

The council created and authorized an independent advisory panel (IAP) to review the Los Rios proposal and suspended its approval for and funding of the project pending the panel's investigation and recommendation. The IAP was to consist of experts in utilities, public health, and security, as well as business leaders, civic notables, and two members of the state legislature. The IAP would hire a professional facilitator to run its process and its own expert to provide independent technical advice.

Utility executives had mixed feelings about the IAP. The IAP included several professionals who would understand and be receptive to the water department's arguments. The IAP's independent technical advisor, Aimee Gronko, was a respected engineer who was familiar with the San Alonso water system and could provide sound technical advice. The IAP process might offer Osborne and her staff a means of making their case for the Los Rios replacement in a dispassionate, systematic way in a forum that would be perceived as neutral. Endorsement by the IAP would settle the issue once and for all, reasoned Osborne. But apart from the professionals and technical experts in the group, the IAP members were citizens with no background in utilities or public health. Winning support from these panelists would be harder for Osborne and her staff, and the laypeople were likely to be more receptive to LRA arguments.

As the IAP and its facilitator began laying out the process, it became clear that the IAP intended to call on Gronko, not Osborne and her staff, as the primary source of technical information on Los Rios. Water department bureaucrats could not participate in the public comment portions of the IAP. To Warner and other LRA members, the water department's restricted involvement in the IAP process was an appropriate counterbalance to the city's earlier public processes. An openly adversarial relationship between the LRA and water department bureaucrats had evolved over the months of controversy, and the LRA made no secret of its suspicion of the department's staff people. Said a leading LRA member:

> We did not choose an adversarial strategy; it was the only strategy that remained when our concerns were ignored. We faced enormous odds in getting our case to the public. . . . The City had the weight of its professional water department and their well-paid consultants behind its decisions. The primary resource that a citizens' group has to overcome this deference to specialist knowledge is to challenge assumptions, identify contradictions, expose cozy relationships, and question the process by which conclusions were reached and issues were framed.

The department and its consultants controlled the earlier public meetings they sponsored, cutting off or dismissing public comments that fell outside the terms that they had set to define the issue. The IAP process was fundamentally different from the public involvement process that Osborne had originally envisioned. Rather than an executive-driven consensus-building process (Dahl 1960), the IAP took on a quasi-legislative role.

Warner and the other LRA leaders recognized the opportunity that the IAP process offered. They contacted panelists in advance of its first official meeting. At the first IAP meeting, the LRA presented each of the panelists with a two-inch binder full of information on LRA's arguments. Considering that the LRA was a voluntary organization with no professional staff, the material that LRA provided to the panel was impressive, rivaling in presentation quality the technical reports generated by Gronko, the water department, and Holtzer-Sanborn. The LRA advanced several arguments. Besides their claims about the aesthetic and historical significance of Los Rios, they challenged the water department's cost estimates and its arguments about water quality, health, security, and regulatory imperatives. LRA leaders requested and were granted an opportunity for a formal presentation before the panel at an upcoming meeting. LRA members attended each panel meeting, demanding that the panel consider alternatives that would preserve Los Rios. Their participation was raucous at times, coloring the proceedings with occasional applause, boos, and catcalls from the gallery.

The water department's first opportunity to address the IAP directly came six weeks into its process. Yob developed a slide presentation that the water department saw as its last chance to sway the panel. Yob's presentation included photographs of debris collected from the reservoir (food containers, dead birds, and dog-scoop bags, among other trash) along with a series of slides that he playfully called "the red clouds of death"—a schematic diagram of the city's water system showing in time-series the hypothetical spread of toxins from Los Rios to more than one-half of the city. It was a potent display.

But the IAP process had become as much a clash of values and identities as one of evidence and arguments. The LRA's report to the panel openly questioned Gronko's qualifications and highlighted her professional connections to water department executives and Holtzer-Sanborn. LRA members questioned Alvarez's participation in the EPA rulemaking process and Holtzer-Sanborn's prominent participation in the water department's planning. One

LRA member suggested that Yob's photographs of debris from the reservoirs might have been doctored. Gronko, water department executives, and Holtzer-Sanborn consultants bristled at the questions about their professional judgment and the charges of conflicts of interest. To these engineers, the LRA was a collection of spiteful, affluent malcontents waging a NIMBY protest.

From Warner's perspective, the LRA had only raised questions about the professionals who were driving the policy process, and the professional engineers were simply angry at their loss of hegemony. The LRA's challenge had introduced a different set of values to the Los Rios decision process. An LRA member put it this way: "Engineers have a certain mindset and see things in terms of engineering solutions. It behooves the citizens to consider other values in this decision. If you value cultural resources, neighborhoods, historical resources, beauty, then you will stop and think about what you are giving up to get the engineering solution."

The city's utility executives were unapologetic. Yob made repeated references to professional values in describing the department's mentality as the IAP process:

> It was the right thing to do. . . . Here was clearly a vulnerable point in the system open to birds, rodents, dog-scoop bags, and now terrorists. I'm an engineer with 20 years in the profession. I'm just stupid enough to keep pushing. That's the engineer in me. From a public relations perspective, we thought it would have looked terrible to back off at that point. . . . My calculus was, "Damn it, this is the right thing to do."

As the IAP process drew to a close, it became clear that popular values would prevail over professional values in this matter. The panel ultimately voted eight against five to reject the water department's Los Rios plan. The next week the city council reversed its decision on Los Rios and cancelled the replacement project.

Fallout

The mayoral campaign was in full swing as the IAP process concluded, and news about Los Rios shared front pages with coverage of the election. One of the leading candidates began to attack the water department and its Los Rios plans. The front-running candidate, councilman Bill Zorn, was on the record as supporting the water department's plans. In fact, Zorn made an impassioned defense of the water department's Los Rios proposal during the meeting at which the city council ultimately rejected it. Zorn won the mayoral election narrowly, anyway.

Despite his support for Osborne's plan to retire Los Rios, the controversy and IAP process had raised serious concerns for Mayor Zorn about a water department whose management seemed to be out of touch with the public and too confident in their professional sensibilities. Those concerns were reinforced when Zorn took office and began working directly with Osborne and her senior staff. Mayor Zorn described his impression of the senior utility administrators in an interview with me: "To say the [water department executives] were condescending is to understate it by a mile. . . . They're offended that someone would even suggest that consideration of a neighborhood amenity is a good idea. Technocrats run amuck. They know they're right, and they don't know why you're even having a conversation."

Zorn was also alarmed at the water department's relationship with Holtzer-Sanborn and the other engineering firms that routinely worked on San Alonso utility projects. "I was invited to a Christmas party hosted by Holtzer-Sanborn. So I went, along with [senior utilities executives]," said Zorn. "What I observed was a disturbing, over-comfortable relationship between my utility managers and these consultants."

Six months after he took office, Zorn fired Osborne. In Osborne's place Zorn appointed Charles Dwight, a manager from another city department who had no experience in engineering or utilities. Zorn explicitly selected Dwight from within city government because he had no loyalties to the engineering profession or to the consulting firms that work with the city. "In the past, the utilities director has been an engineer—a technocrat," Zorn said. "I needed someone I could trust." The new mayor also added full-time engineering staff and slashed the budget for consulting contracts.

Zorn's housecleaning continued after he sacked Osborne. Zorn dismissed Yob, Alvarez, and two other senior utility executives who enjoyed civil service status and so were entitled to large financial settlements from the city on their departure. Osborne and Yob took jobs as consulting engineers with prominent firms in San Alonso, though notably neither took jobs with Holtzer-Sanborn. Alvarez accepted an executive position with a large regional utility in a neighboring state. Eight months after Zorn took office, the finance director was the only remaining senior utilities executive remaining from the prior administration.

Principals and Agents, Clients and Professionals

Jobs are temporary matches of individuals with employers. When elected officials and bureaucrats link to form public administration jobs, their relationships are at once principal-agent and client-professional. The cases in this chapter demonstrate the tensions between the agent roles and the professional roles that administrators play when they take jobs in governments. Both the seller (bureaucrat) and buyer (elected official) of administrative labor carry expectations about their relationship to the job and they behave accordingly. In a principal-agent framework, bureaucrats are not expected to initiate or carry out significant policy innovations without prompting from elected officials, except to the extent that the policy innovations anticipate elected officials' preferences (Bendor, Taylor, and Van Gaalen 1987). In a client-professional framework, bureaucrats are expected to apply their judgment and initiate, advocate for, and carry out policy innovations. Put another way, a client-professional framework is conducive to bureaucratic policy entrepreneurship. Whether the buyer and seller of labor see the relationship as a principal-agent or a client-professional relationship shapes the political processes and policy outcomes that follow. The experiences of agency heads related in this chapter show how policy entrepreneurship (or lack thereof) can turn bureaucrats into glorious heroes, tragic heroes, or antiheroes.

At first glance, principal-agent versus client-professional might seem like a distinction without a difference. From the elected official's perspective, both involve information asymmetries, potential adverse selection, and moral hazards. The key difference between the two relationships is evident from the bureaucrat's perspective: the possibility of voluntary exit to another job. The potential for an administrator to leave her current job for another employer may change her institutional incentives in two important ways. First, the severity of disciplinary sanctions available to the elected "principal" (e.g., restricted authority, lower pay, or job termination) declines substantially if the "agent" can find a similar or better job from another employer. Second, the potential for career advancement through exit creates an incentive for the bureaucrat to develop a reputation in his current position that will make him a strong candidate for another position. That an exit alternative changes the incentives for a bureaucrat in relation to his elected officials may seem so obvious as to be hardly worth stating. Yet surprisingly, political scientists' principal-agent models have paid virtually no attention to this possibility.[6]

Bureaucrat's Role Orientation

		Principal-Agent	Client-Professional
Elected Official's Role Orientation	*Principal-Agent*	II. Cook* (Case A) Dwight** (Case C)	I. Jensen (Case A) ▲
	Client-Professional	III. Alesky (Case B)	IV. Osborne (Case C)

Figure 2.1 Bureaucratic role orientations in three cases
*Succeeded Jensen as Greenport police chief.
**Succeeded Osborne as San Alonso utilities director.

In *Bureaucracy*, James Q. Wilson defines professionals as individuals "who receive some significant portion of their incentives from organized groups of fellow practitioners located *outside the agency*" (1989, 60; italics added). In this sense, responsibility to an external peer community is the very essence of bureaucratic professionalism. In the same text, Wilson distinguished professionals from "bureaucrats" whose incentives were controlled by organizational principals—that is, elected officials. In a revision of figure 1.2 in chapter 1, figure 2.1 illustrates the possible intersections of bureaucrats' and elected officials' conceptions of their relationships. Figure 2.1 places each of the agency heads profiled in this chapter into the cell that best depicts his or her situation.

Matches and Mismatches

Calvin Jensen's tumultuous tenure as chief of police in Greenport occupies quadrant I in figure 2.1. Jensen was a highly educated, decorated, and accomplished police administrator who climbed diagonally to successively higher-status jobs before arriving at Greenport. Jensen approached his job as a professional serving a new client with his expertise in law-enforcement policy and management. But the mayor regarded Jensen as an agent hired to carry out his directives and quickly reasserted his authority over the new chief when he perceived a threat from Jensen's reforms. A frustrated Jensen quit Greenport and took a different job, perhaps in anticipation of an impending dismissal. With bureaucrat and elected official approaching the job with fundamentally different understandings of their role, jobs in quadrant I are likely to show a high degree of innovation, but also may be dogged by controversy and instability.

Jensen's successor in Greenport was Jerry Cook, whose leadership of the police department put him in quadrant II of figure 2.1. Both Cook and the mayor regarded the police chief as an at-will appointee of the mayor, with a responsibility to carry out mayoral directives. This shared understanding in quadrant II fosters stability in the job and increases bureaucrats' accountability to elected officials. But for better or worse, jobs in quadrant II are unlikely to generate significant policy innovation, or at least are likely to innovate slowly. Moreover, when bureaucrat and elected official alike perceive the bureaucrat's role to be dependent on the will of the elected official, there is a greater danger that elected officials may abuse their authority over the bureaucracy. Cook's acquiescence in the cover-up of an emerging scandal demonstrates the potential for political corruption in a quadrant II arrangement.

A career-long employee of Mount Brantley schools, Superintendent Jude Alesky approached the superintendency as an agent with a duty to serve the district and its board. In his interview with me, Alesky made frequent references to the desires of the community and the board. His practice of planning in advance of his board's ideas and questions conforms to Bendor, Taylor, and Van Gaalen's (1987) model of an agent who anticipates his principal's preferences. For their part, Mount Brantley's board members speak of Alesky as a "professional" openly and without prompting; the board instinctively looks to Alesky for policy leadership. Historically, Mount Brantley has hired superintendents from outside based on their credentials and educational expertise, and the district's long-serving board president noted that Alesky's relationship with the board was much like his predecessor's.

Alesky and the Mount Brantley school board fit well into quadrant III of figure 2.1. With their mutually deferential postures, Alesky and his board enjoy extraordinary stability in a profession where rapid turnover of bureaucrats and elected officials is the norm. Alesky is deeply loyal to the district that he serves. But as in quadrant II, bureaucrats in quadrant III are unlikely to initiate important policy innovations and so, for better or worse, may lag their peer institutions or stagnate with respect to policy innovation. The exogenous force of the NCLB Act was necessary to prompt Mount Brantley schools to adopt new and improved standards, curricula, and evaluative techniques. However, once NCLB was imposed, Mount Brantley was poised for smooth implementation of its mandates.

In San Alonso, Director Carmen Osborne enjoyed a client-professional relationship with the city's elected officials before September 11, 2001, catapulted the Los Rios project to the top of the department's capital priority list. Osborne was accustomed to providing technical advice to San Alonso's mayor and city council, who were generally deferential to their professionals on matters of policy. Osborne and San Alonso's elected officials initially occupied quadrant IV of figure 2.1. The department enjoyed a high degree of innovation and technical expertise, as would be expected in quadrant IV. But elected officials' deference to professional administration, coupled with agency executives' penchant for pushing innovations, can lead to a bureaucracy—a technocracy, perhaps?—that is insensitive to citizens and elected officials.

Osborne's sense of professional responsibility compelled her to press for the controversial Los Rios replacement. Over several months, a creative and resourceful citizen group mobilized opposition to the water department's plans sufficient to cause San Alonso council members who had previously supported the Los Rios replacement to equivocate. Osborne and her staff clung doggedly to their proposal, even as public and council opposition grew. To the senior engineers running San Alonso utilities, steadfast support for their Los Rios plans was a principled stand for the city's future that would win over the majority of San Alonsans and their legislators. But to the citizen members of the Los Rios Alliance, Osborne's recalcitrance betrayed the utility department's arrogance and insensitivity to democratic demands. An intervening city election and sustained opposition ultimately doomed the utility department's plans and Osborne's tenure as director of utilities.

The newly elected mayor of San Alonso replaced his utilities director with someone from within city government. Moreover, the new mayor selected an executive who was not an engineer and had no prior experience in the utilities industry, but rather was promoted to the post from another city job. Mayor Zorn's explicit goal in purging the utilities department's executive staff and appointing Dwight was to reduce the agency's accountability to the professional, "technocratic" community and increase its accountability to its elected principals. With reference to figure 2.1, the Los Rios controversy shifted the San Alonso utilities director job from quadrant IV to quadrant I. Subsequently, Osborne's firing and Dwight's hiring shifted the job from quadrant I to quadrant II.

The matches and mismatches related in this chapter's cases and depicted in figure 2.1 underscore just how difficult it is to sustain effective executive leadership in an agency over time. Organizations' relative needs for stability and innovation are likely to change as the economic, demographic, and political environments in which they operate change. Executives who manage their agencies effectively under stable conditions may struggle to innovate or even resist innovation when conditions demand it. Innovative, entrepreneurial bureaucrats may not be effective under conditions that require greater stability or deference to elected officials. The most effective executives may be those whose styles and personalities match the organizations that they lead and the environments in which they must operate (Greiner, Cummings, and Bhambri 2003). For agency executives, sustaining success as environments evolve or fluctuate can require what Robert E. Quinn (1996) has called "deep change," which "requires new ways of thinking and behaving" (3). Administrators accustomed to approaching their jobs as agents to elected principals or professionals to elected clients must sometimes learn to play the other role.

At a normative level, bureaucrats may perceive either democratically responsive or professionally innovative policies as "the right thing" for their communities. A conscientious administrator may think of the government he serves as "the boss" or "the client" (Wilensky 1964); either is at least potentially consistent with the altruistic public service aims that scholars of public administration have observed (Staats 1988; Wilson 1989; Perry and Wise 1990; Brehm and Gates 1997; Crewson 1997; Houston 2000; Wright 2001).

Toward a Theory of Bureaucratic Ambition

The cases in this chapter are meant to be illustrative, not demonstrative. They offer context and a feel for the analytical and normative issues at hand, but not clear or consistent causal explanations. Just so, describing public administration jobs as principal-agent or client-professional is interesting at a descriptive level but it offers little theoretical leverage on bureaucratic policy entrepreneurship. How are the tensions between these roles resolved? Under what conditions are administrators likely to take entrepreneurial risks? When will they avoid such risks? And how do these conditions affect democratic governance? The chapters that follow develop a theory that seeks to answer these questions by linking bureaucratic politics to bureaucratic ambition.

CHAPTER THREE

A Theory of Bureaucratic Ambition

Why Bureaucratic Entrepreneurship Happens (or Doesn't)

> How many people can play this role, take the risks that being a leader entails, when they have families to support, children to put through college, mortgages to pay? How many people are willing to play this role when every aspect of your professional *and* private life can become the stuff of front-page stories, editorials, and columns such as yours? The best people, the people we want running our agencies (or should want doing this job) have options and they're exercising them. They have good skills, are eminently employable, they can go elsewhere, and they have.
>
> A RECENTLY FIRED AGENCY EXECUTIVE IN A LETTER TO THE EDITOR
> OF A CITY NEWSPAPER

Despite numerous anecdotal accounts and case studies, we know little about why some bureaucrats emerge as policy entrepreneurs while others do not. Greenport's two police chiefs, Calvin Jensen and his successor Jerry Cook, approached the same job with very different decisions: Jensen was entrepreneurial and Cook deferential, each in the extreme. The concept of a policy entrepreneur is a useful component of a theory of bureaucratic politics since it underscores the role of purposive, individual behavior in explaining policy innovation. But "bureaucratic policy entrepreneurship" is not a very satisfying explanation for innovation if the label is simply applied descriptively in post hoc fashion. It is neither profound nor useful to point out that some bureaucrats are bold, even rash, innovators if we can say nothing about what makes them entrepreneurial when others are not.

In this chapter, I lay out a theory of bureaucratic ambition that explains how administrators' motives and career opportunities combine to drive (or to not drive) policy entrepreneurship. Here bureaucrats are cast as heterogeneously motivated individuals facing varying career opportunities. I argue that bureaucrats' motives and career opportunities lead them to pursue more or less professionally innovative policies more or less vigorously.

Bureaucratic Policy Entrepreneurship

By definition, bureaucratic policy entrepreneurs are individuals who invest time and energy pursuant to policy innovation by connecting latent demand for public policies with a government supplier, just as commercial entrepreneurs do (Kingdon 1984; Schneider, Teske, and Mintrom 1995; Roberts 2005). "By implication," writes Paul Manna (2006) in his book on education policy, "entrepreneurs are not mere bystanders but advocates who fight to push their ideas onto the agenda." (28). Policy entrepreneurship is a useful component of a theory of bureaucratic politics because it underscores the important role of purposive, individual behavior in explaining policy change. But in order for bureaucratic policy entrepreneurship to be a useful theory of policy change and not simply a post hoc description, we must understand why bureaucratic policy entrepreneurship happens. My theory of bureaucratic ambition aims to do just that. When stepping into the political arena, a public administrator must make two related decisions: (1) which innovations (if any) to pursue; and (2) how hard (if at all) she should try to change policy. The theory developed here addresses both of these decisions.

Professional Innovation

Not all policy change is equal. Which innovations do bureaucrats choose to pursue? The first phenomenon of interest here is the *professional innovations* initiated by an administrator. In using this somewhat awkward phrase, I seek to link the concepts of innovation and professionalism. *Innovation* means the introduction of a new policy to an agency.[1] *Professional innovation* means the import of policy ideas from the broader profession into an organization.

It is important to bear in mind that innovation is different from invention: the former is the process of introduction, while the latter is the process of creation. All inventions are innovations, but most innovations are not inventions. The phenomenon of interest in this study really is the diffusion of policies across agencies, rather than policy conception. A government policy or program may be conceived and first deployed anywhere, but when an agency head introduces to his agency a policy that he learned about through professional training, conferences, or journals, he is introducing a policy that is new to his organization, and therefore innovating.

But defined as simply "newness," innovation is a rather blunt theoretical instrument: if an innovation is simply a new policy, a policy is either innovative or noninnovative. Such a binary definition of innovation implies that any policy change, however paltry or innocuous, is an "innovation." A police chief might apply a more fashionable logo design to the sides of his agency's patrol cars, or deploy officers on bicycles, or equip and train his officers with new, nonlethal weapons, or introduce a municipal curfew ordinance. "Innovation-as-newness" implies that any of these policies is an innovation.

The policy innovations that generally interest students of the public policy process are highly salient or otherwise important ones. In the present study, the professional innovations of interest are those that represent the predominant norms of an administrator's professional community. This fairly restrictive definition departs from popular understandings of the terms *innovation* and *professional*. I do not mean to imply any normative dimension to professionalism or innovation. In some settings the word *innovation* is used as a generic laudatory term describing invention, ingenuity, or any fruitful change. But when innovation is understood as simply the introduction of a new policy, "innovation is not inevitably good," as James Q. Wilson has observed. "There are at least as many bad changes as good" (1989, 227). Similarly, in popular usage, the word *professional* is often used loosely to describe a personal dedication to excellence, with perhaps a detached demeanor. The present inquiry applies the narrower public administration definition of *professional*, which mainly means adherence to standards set by external reference group of peers. Professionalism is also not necessarily good, Wilson reminds us: "Professionalism and nonprofessionalism can each lead to good or bad outcomes" (1989, 64).

Political Advocacy

The second important decision that an administrator must make in the policymaking arena is: how vigorously to pursue policy change? Studies of policy entrepreneurs to date tend to use the term *entrepreneur* either descriptively or in a binary fashion, depicting some individuals as "entrepreneurs."[2] The implication is that individuals who do not so vigorously pursue policy change are "nonentrepreneurs." Unfortunately, it is difficult to say with any precision when an observed individual is a policy entrepreneur and when she is not. A bureaucrat (or politician or citizen or lobbyist) may be more or less entrepreneurial, and so it is more useful to think of bureaucrats' advocacy on behalf of policy innovations as continuous than to see them as binary. Thus public administrators' *political advocacy* is the second phenomenon that my theory seeks to explain. Bureaucrats exert varying degrees of effort at policymaking. The summation of a bureaucrat's efforts might (or might not) earn him the title of entrepreneur, but that is a distinction I do not attempt to make.

A bureaucrat's political advocacy is observable in various kinds of activities, whether or not he ever actually achieves his policy aims. Bureaucrats may initiate new policy from within the agency through rulemaking, personnel decisions, and policy evaluation. In the legislative phases of the policy process, administrators may introduce policy alternatives, place items on the legislative agenda, participate in official proceedings, organize legislative coalitions, build support with appeals to the public and interest groups, communicate through the media, or lobby legislators directly through informal contact. In this study, political advocacy is measured as the contacts that bureaucrats make with people outside of their agencies in order to build political support for their policy initiatives. These efforts at advocacy are costly and sometimes risky, and so represent the "investment" that bureaucratic policy entrepreneurs make in pursuit of innovation.

Mezzo-level Bureaucrats

The subjects of this study are professional public administrators who direct operational divisions of government. These individuals occupy the "mezzo-level" of administration, below elected executives and above the line personnel who execute programs. Uniquely situated to influence both policy design and execution, these mezzo-level administrators are identified as bureaucratic policy entrepreneurs at the federal (Carpenter 2001), state (Rabe 2004), and local (Schneider, Teske, and Mintrom 1995) levels. Mezzo-level bureaucrats have frequent contact with elected officials and can sometimes become high-profile political actors themselves. Applied at the local level, these mezzo-level administrators are Wirt's (1985) "professional executive officers," whose careers are largely devoted to specific public administration professions, such as city managers, school superintendents, police chiefs, and fire chiefs. These individuals are professionals in the sense that they receive specialized training, generally belong to professional societies, and participate in career systems that are defined by their professions. Explicitly excluded from this study are individuals occupying elected offices that direct administrative agencies, as many county sheriffs or tax assessors do. Elected officials' career opportunities and incentives are different from those of professional administrators, and so my theory does not apply to elected administrators.

The policies of interest in this study fall either in the legislative phases of the policy process or might reasonably be of interest to elected legislatures and executives. A policy issue need not reach the formal agenda of the legislative body for legislators to be interested in it or potentially interested in it. Put somewhat formally, this study's immediate dependent variables are the professional innovations advanced and the level of political advocacy by bureaucrat i in government j during timeframe $(t-x)-t$.

Professional Careers and Political Behavior

As Schlesinger (1966) observes in *Ambition and Politics*, political institutions in the United States channel and condition the behavior of politicians: parties and local elected offices provide stepping stones to state and perhaps national office. In this way, institutions create opportunity structures within which ambitious politicians fashion careers. Schlesinger argues that a political "amateur" or a politician who has limited, "discrete" ambition will pursue pet issues and/or serve narrow interests, with little regard for the ways that the broader electorate perceives his behavior. By contrast, the progressively ambitious politician will hone a reputation with broader appeal to improve her chances for upward advancement in the opportunity structure. For example, if a representative from rural southeast Missouri's Eighth Congressional District is a political "amateur" who plans to serve for only a few terms before returning to some other career, she is likely to pursue policies in which she has a strong personal interest. If she hopes to hold her current seat in Congress indefinitely, she is likely to pursue agricultural policies narrowly and vigorously to satisfy her district constituents pursuant to reelection. If the same representative plans to run for governor or some other statewide office in Missouri, she will pursue a broader slate of policies that might appeal to the urban and suburban voters in and around St. Louis and Kansas City. Crafting such a broadly responsible reputation will improve the representative's chances of becoming governor, even if it diminishes somewhat her chances of reelection in her southeastern Missouri district.

Just as the elected politician's career opportunities are defined by government institutions, so too are the bureaucrat's. I argue that a similar logic shapes bureaucrats' political behavior. Where public administrators are concerned, there is no distinction between "amateurs" and "professionals": the mezzo-level bureaucrats that serve U.S. local governments are now, by and large, career professionals (Mosher 1968; Wirt 1985; Green 1989). Professional career systems powerfully shape bureaucrats' political behavior. My basic claim is that public administrators are aware of the labor markets in which they work and their potential paths to advancement and so make rational decisions about which policies to pursue based in part on their career interests.

But of course, as anyone who has spent any time in a public agency knows, administrators do not all seek career advancement (or any other specific goal, for that matter) uniformly and monotonically. Some bureaucrats are energetic and assertive, others are shiftless or docile. Ambition for career advancement emerges within career opportunity structures, but varies according to individuals' personalities. Fortunately, the field of personality psychology offers a means of understanding how individual psychology plays out in organizational settings. This study takes up a particular element of personality, human motivation, as a cause of public administrators' behavior. Motivation varies by individual; hence, the expression of personality as career ambition varies across individuals. Faced with similar career opportunities, people with different personalities may behave differently. The theory advanced here thus lies within the "rational-choice" tradition. My central claims are about individual decisions made by bureaucrats and their employers to maximize utility given the conditions and constraints of an institutional framework.[3] In language that approximates traditional rational-choice terms, a theoretical account that includes heterogeneous motivations allows us to consider variation in the "utility functions" that inform individuals' decisions.

As emphasized earlier, then, my central argument is that ambition—psychological motives manifested in a career opportunity structure—drives administrators' political behavior in predictable ways, with important consequences for policy innovation and democratic governance.

Jobs, Careers, and Opportunity Structures

Jobs are temporary matches of individuals with employers. A job forms when an individual accepts an employer's offer to exchange labor for pay. For public administrators, the employers are governments. But individuals and agencies do not latch on to one another at random, like so many atoms in Brownian motion. Bureaucratic jobs exist within an opportunity structure. *Opportunity structure* describes a profession's educational and/or apprenticeship requirements, as well as jobs and paths to advancement within a profession. Opportunity structures present individuals with both possibilities and constraints, for while multiple paths are available for advancement in a profession, the number and types of paths available vary across professions in ways beyond the control of most individuals. In this sense, public administration career-opportunity structures are *institutions*, according to Douglass North's familiar definition of the term: "[the] rules of the game in a society, or, more formally, the humanly devised constraints that shape human interaction" (1990, 3). Public administration career-opportunity structures are not organic phenomena. Opportunity structures in public administration are to a greater or lesser extent constructed by government organizations and/or professional societies. Indeed, the very existence of government agencies creates public administration career-opportunity structures. Civil service laws, as well as statutes requiring educational credentialing, proficiency examinations, and so forth further define who can and cannot pursue a professional career. That career-opportunity structures are synthetic does not necessarily mean that they are designed to channel professional careers. Legally mandated state engineering examinations clearly are intended to shape professional careers. As a counterexample, consider soil conservation districts. Soil conservation districts are created to coordinate and implement erosion control and sedimentation management policies. At the same time, the proliferation of soil conservation districts creates job opportunities for soil conservation management. As the number of soil conservation districts expands, so does the number of administrative jobs in soil conservation. Opportunities to pursue professional careers in soil conservation management develop when enough independent "client" agencies offer administrative jobs in soil conservation.[4] If soil conservation policy were vested in a single national authority, the career-opportunity structure for soil conservation managers would be different. Creation of or alteration to career opportunities is a by-product of these institutions' formation.

Bureaucratic jobs within an opportunity structure vary in status. Many low-status jobs exist in a profession; high-status jobs are few. A job's status is a function of many factors, including salary, benefits, and prestige. A job's reputation as a high-profile "stepping stone" to even-higher-status jobs may add to its status. However, for purposes of this study, the main indicator of a local public administration job's status is agency size, since larger agencies tend to offer higher salaries, benefits, and prestige.[5] At any given point in a professional's career, she occupies a status position within the profession's opportunity structure. The distinction between job title and status is important: in 2007, Los Angeles (population 3.7 million) and Paducah, Kentucky (population 26,000), both employed a Chief Bratton to head their respective police departments. Each chief's professional status was quite different, however: L.A.'s *William* Bratton was an internationally recognized figure who commanded a force of more than ninety-three hundred sworn officers; Paducah's *Randy* Bratton commanded about seventy officers and enjoyed more limited fame.

Opportunity structures are observable in the predominant patterns of career advancement within professions. Career-opportunity structures for professional public administrators vary considerably. Administrative careers in the U.S. armed services are relatively closed: these jobs generally require entry into the officer corps early in an administrator's career, along with highly specialized and continuing education. Local government parks directors offer comparatively open opportunities: the skills and education required for their jobs are ubiquitous, with many applications in the private sector. The costs of entry to and exit from local government parks management is relatively low.

Paths to advancement vary across career-opportunity structures. Professions with vertical advancement may be thought of as featuring vertical career "ladders" for administrators, as in the U.S. armed services.[6] Where advancement to high-status jobs typically entails changing employers, career progress occurs along diagonal career "ramps" for administrators, as is the case for many public school superintendents. Figure 1.1 depicts two professional administrators' careers that demonstrate typical "ladder" and "ramp" advancement patterns. Peter Pace's ascent from rifle platoon leader to chairman of the Joint Chiefs of Staff took him to posts around the United States and around the world, but progressed entirely within the U.S. Marine Corps. On the other hand, the path that took Dennis Rubin's administrative career from station commander in Fairfax, Virginia, to fire chief in Washington, DC, included changes in employer with each change in title.

As previously noted, for professional public administrators, the very arrangement of government institutions defines the paths to professional advancement that bureaucrats may take. A college student who aspires to lead the U.S. military forces some day (a young Peter Pace?) would follow a fairly prescribed career path that is defined by the structure of the U.S. armed services. A similar new professional who aspires to run a large city fire department (a young Dennis Rubin?) would consider a different career path, defined by the multiple institutions that provide fire protection in the United States. It is easy to imagine that an ambitious young firefighter's career plans might be much different if fire protection in America were provided exclusively by a U.S. Federal Bureau of Firefighting. Career-opportunity structures vary widely across public administration professions in the United States, from almost purely vertical (e.g., the U.S. Navy) to overwhelmingly diagonal (e.g., college and university presidents). As can be seen in chapter 4, typical career paths of police chiefs look significantly different from those of water utility managers.

The geographic extent of an opportunity structure varies by profession. Today the market for many municipal department heads in the United States is effectively national (Green 1989). Low communication and transportation costs have broadened the geographic scope of the market for most local government administration jobs.[7] The cost of exit to a new position that is close to the job changer's present home is lowest; movement to far-flung employers is costlier. Changing jobs involves transaction costs. For some the cost of advancement may be low, as when an individual moves vertically within an organization with no geographic move involved. But movement to a job outside a bureaucrat's current region may be very costly, especially for those with children and/or working spouses. Exit from an organization also may involve loss of pension or other benefits.

There is no obvious reason why career-opportunity structures should vary so widely across public administration professions, and the causes of that variation have received relatively little attention from political scientists and public administration researchers. Bureaucratic career paths may evolve in some historically contingent or path-dependent way. Alternatively, form may follow function: a profession's substantive task may lead it to design or evolve one or another career-opportunity structure. A satisfactory exploration of these possibilities is beyond the scope of the present study; for the present inquiry, career-opportunity structures are assumed to exist exogenously from the administrators who progress through them.[8]

Professionalism

At one point or another, virtually all Americans receive services from professionals. Most of us are ignorant of the fundamental principles (much less the technical details) that professionals follow when providing their services. Aware of our own ignorance, we rely heavily upon educational credentials, licensure, and professional certification when buying professional services. When I have an illness or injury, I take comfort in seeing my doctor's Ivy League medical school diploma prominently displayed in his office and in seeing his name on a list of local board-certified physicians. Of course, like most patients, I have little idea of what happens in medical schools or why the University of Pennsylvania's is rated highly by *U.S. News and World Report*. I know next to nothing about how a physician becomes "board certified." But these credentials inspire confidence and make my doctor a more attractive physician than others who attended little-known medical schools and who lack board certification. Just so, most of us want to know that our lawyers, architects, and accountants received sound education in their fields and passed their licensure examinations. Professional schools, professional societies, and professional accreditation regimes—in short, professions themselves—exist in large part to provide signals of credibility to buyers in the market for knowledge-based service.

A patient's relationship with a doctor is a principal-agent relationship on one level, for the patient (principal) pays the doctor (agent) to provide a service. Insofar as the patient-doctor relationship is a principal-agent relationship, the patient expects the doctor to follow his instructions and prescribe the treatments that he prefers. On another level, a patient's relationship with a doctor is client-professional relationship, for the doctor's profession limits his willingness to follow the patient's instructions. A healthy patient who wishes to gain strength rapidly may ask for his doctor to prescribe anabolic steroids and human growth hormone. With his knowledge of medicine, he is likely to refuse the patient's request and instead prescribe a high-protein diet and an exercise regimen. But in addition to his concerns for his patient's health, the doctor is unlikely to comply with the patient's wishes for fear of criminal culpability and damage to his professional licensure and reputation —and thereby his ability to attract patients in the future. It is easy to imagine that the doctor's decision calculus might be different if his patient is the one and only patient he treats or ever will treat. Since he must consider his need to treat other patients in the future, the doctor's career concerns cause him to put his professional *principles* before the wishes of his patient-*principal*.[9]

Public administration professions operate similarly (Mosher 1968). Like a patient, a school board expects its superintendent (agent) to follow its orders, but also to offer advice and direction, and to apply her professional judgment over policy matters. Just so, presidents pick military chiefs of staff, governors pick state police commanders, mayors and city councils pick fire chiefs to follow orders in a principal-agent sense, but also to apply their own knowledge and training in a client-professional sense. A superintendent's willingness to follow a school board's directives depends in part on her professional judgment, but also on the extent to which she might want to work for another school district in the future.

Selection and Adaptation

When selecting an agency head, elected officials apply different criteria to candidates, depending on whether the organization promotes its top professional administrators from within or hires them from outside. The influence of professions and professional norms on the hiring process is strong when an organization hires an executive from outside. These processes and standards of professionalism are either less significant or absent when governments promote top administrators from within. For agencies promoting administrators from within, a reputation for predictability and adherence to local norms is more important than a professional reputation.

Meanwhile, bureaucrats ambitious for career advancement observe the behavior of those who successfully advance in a profession or organization, and then mimic this winning behavior. For an administrator who is "diagonally" ambitious for a job outside his current agency, adaptation means building a professional reputation, since credentials and a reputation for innovation are important selection criteria for higher-status agency heads. Professional administrators "are aware that their careers may be advanced if they are successful in terms of financial management and efficient administration," as Clingermayer and Feiock have argued. "Even if their accomplishments in these areas are not appreciated by their own city council, managers know that other city governments will be favorably impressed and may seek to hire them at higher salaries" (1997, 232). Meier and O'Toole's study of Texas school superintendent salaries confirms that effective management leads to higher public executive salaries (2002). On a diagonal career path, then, a bureaucrat seeks to introduce professionally fashionable policy innovations to her agency. For administrators seeking advancement within their current agencies, successful adaptation means building a reputation for adhering to organizational norms. I discuss the processes of government selection and administrators' adaptations further in chapter 4.

Motives

Professional bureaucrats, like all political actors, bring different motives to their jobs. Many political scientists despair of finding theoretically useful measures of utility, and so typically assume utilitarian goals for which political actors strive, such as election (Downs 1957), reelection (Mayhew 1974), budget maximizing (Niskanen 1971), or career advancement (Schlesinger 1966; Dewatripont, Jewitt, and Tirole 1999a). Applied universally, these assumptions depict a theoretical world populated by homogenous agents who are single-mindedly pursuing a universal goal. Authors of these theories usually admit that exceptions to such assumptions are many, but reason that their assumed goals hold true in the main, or at least that the implications of their assumptions are consistent with observed outcomes.

However, as noted in chapter 1, theories of bureaucratic political behavior that rely on assumptions of uniform, monotonic utility rest on shaky empirical soil. Moreover, models that assume budget maximizing (or any other goal, for that matter) as a universal aim cannot account for variation in bureaucrats' level of political activity under similar institutional conditions. These limitations have prompted some scholars to craft theoretical accounts for variation in individual administrators' "utility functions" by creating categories of bureaucrats. Gailmard and Patty (2007) classify bureaucrats as "slackers" or "zealots," and Downs (1967) offers a taxonomy of bureaucratic motivation that includes "climbers," "conservers," "zealots," "advocates," and "statesmen."

In this study I drill deeper still into the concept of utility. Beneath the level of an individual's proximate interests in specific political issues (e.g., budget maximizing or zeal for environmental protection), I argue that individuals are driven by motives embedded within their conscious and unconscious selves; that is, by their personalities. Theorizing about motives requires introducing a psychological dimension to this inquiry. To do so, I turn to Winter's (1978, 1996) three-dimension motive scheme, in which the achievement, affiliation, and power motives interact to drive behavior in organizational situations. Briefly, the three motives are:

Achievement—a concern for attaining a standard of excellence
Power—a concern for having an impact, control, or influence on others
Affiliation—a concern for establishing, maintaining, or restoring friendly
   relationships among people

These motives are stable psychological characteristics, but the situations in which individuals work may change the ways that motives affect behavior. I aim to show how motives translate into ambition for career advancement and political behavior.

In the public administration arena, individuals with strong achievement motivation may seek career advancement pursuant to or as a consequence of accomplishing excellent performance. A civil engineer with strong achievement motivation may seek progressively higher status positions in highway administration as a means of maximizing his ability to build more and better roads. Individuals with strong power motivation may seek career advancement in order to gain fame and/or authority over others. An engineer with strong power motivation might build more and better roads (or at least claim to have done so) as a means of attaining more visible and influential positions in highway administration.

Ambition for career advancement is a result of high levels of the achievement and/or power motives, though for different reasons: In the words of the old proverb, people high in the achievement motivation might "build a better mousetrap so that the world would beat a path to their door." In contrast, power-motivated people would try to get the world to come to their door without having to build the better mousetrap first (Winter 1996, 153).

The affiliation motive indicates a concern to establish and maintain close relationships with others, and is not directly associated with career ambition. It is possible that affiliation motivation causes some bureaucrats to forge stronger relationships with fellow professionals. However, taken alone, affiliation motivation is unlikely to drive ambition for career advancement among professional bureaucrats. I discuss human motivation and this three-motive scheme further in chapter 5.

By invoking personality psychology I do not mean to negate bureaucrats' free will. Good administrators are not divinely guided Joans of Arc, and bad administrators are not villainous Leopolds and Loebs, driven by desires beyond their control. Rather, as noted earlier, analysis of motives offers a means of drilling deeper into the "utility functions" that underlie administrators' rational political choices. Motives may operate at an unconscious level, but decisions that are rooted in motives remain just that: decisions. Hunger provides an apt analogy. I do not decide to be hungry; my physiological needs create the sensation of hunger when I have not eaten for several hours. But I decide rationally when and how to satiate my hunger. I may deliberate for hours over a choice of restaurant, carefully weighing cost, flavor, nutritional value, and caloric impact. Alternatively, I may carelessly reach for a bag of corn chips while reading a book. The former is a conscious process, the latter unconscious or semiconscious while my mind stays fixed on the book. In either case, the decision to eat is a rational response to my hunger. That decisions are not entirely conscious does not make them irrational. As Herbert Simon (1997) has argued, an individual's decision is rational if it is goal-oriented, whether or not it is the product of conscious, deliberative thought.

Ambition

Motives find traction in social settings: ambition occurs when the motivational rubber meets the opportunity road. In the present study, the individuals are public administrators and the social settings are professional job markets. I define *ambition* narrowly, in the sense of Schlesinger's (1966) "progressive ambition": a desire for career advancement to higher-status positions. As with my definition of *innovation*, this restricted definition of *ambition* differs from some common uses of the term, which in everyday language sometimes is used generically as a desire for any goal ("his ambition was to preach the Gospel"). *Ambition* also sometimes connotes a selfish, single-mindedness approaching malevolence ("fling away ambition: by that sin fell the angels!" wrote Shakespeare).[10] In this study, *ambition* refers only to a desire for career advancement, with no attendant pejorative.

There is a continuous spectrum of bureaucratic ambition; all professionals are more or less desirous of career advancement within an opportunity structure. In statistical terms, ambition is not a discrete, categorical variable, but rather continuously distributed. At one end of the ambition continuum are individuals with little or no desire to attain high job status; at the other end are individuals with very strong desire for high job status. Ambition in this sense is only partially observable in behavior: career advancement does not necessarily follow a desire for advancement as night follows day. An individual who occupies a top-tier job in her profession may have gained that position due to her ambitious pursuit of it. On the other hand, an individual might be highly ambitious but might not advance if the opportunity structure she faces does not allow her to advance. An ambitious female pilot would have had little chance of advancing to the upper echelons of U.S. Air Force administration in the 1960s, for example. Just so, a highly ambitious individual may fail to attain high status because he lacks other qualities that are required for advancement in his profession, such as social grace, intelligence, or good health. Meanwhile, an individual without great ambition might gain a high-status job by accident or nepotism.

Human motivation is not the only force that affects career ambition. Administrators' perceptions of their ability to advance in their opportunity structures, too, can affect ambition. Administrators may perceive their gender, age, race, or other attributes as either beneficial or detrimental to their odds of advancement and therefore may strengthen or temper their ambition.

Ambition and Policy Entrepreneurship

Administrators adapt to the career-opportunity structures in which they work, and their policymaking decisions reflect their career interests. As observed at the beginning of this chapter, administrators in the political arena face two related decisions. First, the bureaucrat must decide what policies to pursue in his agency. Second, the bureaucrat must decide how vigorously to advocate for policy innovations. The theory advanced here addresses both of these decisions.

Which Policies to Advance?

I argue that when making political decisions, ambitious administrators will introduce policies that are rewarded by the labor markets in which they work. Governments that hire executives from outside provide diagonal advancement opportunities for bureaucrats with reputations for professional innovation and give their outside hires tacit (and occasionally overt) license to innovate. Diagonally ambitious bureaucrats seek to be attractive to other governments, especially larger, more prestigious and rewarding governments (Dewatripont, Jewitt, and Tirole 1999b). For this reason, ambitious bureaucrats may have reason to minimize budgets as a means of developing reputations for efficiency (Young 1991; Campbell and Naulls 1991), rather than maximizing their budgets as principal-agent models typically assume. The bureaucrat with diagonal ambition will cultivate a professional reputation and will seek to associate herself with innovative policies that would be attractive to higher-status employers. Indeed, association with failure at the *"right"* policy (e.g., community policing for a police chief) may be better for a diagonally ambitious administrator than success with the *"wrong"* policies (e.g., racial profiling). Ramp-climbing public administrators take risks in pursuit of policy changes because "even if they failed in their new job, they might expect to go on to even better jobs elsewhere, provided only that they failed for the right reason—that is, failed while striving to attain some goal that was approved of by their profession," observes James Q. Wilson in *Bureaucracy*. "For such executives, nothing succeeds like failure" (229–30).

The ambitious and diagonally mobile administrator recalls the bureaucratic champions of progressive policies with generalized benefit that are described in Alford's *Bureaucracy and Participation* (1969) and Schneider, Teske, and Mintrom's *Public Entrepreneurs* (1995). Fluoridation of drinking water is one such policy, and fluoridation is championed by public health and public utilities administrators, with the encouragement of their most important professional organizations (Alford 1969). Schneider, Teske, and Mintrom cite Paul Leonard, the borough manager of Perkasie, Pennsylvania, as a "public entrepreneur" for his simultaneous introduction of trash disposal fees and curbside recycling (1995). Leonard's high-profile, aggressive initiation of these policies in a small town (Perkasie's population was 6,200 at the time) built his reputation as an innovator. Leonard's exploits in Perkasie landed the tiny town on the front page of the *Wall Street Journal* (158). Apparently Leonard's reputation building has been fruitful in career terms: since the 1995 publication of *Public Entrepreneurs*, he has moved on from Perkasie to become assistant manager of North Miami Beach, Florida (population 42,000), and then manager of Upper Dublin Township, Pennsylvania (population 26,000).

Atop a vertical career-opportunity structure, a bureaucrat in a mezzo-level position has little or no room to advance and so will have little reason to build a reputation for innovation. Bureaucrats leading vertical public agencies will not be strongly interested in professional innovations. Regardless of their career paths, low-ambition bureaucrats are less likely to pursue professional innovations than their more ambitious peers are. Meanwhile, less ambitious administrators can be more faithful agents to their elected principals than their more ambitious peers because they have less incentive for loyalty to their external professional communities.

How Hard to Push?

By definition, bureaucratic policy entrepreneurs incur costs in pursuit of innovation, including time away from routine administrative duties and personal interests. When she enters the policymaking arena, the bureaucrat also risks alienating her elected superiors, which can weaken her future efforts to influence policy, may cost her perquisites of employment, or, in serious cases, her job.

I argue that administrators consider—albeit unconsciously, perhaps—the benefit of a public policy in terms of the impact that the policy will have on their careers. Administrators with low ambition value the benefits of their current posts greatly and discount greatly the benefit of building their reputations for potential future positions. Hence, a low-ambition bureaucrat perceives little benefit from policy innovation in the absence of some external pressure to innovate. Low-ambition bureaucrats perceive benefits from policy advocacy only to the extent that participation will preserve their current jobs. An ambitious agency head tends to discount the value of her current position relative to potential future jobs and so perceives significant advantages in building her reputation through innovation. A critical point here is that a highly ambitious bureaucrat may foresee a benefit from policy change even in the absence of or an overt demand for change, whereas a less ambitious one may not.

How much benefit or harm an innovation can bring to a bureaucrat's career depends on the career-opportunity structure that he faces. If an administrator's profession offers many opportunities for advancement outside his current agency and favors professional innovation, then he stands to gain quite a lot from successful policy advocacy. If the bureaucrat's career opportunity structure offers few opportunities for advancement, or if the bureaucrat's advancement prospects bear little relationship to innovation (as in a pure seniority-based system), then she is unlikely to gain much benefit from innovation. Administrators who are approaching retirement have less to gain, and perhaps more to lose, as a result of innovation. Administrators' personal circumstances may affect their costs and risks of policy advocacy. Demotion or dismissal is costlier to individuals for whom movement to another community is undesirable (Green 1989; Nalbandian 1991). Administrators who have no immediate family and few or no personal ties to a community perceive less cost. Similarly, administrators who have working spouses, children, or strong social ties to a community may discount the benefit to be gained from promotion if promotion might require a significant geographic move.

Figure 3.1 depicts graphically this model of bureaucratic political advocacy. In this graph the vertical axis represents the perceived career utility of advocacy; the horizontal axis represents the level of advocacy that a bureaucrat undertakes pursuant to some innovation. A marginal cost (MC) of advocacy is graphed across the range of advocacy from lesser to greater. Two marginal-benefit (MB) curves are depicted in each graph, one for a bureaucrat who has high ambition and another for one with low ambition.

Figure 3.1 assumes a reasonably open career-opportunity structure with multiple employers and featuring diagonal, "ramped" professional advancement—perhaps the U.S. market for public school district superintendents. In this graph, the marginal cost of political advocacy is depicted as upward sloping, with an increasing slope. This shape of the MC curve suggests that both the direct costs (time, energy) and the risk of job loss increase as advocacy increases. The two MB curves represent the benefits of policy advocacy perceived by administrators with high and low ambition. For the less ambitious administrator, the MB_{low} line is low and flat, since the benefits of policy advocacy in this situation are limited to this bureaucrat's current job; this administrator attaches little value to the potential gains from advancement in the profession. The more ambitious bureaucrat's MB_{high} line initially slopes steeply upward, but then slopes downward at higher levels of political advocacy. This line suggests that the high-ambition bureaucrat perceives significant benefits to be gained by reputation building, though with diminishing returns at very high levels of advocacy, perhaps reflecting a concern for being branded a zealot.

The bureaucrats depicted in figure 3.1 will engage in political advocacy if the marginal benefit of participation is greater than its marginal cost. A highly ambitious bureaucrat is relatively active, engaging in policymaking to the point where $MC = MB_{high}$. Some degree of political advocacy is probably inevitable even for bureaucrats with low ambition, and so in figure 3.1, MB_{low} is greater than MC at very low levels of political advocacy. However, MC slopes upward at higher levels of political advocacy, so MB_{low} lies below MC at most of the range advocacy in the figure.

Exogenous forces can cause the benefits and costs of political advocacy to shift up and down across the range of the profession. A major security crisis

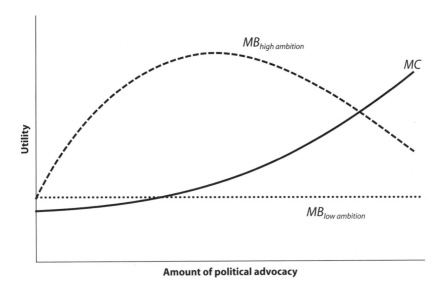

Figure 3.1 Ambition and policymaking activity
"Utility" means happiness or satisfaction that a bureaucratic agency head enjoys at various levels of political advocacy.

like the terrorist attacks of September 11, 2001, could provide a vast, new, multifaceted political resource for bureaucrats, particularly those heading agencies related to public safety and health, such as law enforcement, fire protection, emergency medical services, public health, and utilities. Administrators of these agencies in the immediate postcrisis environment might find it easier to mobilize citizens and interest groups and they might have less difficulty in getting their proposals on the legislative agenda (Birkland 1997; Kingdon 1984). In a federal system, changes in policy at other levels of government can also affect the costs and benefits of political advocacy for a bureaucrat (Posner 1998; Manna 2006). A crisis or change in policies at other levels of government could reduce the cost of political advocacy for an agency head. Such a downward shift in *MC* is illustrated in figure 3.2, a revision of figure 3.1. Similarly, fiscal stress or another threat to an agency can increase the perceived benefits of political advocacy for its administrator. For example, city administrators facing a fiscal crisis and potential takeover from a state or county government would stand to gain more by introducing revenue-generating programs, such as user fees, than they would under normal or

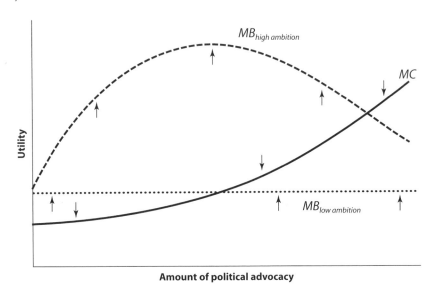

Figure 3.2 Shifting costs and benefits
"Utility" means happiness or satisfaction that a bureaucratic agency head enjoys at various levels of political advocacy.

prosperous conditions. This upward shift in the *MB* curves is illustrated in figure 3.2. The consequence of the shifts in figure 3.2 is higher levels of policy advocacy among low- and high-ambition bureaucrats alike.

A bureaucrat's ambition fuels political advocacy only if there are higher-status jobs available to him. Bureaucrats at the beginning or middle of their professional careers and those leading small or medium-sized agencies may have many years of potential advancement at stake in policy matters. Administrators holding high-status jobs have fewer potential job destinations that offer still higher status. As a bureaucrat's career progresses there are fewer and fewer advancement alternatives, so the potential career payoff for political advocacy falls as a bureaucrat's job status increases. The influence of ambition on bureaucratic political advocacy falls as job status increases due to the declining career benefits of political action for high-status bureaucrats. Meanwhile, normal day-to-day work for agency heads in large governments requires a significant degree of policy advocacy, even for the less ambitious. Therefore, in positions with very high status the disparity in political advocacy between ambitious bureaucrats and their less-ambitious brethren shrinks.

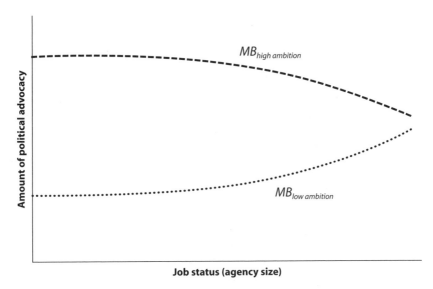

Figure 3.3 Declining influence of ambition on political action

Figure 3.3 illustrates graphically the attenuation of ambition's effect on political action as bureaucratic job status increases.

Advancement

Because of governments' selection practices and individuals' adaptation, different kinds of bureaucrats tend to advance in different opportunity structures. I argue that, in public administration professions that have multiple government employers, the pool of bureaucrats will not be a representative sample of the regional population but rather will be homogenous in ways relevant to bureaucratic work (e.g., education, experience, psychological profile). Career opportunity structures thus act as "filters," systematically promoting certain types of administrators to high-status posts and holding down or eliminating others from the profession. The kinds of individuals that secure significant policymaking roles within a particular government bureaucracy therefore depend on the dominant pattern of career advancement for that government.

Bureaucrats adapt to their career systems by seeking organizations in which they can best attain career success, given their personalities. Individuals with strong achievement motivation are more likely to advance in diagonal opportunity structures than in vertical opportunity structures. The achievement motive reflects a concern for excellence, and so achievement-motivated bureaucrats are more likely to promote innovations that diagonal opportunity structures reward through selection. Vertical opportunity-structures may frustrate achievement-motivated individuals to the extent that these opportunity structures may select longevity, shrewdness, and "playing by the rules" over innovation. Achievement-motivated individuals may adapt to such circumstances by leaving for other organizations or professions.

Either diagonal or vertical opportunity structures will allow advancement for individuals with high power motivation. The power motive reflects a concern for influence or impact on others. Movement to large, high-status jobs may satisfy this concern for influence and impact, whether the administrator arrives at his post vertically or diagonally. However, governments that routinely promote from within will select individuals who adhere to local preferences and thrive in hierarchical organizations. In the absence of strong achievement motivation, power-motivated individuals will seek out and remain in such vertical career opportunity structures because they satisfy the power motive without a need for professional innovation. As Winter (1996) might put it, a vertical opportunity structure allows the power-motivated bureaucrat to exercise authority without having to "build a better mousetrap."

Broad patterns of bureaucratic policy entrepreneurship develop as individuals advance (or fail to advance) through these opportunity structures. Where many diagonal advancement opportunities exist, achievement-motivated bureaucrats are likely to advance by advocating for professional innovations. Where advancement opportunities are few or primarily within the bureaucrat's current government, power-motivated bureaucrats are likely to advance by adhering to organizational norms with relatively little professional innovation. In short, diagonal mobility fosters entrepreneurship, while vertical advancement inhibits it.

Public administration career-opportunity structures are not organic phenomena but rather consequences of synthetic rules and customs. That opportunity structures so affect the psychological composition of governments' executive ranks implies that bureaucratic policy entrepreneurship is partly a consequence of institutional design. In other words, through government agency design, hiring, and promotional policies, it is possible to exert some control over the vigor of political advocacy and the character of policies that emerge from the executive ranks of public agencies.

Hypotheses

A few key hypotheses follow from the theory elaborated here. These hypotheses will guide the analyses in the chapters that follow.

Hypothesis 1: Bureaucrats on diagonal career paths (who arrived to their current positions from outside) are more likely to initiate professional innovations than are bureaucrats atop vertical career paths (who were promoted to their current positions from within).

Hypothesis 1 relates career path to professional innovation and is investigated in chapter 4. If governments hire agency executives on the basis of their reputations, then we might expect (as presumably those employers do) bureaucrats to continue pursuing similarly innovative policies in their new agencies. Hypothesis 1 is purely institutional, as it relates agencies' personnel policies and professional career paths to innovation.

Hypothesis 2a: Bureaucrats' policymaking activity increases as their ambition increases. That is, a bureaucrat's policymaking activity increases as his or her achievement and/or power motive increases.
Hypothesis 2b: The influence of ambition on bureaucrats' policymaking activity falls as job status increases. That is, the difference in political activity between more and less ambitious bureaucrats shrinks as job status increases.

Hypotheses 2a and 2b, explored in chapter 5, introduce a psychological dimension to the investigation. In identifying ambition as a variable, these hypotheses imply that individuals gain different degrees of utility from career advancement. Ambitious bureaucrats expend more energy on policymaking and take risks in order to hone a policy reputation. Hypothesis 2b posits declining returns to political advocacy as bureaucrats advance to higher status jobs (depicted graphically in figure 3.3). "The man with progressive ambitions is the hero," as Joseph Schlesinger (1996) observed. "If anyone is going to search for solutions, it is the man whose career depends on finding solutions" (209). Hypotheses 2a and 2b may lack Schlesinger's flair, but they recapitulate his claim.

Hypothesis 3a: A bureaucrat's probability of career advancement in a diagonal opportunity structure increases as his or her achievement motivation increases.

Hypothesis 3b: A bureaucrat's probability of career advancement in a vertical opportunity structure increases as his or her power motivation increases.

Hypotheses 3a and 3b depict bureaucratic career opportunity structures as personality filters that systematically favor some motive profiles over others. Together with the other hypotheses, hypotheses 3a and 3b imply that different career-opportunity structures tend to channel different kinds of individuals to positions of influence, that these individuals advocate more or less ardently, and that these individuals promote different kinds of policies. Chapter 6 takes up these two hypotheses.

Investigating Ambition

Evaluating these claims about bureaucratic ambition requires gathering data on individual administrators' career paths, political activity, and motives. To that end I employ a survey of local public administrators in two local government professions: law enforcement and water utilities. By studying these two very different professions I seek to demonstrate the theory's validity across substantive policy areas. I chose to survey police chiefs and water utility managers because these professions are ubiquitous throughout the United States. Data from this survey allow flexible statistical analysis of relationships between many variables of interest in this study. The sampling strategy and administration of the survey were intended to maximize its validity and generalizability within cost and time constraints. Here I outline the study's survey methodology in very broad terms. Appendix A relates additional details on sampling methodology.

Sampling

The survey's sampling frame was defined for each profession using U.S. federal government catalogues of local government agencies. The survey employed a stratified sampling method to draw representative data from agencies of many sizes. A great majority of American local government agencies are very small and serve small proportions of the total U.S. population; hence, a simple random sample would likely offer little data on large and medium-sized governments. Since large and medium-sized governments serve the majority of the U.S. population, stratifying to ensure their inclusion in the sample is important for drawing conclusions about the nation as a whole (Dziegielewski and Opitz 2004). The very smallest police and water agencies were excluded from the frame because they serve very small proportions of the U.S. population and require very limited administrative and policymaking responsibilities of their agency heads. Moreover, many of these very small agencies are "semiprofessional," in some cases operated by volunteers. For police, agencies employing fewer than three full-time sworn officers were excluded. Also excluded were water utility systems serving populations below 3,300. While these very small agencies compose a substantial share of the total agencies in each profession, collectively they serve a very small share of the total U.S. population. Stratification also ensured that data are gathered from agencies occupying every stratum of these professions. Weights are applied in the analytical phases of the study as appropriate to correct for the nonrandomness introduced by the stratification process.

To gain maximum generalizability with limited resources, this survey emphasized response rate and measurement validity rather than a large sample size. When the sample is properly randomized, a smaller sample size with a high response rate reduces the risk of nonresponse bias that can occur in large sample surveys with poor response rates (Groves et al. 2004). Moreover, because I contacted each respondent directly, I can be confident that the respondents were the agency heads themselves and that the questionnaires were not simply passed off to other employees. This element of the study design is critical since understanding the behavior of individual agency heads is central to this research. The result is a relatively small dataset that offers a high degree of sampling confidence and measurement validity. My aim with this "medium-N" approach is to give the reader confidence that the study's findings are robust—conventional sensibilities about statistical power notwithstanding.

Instrument

Similar survey instruments were developed for each profession. For water utility managers, the instrument was an Internet-based questionnaire. For police chiefs, the survey included a brief telephone interview and an Internet-based questionnaire. The telephone portion of the police survey included two psychological probes to capture motivational data (discussed further in chapter 5). With the exception of the psychological probes, the survey was designed to capture behavioral data, rather than attitudes or opinions. In focus-

Figure 3.4 Geographic distribution of survey respondents
Each dot represents one survey respondent (dots randomly distributed within state).

ing on what respondents did or planned to do during a proximate period, the survey captured administrators' political decisions, not their attitudes on various policies or their ideas about the political role of administrators in their positions.[11] The instrument also directly asked about respondents' career paths, current and past jobs, and family circumstances, rather than asking respondents to report the relative importance of each of these variables in their decision making. By asking about respondents' concrete circumstances and actual behavior during recent events, these questions help avoid nonattitudes, motivated misreporting, and other cognitive effects that question wording can have on attitudinal reporting. The survey instrument is discussed further in chapters 4 and 5.

Response

The overall response rate to the survey was 50.3 percent. Responses were well distributed by size across the sample, providing good representation for small, medium, and large agencies. Responses also were well distributed geographically, though administrators from Midwestern agencies responded at higher rates and those from Northeastern agencies at somewhat lower rates.[12] Figure 3.4 shows the general geographic distribution of survey respondents.

Ambition and Bureaucratic Politics

As a professional in a labor market, a bureaucrat ultimately serves two masters: the employer that pays her salary today and the universe of employers who might potentially pay her salary in the future. I have argued that, to the extent that she is ambitious, a bureaucrat will tend to value the latter over the former. As Albert Hirschman (1970) argued, the availability of an exit alternative fundamentally changes the decision logic of a political actor. On diagonal career paths, bureaucrats tend to emphasize their professional principles in their political behavior, while those on vertical career paths seek to satisfy their elected principals. By the same token, governments that hire administrators from outside select on the basis of professional reputation and so seek professional expertise (principle) over strict accountability (principal).

I have also argued that ambition fuels bureaucratic political advocacy. Ambition determines the utility that a bureaucrat gains from advocacy and so causes him to seek or avoid risks in the political arena. Strong achievement and/or power motivation drives greater bureaucratic political advocacy: these motives are the psychological wellsprings of ambition.

Taken together over time, these two claims about bureaucratic ambition imply that career-opportunity structures systematically favor some kinds of bureaucrats over others. Greater political advocacy in pursuit of professional innovation is rewarded with an increased probability of movement to higher-status agencies that offer diagonal advancement opportunities. Advocacy and innovation are less important for advancement in vertical opportunity structures. Over time, patterns of political action from the bureaucracy develop: more politically active, more innovative, but less accountable administrators show up in diagonal organizations and less active, less innovative, but more accountable administrators are to be found in vertical organizations. In the chapters that follow I evaluate this theory empirically and consider its implications for democratic governance in an age of professionalized public administration.

CHAPTER FOUR

The Market for Bureaucratic Entrepreneurs

Career Path and Professional Innovation

> When I became chief my top priority was CALEA accreditation. . . . We open ourselves up for inspection from an independent body, which comes and looks at everything we do, from the logos on our police cars to how we handle evidence and complaints. In our city it's a very diverse community. We've had strained relationships with the minority community. I thought that this would be one way of sending a signal that we are open, transparent, and that we conform to national and international standards for community policing.
>
> CHIEF OF A LARGE CITY POLICE DEPARTMENT PLANNING TO
> LOOK FOR ANOTHER JOB WITHIN FIVE YEARS

> I don't really have any specific proposals planned for the council this year. I guess my goal for the next twelve months is to get by and make the best of it.
>
> CHIEF OF ANOTHER LARGE CITY POLICE DEPARTMENT PLANNING
> TO RETIRE WITHIN FIVE YEARS

Policy entrepreneurship occurs when an individual introduces a policy in-novation that satisfies some public demand. Like their commercial coun-terparts, policy entrepreneurs must assume some costs or takes some risk in pursuit of innovation with the expectation of some future payoff. For business entrepreneurs, the payoff is clear: commercial innovators emerge in a market to capture profits. Entrepreneurial elected officials who champion policy in-novations may seek reelection or election to higher office. The "profits" avail-able to an entrepreneurial public administrator are less clear. Indeed, the very idea of "bureaucratic ambition" seems almost oxymoronic in light of the common depiction of bureaucrats as impersonal, myopic, rule-bound satisficers. Classic Weberian bureaucratic organization is in fact supposed to ensure compliance with rules, roles, hierarchical accountability, and standard operating procedures (Weber 1978). Bureaucratic policy entrepreneurs risk sanction, including possible removal, if they deviate from organizational norms or pursue policies disfavored by their elected superiors. With their livelihoods on the line and families relying on them, bureaucrats have ample disincentives to initiate innovations without prompting from their elected masters. It is hardly surprising that the stereotypical bureaucrat is conservative and risk-averse, for public administrators seem unlikely candidates to emerge as policy entrepreneurs.

Yet many do. Despite the costs and risks, professional public administrators are among those whom scholars of the policy process identify as policy entrepreneurs most frequently. For better or for worse, working with or around or against their elected officials, many bureaucratic policy entrepreneurs are successful innovators. Others are sanctioned or fired for their efforts, as the cases in chapter 2 illustrate. Why do some administrators take such risks in the name of innovation, sometimes even in the face of explicit opposition by interest groups and elected officials? Why do others proceed more cautiously and forego opportunities for innovation?

This chapter explains how government hiring and promotional practices encourage or inhibit bureaucratic policy entrepreneurship and professional innovation. Analysis of American police chiefs and water utility managers shows that administrators' career paths predict their introductions of professional innovations to their agencies. I also examine a familiar alternative hypothesis along the way: that bureaucrats' professional socialization, not career path, explains the adoption of professional innovations. The picture that emerges is mobile bureaucrats as something like professional policy pollinators, bringing innovations from profession to governments as they move from one to another.

Bureaucratic Mobility and the Market for Innovation

Bureaucratic jobs form when a government employer offers to pay an individual for her services and that individual accepts the job. The set of all governments and all individuals offering services form a market for professional bureaucratic labor. For the individuals seeking employment, the marketplace offers varying salaries, perquisites, and prestige. For governments looking to hire bureaucrats, the marketplace offers varying degrees of professional expertise and innovation. I argued in the last chapter that governments'

hiring and promotional practices create opportunity structures in which bureaucrats may advance. Opportunities that involve moving from one government to another tend to reward individuals with favorable professional reputations. Professional reputations are not so important where advancement
opportunities are predominantly within an agency. Ambitious administrators
adapt to these conditions by pursuing (or not pursuing) professionally fashionable innovations. In this way, bureaucratic labor markets are markets for
professional innovation. Bureaucratic policy entrepreneurs are most likely to
emerge where government demand for innovation meets a supply of mobile,
professional administrators.

Selection

When selecting a chief bureaucrat, elected officials apply different criteria
to candidates depending on whether the candidates are internal or external
and whether the organization typically promotes from within or hires from
the outside. In general purpose municipal governments like cities, towns and
counties, agency heads are hired by the mayor, legislative council, or city
manager. In special purpose governments like school districts and utility districts, the elected board or commission hires its chief executive. The elected
officials or governing boards of these governments are buyers of bureaucratic
labor. When shopping for their agency heads, some governments routinely
hire from outside the organization, some routinely promote from within, and
some use each approach from time to time.

The influence of professions and professional norms on the hiring process is particularly strong when the organization hires a chief executive from
outside (Carlson 1961; Rosenthal and Crain 1968; Wilson 1989). In most cases
elected officials have only minimal knowledge of the fields for which they are
hiring administrators. Like the patient who looks for a board-certified, Johns
Hopkins–educated surgeon, elected officials use professional credentials and
reputation as signals of job candidates' qualifications for administrative positions. Local governments hiring agency executives from outside their organizations typically hire executive search consultants who specialize in the professions at hand (Ammons and Glass 1988).[1] In the process of researching this
book I observed the hiring processes of a number of local governments looking for chief executives from outside, including two cities recruiting chiefs for
their police departments, two school districts searching for new superintendents, and a large utility hiring a general manager. These governments em-

ployed executive search consultants, who were themselves former police chiefs, school superintendents, and a civil engineer, respectively. These search consultants were central to the recruitment and hiring processes: they helped identify candidates and vetted them for qualifications. The search consultants were deeply involved in crafting job descriptions and in narrowing the initial field of applicants to a smaller pool of candidates. Perhaps more significantly, the search consultants worked directly with the search committees and elected officials who made the ultimate hiring decisions. In this way the consultants were influential in framing issues and establishing evaluative criteria (Schall 1997b). Elected officials relied heavily on the advice of their search consultants and the candidates' credentials and reputations. Recommendations from fellow professionals figured significantly in the selection process, as did media accounts of the candidates' work in their former governments.

A professional reputation earned through higher education, accreditation, and past work experience is thus especially important for external candidates. As an architect relies on his advanced degree and portfolio of designs to win new and bigger clients, so a public administrator who is seeking to move from one agency to another must rely on the "portfolio" of policies that she has proposed, developed, and administered to secure higher status jobs. Professionally innovative administrators, like innovative architects, will be appealing to higher status employers. Architects and administrators who are known for thrift and efficiency are more likely to advance than those who consistently exceed budgets and come to their clients with repeated requests for additional funds. By the same token, professional reputations can stymie career advancement: if an architect's designs are considered passé or too radical by his peers he will have trouble winning big contracts; if an administrator's policies and practices are widely considered obsolete or fanatical by her peers, she will not easily advance to higher status posts. A severely damaged reputation can block career advancement entirely: a disastrous structural failure can ruin an architect's career, and an abject, high-profile policy failure can ruin a public administrator's career.

Cultivating a favorable professional reputation therefore requires compliance with the profession's contemporary sensibilities. In this sense, building a professional reputation means pleasing professional peers, not necessarily pleasing any one client or "pushing the envelope" with radical policies and practices. Truly pioneering bureaucrats may advocate for policies so novel that their professions have not yet recognized their innovations, but may to herald them as admirable in the future. For example, a police chief I interviewed as part of this study mentioned plans to deploy military-style unmanned aerial drones for neighborhood surveillance in his city. This technology was "on the cutting edge," he told me, and though unmanned surveillance drones were not yet used by American police departments to his knowledge, he was certain that they would become commonplace over the next twenty years. Such a policy might be innovative, but it is not a *professional* innovation inasmuch as the law enforcement profession at large has not yet embraced unmanned aerial surveillance drones as a favored policy or practice.

Professional societies' slates of favored policies are not static, but rather reflect the dominant sensibilities of the times. Professional groups evolve in their positions about important issues, sometimes radically. In 1943 the National Association of Real Estate Boards (NAREB) encouraged its member real estate agents to reinforce racial segregation in housing (Burns 1994, 55); in 2005, the Code of Ethics of the National Association of Realtors (formerly NAREB) explicitly prohibits racial discrimination by its members (NAR 2005, 4). Similar shifts abound in public administration professions. Prior to the 1980s, for example, the American Water Works Association (AWWA) manual of practices on setting water rates discouraged the use of pricing as a means of managing demand or promoting resource conservation (AWWA 1972). Facing changing financial, environmental and regulatory conditions, AWWA has changed its tune: the 2000 edition of its manual of practice devotes five chapters to conservation rate design (AWWA 2000). Employers and administrators alike look to such shifts as a means of identifying important and progressive policies. Vetted by regional and national professional organizations, professionally trendy policies are likely to appeal to a broad local government "clientele." Governments hiring professional administrators from outside will tend to favor candidates who adhere to predominant professional norms, and who apply the favored policies of the profession in their agencies. While it is certainly possible that an individual may be promoted from within a government with the expectation of initiating changes, external hiring explicitly or implicitly suggests a demand for innovation (Carlson 1961), and so local governments scrutinize applicants through the prism of professionalism when they hire from outside.

These processes and standards of professionalism are either absent or less significant when elected officials promote mezzo-level administrators from within. A search consultant is not necessary to identify or vet internal candidates. References and recommendations also are not essential for internal promotions. An internal candidate is a "known commodity" and so elected officials need not rely on outsiders' assessments of his or her quality. Agencies with a custom of hiring executives from within the organization almost certainly have fewer candidates for the job—perhaps only one. I interviewed several chiefs of police serving in vertical organizations who described their efforts to identify potential future chiefs among the lower level officers in their departments. In many public organizations, grooming a successor is part of an agency head's job. Senior administrators in line to become agency heads are identified early—sometimes several years in advance—and given assignments in posts throughout the organization in order to "give them a thorough understanding of the way we do things," as one chief of police told me. This years-long process of inculcating and socializing candidates for advancement creates loyalties to existing norms, and so strengthens organizational hierarchy (Kaufman 1960). Hiring an agency head is a virtually automatic process in some organizations: the next school superintendent is simply whoever the deputy superintendent is today (Carlson 1961). Administrators selected through such internal promotional processes generally arrive at the agency head position through adherence to agency norms and local sensibilities; professional reputation is not so important (Schall 1997a).

Adaptation

As governments set and adjust their standards and processes for selecting agency heads, a simultaneous adaptation process occurs among public administrators. Bureaucrats ambitious for career advancement observe the behavior of those who successfully "get ahead" in a profession or organization and then mimic this winning behavior (March and March 1977). For the diagonally ambitious, adaptation means building a professional reputation pursuant to higher-status jobs (DiMaggio and Powell 1983). A bureaucrat who seeks career advancement via movement to another government will be very active in her profession and will seek to introduce professionally fashionable innovations to her agency.

An administrator who was hired from outside arrives with a perceived mandate for innovation, her hiring having been due in part to her reputation for professionalism. Governments may select external candidates precisely because they are likely to bring change to their agencies (Carlson 1961; Wilson

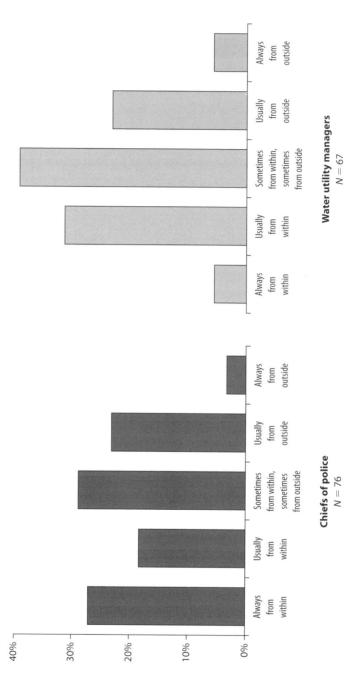

Figure 4.1 Agency administrator hiring practices

Reported history of hiring practices for agency head position, poststratification weighted by agency size.

1989). Moreover, the possibility of finding a job in another agency gives an administrator a degree of security because loss of his current job does not necessarily mean the end of his professional career. For administrators not interested in potential movement to a job in another government, adaptation means adhering to organizational norms (Kaufman 2006). A bureaucrat who has advanced vertically within an organization and who is not seeking job options elsewhere is not so interested in pursuing professionally innovative policies and likely has no specific mandate for innovation.

If internal promotions are endorsements of existing organizational norms, values, and practices, then it follows that a *principal-agent* relationship between elected officials and bureaucrats is likely to hold where agency heads are promoted from within. Meanwhile, a *client-professional* relationship— and perhaps bureaucratic policy entrepreneurship—is likely to emerge under conditions of bureaucratic job mobility. Mobile administrators will carry professionally fashionable innovations where they go; hence, those on diagonal career paths (who arrived at their current positions from outside) are more likely to initiate professional innovations than are bureaucrats atop vertical career paths (who were promoted to their current positions from within).

A variety of career paths are available to police chiefs and water utility managers, but the career opportunity structures available in municipal law enforcement and water utility management are quite different, as the survey results on agency hiring and promotional practices displayed in figure 4.1 indicate.[2] Advancement to agency head status in police departments is more vertical than it is in water utilities, with 45.3 percent of respondents' agencies "always" or "usually" promoting the chief of police from within the organization, compared with 35.2 percent for the more normally distributed water utilities. Twenty-seven percent of police chiefs reported that their agencies always promote the chief from within. The rest of this chapter analyzes the ways that differences in police chiefs' and water utility managers' career paths affect their introduction of professional innovations to their agencies. The public administration professions examined here are quite different in function and organization, and I analyze innovation in each profession separately.

Police Agency Accreditation

Professionalism in the bureaucracy means, in part, accountability to an external group of peers. Forty years ago, James Q. Wilson (1968) declared in a

Public Administration Review article that municipal law enforcement was not a "profession" because there was no recognized external group of practitioners that provided standards of practice for police officers. Police work was a "craft," or perhaps a "guild," argued Wilson, because officers were accountable first and foremost to their fellow officers *within* their agencies. In the wake of the civil rights era, however, reformers sought to professionalize U.S. local law enforcement. Policing has evolved considerably in the decades since: several professional organizations, state and national programs, and educational institutions were established in the 1970s to transform police work into a profession (Staufenberger 1977). These efforts culminated when a coalition of law-enforcement professional societies formed the Commission on Accreditation for Law Enforcement Agencies (CALEA) in 1979.

Accreditation through CALEA requires police agencies voluntarily to adopt a comprehensive set of standards, practices, and plans developed by the commission. To secure accreditation, agencies must comply with the procedures laid out in CALEA's *Standards for Law Enforcement Agencies* (2006b). Accreditation entails developing and adopting more than four hundred written policies and procedures. Developing and adopting these procedures typically takes several months of "self-assessment" led by senior officers in the agency seeking accreditation. The accreditation process continues with an on-site assessment of the applicant agency by panel of outside experts appointed by CALEA. Finally, the commission reviews the self-assessment and outside assessments before granting a three-year accreditation. CALEA accredited its first agency in 1984, and the number of agencies accredited by CALEA has grown steadily since then. In 2009, 741 law-enforcement agencies in the United States were CALEA-accredited, and another 214 were in the process of seeking accreditation.[3] Several U.S. state governments also now offer state-level accreditation programs similar to but separate from CALEA.

CALEA characterizes its accreditation program this way:

> The overall purpose of the commission's accreditation program is to improve delivery of law enforcement service by offering a body of standards, developed by law enforcement practitioners, covering a wide range of up-to-date law enforcement topics. It recognizes professional achievements by offering an orderly process for addressing and complying with applicable standards. Successful completion of the accreditation program requires commitment from all

levels of the organization, *starting with the chief executive officer.* To foster commitment, a decision to participate should be voluntary. (CALEA 2006a; italics added)

Observing the ways that organizations like CALEA were providing external standards of ethics and practice for police departments, Wilson, who in 1968 had declared municipal policing to be not professional, recognized it as a profession in his 1989 book *Bureaucracy.*

A handful of studies have sought to gauge the impact of CALEA accreditation on the police department policies and outcomes. The results of these studies are mixed. Burlingame and Baro (2005) found that CALEA-accredited police departments employ higher percentages of female officers than non-accredited agencies. Giblin (2006) found that CALEA-accredited agencies are more likely to have crime-analysis units than nonaccredited agencies, and he attributes the difference directly to the professionalizing influence of CALEA. However, McCabe and Fajardo (2001) found very few significant performance differences between accredited and nonaccredited police departments and no differences in the racial or gender compositions of accredited and nonaccredited agencies. Similarly, Alpert and MacDonald (2001) found that accreditation had no effect on the frequency of police use of force incidents. In short, CALEA appears to offer some potential benefits for law enforcement, but the connection between accreditation and performance is tenuous. Moreover, for forty-five dollars anyone may purchase CALEA's *Standards for Law Enforcement Agencies,* and any agency can adopt CALEA's specified policies without pursuing accreditation or engaging with CALEA at all. If the point of accreditation is simply to adopt the leading policies of the law-enforcement profession, then any agency might adopt all of the ostensibly beneficial policies that come with CALEA accreditation without bearing the costs of the accreditation process. Why, then, would a sensible police chief bother with accreditation?

Observing this puzzle, other scholars have considered CALEA as an organizational or political outcome—an effect, rather than a cause. Mastrofski (1986) suggested that accreditation is more symbol and ritual than substance and that the decision to seek accreditation is driven by police administrators' desire to "wrap themselves in the cloak of professionalism" (72). Sykes (1994) argued that police administrators seek CALEA accreditation to affirm their existing policies, rather than to drive innovation in their agencies. Carter and Sapp (1994) found that police chiefs seeking agency accreditation mention recognition from peers and the public and higher status in the law-enforcement communities as reasons for pursuing accreditation. Similarly, Hougland's (2004) survey of administrators' attitudes found that police chiefs rank "increased professionalism" as the top reason for seeking accreditation, ahead of "improved policies" and "reduced liability." *Professionalism itself*, not merely professionally sanctioned policies and procedures, seems to be central to the CALEA enterprise.

Agency accreditation through CALEA is useful for the ambitious police chief. George Turner, for example, put accreditation and professionalism at the heart of his application when he sought the position of chief of police of Brooksville, Florida, in 2007 (Frank 2008). Accreditation through CALEA is widely recognized by officers and police leaders throughout North America, and it is comprehensive in scope. Detailed management initiatives and picayune operating procedures may be important for effective administration of a police agency, but they are not necessarily strong resume items. By contrast, CALEA accreditation is a simple and potent signal of professional quality to buyers of executive labor: this single line on a resume captures a sweeping range of professionally favored policies and practices, much like board certification distinguishes a surgeon. Moreover, unlike state-level accreditation programs, CALEA's imprimatur carries its value across state lines and so broadens the potential market for the head of a CALEA-accredited department. Thus, accreditation is valuable to top administrators as a mark of professional accomplishment in ways that transcend the policy benefits that accreditation brings to agencies. In other words, career mobility and ambition for advancement provide reasons for a chief of police to seek CALEA accreditation, even when its costs are substantial and its direct benefits negligible. George Turner made good on his promise after he got the Brooksville police chief job, launching the CALEA accreditation process shortly after taking over the city's police department. Turner's hiring can be interpreted as a validation of his program of professionalism by Brooksville's city manager and council, as well as an example of the market value that CALEA offers an ambitious police chief. Evidently, CALEA itself has recognized the link between accreditation and job mobility: since 2004, the commission has given the Jim Cotter Award to police chiefs who bring accreditation to three or more different agencies.

Analysis of Mobility and CALEA Accreditation

Police chiefs' initiation of CALEA offers an excellent way to look at the relationship between bureaucratic job mobility and the influence of professionalism on agency policies. Agency accreditation is the very hallmark of professionalism in the bureaucracy: it aligns the policies of the agency with the strictures of the profession and a set of incentives established by an organization external to that agency. Evidence that police chiefs who are hired from outside are more likely to initiate CALEA accreditation than those promoted from within would affirm a depiction of administrators as professionals selling professional innovation in a market for expert labor.

Data from the survey of police chiefs described in chapter 3 are used in the analysis presented here. To capture the dependent variable—initiation of the CALEA accreditation process—respondents were asked if the agencies where they currently worked were CALEA-accredited or in the process of securing accreditation. Respondents from accredited agencies were then asked whether accreditation was initiated under their leadership or by a previous chief. Respondents whose agencies were not accredited were asked if they planned to initiate CALEA accreditation in the future. Chiefs who personally initiated or planned to initiate CALEA accreditation were coded 1 for *CALEA accreditation*. Chiefs whose agencies were not accredited, who were not in the process of accreditation, who did not plan to initiate accreditation in the future, or who did not initiate accreditation themselves were coded 0. Independent review of CALEA's participant list on the organization's Web site confirmed the respondents' reported participation in the program.

The key independent variable investigated here is the past career path for the chief of police. Respondents were asked about their employment history, including whether they arrived at their current jobs via internal promotion or external recruitment. I counted a police chief as hired from outside if he or she arrived at the current position from a management job in another government; if he or she was promoted to the current position from within the government in which the chief currently works I counted that as promoted from within. In other words, the respondent is coded as having advanced diagonally only if hired for the current job from outside, not if the chief was hired from outside for a lower-level position in the respondent's current government. This measure of *diagonal career path* helps assure that a bureaucrat's reputation built in a prior government informed the decision to hire him. A sizeable majority of the police chiefs reported arriving at their current jobs from outside the agency: 59 percent, compared with 41 percent promoted from within.[4] Governments sometimes hire administrators from outside to senior administrative (but not agency head) positions and then promote these senior administrators to top administrative posts after a few months or years. Under the coding scheme used here, these individuals would be counted as "vertical" climbers. To the extent that bureaucrats were hired from outside with the expectation of being promoted eventually, this coding method may understate the number of diagonal climbers and so blur the distinction between vertical and diagonal climbers. Since the analyses presented in this chapter focus on behavioral differences between vertical and diagonal climbers, any bias introduced by the vertical/diagonal coding scheme would tend to operate in favor of the null hypothesis (no difference).

The analysis includes some controls for institutional variables that might affect administrators' initiation of CALEA accreditation: the presence or absence of *full-time elected officials* and the presence or absence of a *city manager*. These institutional features are frequently cited in the literature on urban politics as important determinants of bureaucratic power. We might expect more of a client-professional relationship (and therefore professional innovation) between elected officials and administrators where elected officials are part-time amateurs. More of a principal-agent relationship might be expected under elected officials who work full time and draw larger salaries. Alternatively, full-time elected officials might make CALEA accreditation more likely if the presence of full-time elected officials requires agency heads to appeal to external professional standards in order to justify a policy agenda. One chief of police told me that he used CALEA accreditation in precisely this way. We would expect that the presence of a city manager would reduce innovation by an agency head since the city manager acts as something of a political gatekeeper between agency heads and elected officials in council-manager governments.

I control for agency size using the natural *log of full-time sworn officers* employed by the agency. Larger agencies have greater resources and so might be better able to bear the considerable costs associated with the CALEA accreditation process. A very large range of agency sizes is included in the sample because it is stratified by size. The log transformation compresses the distribution of agency size for better statistical modeling and is theoretically consistent with the nonlinear nature of agencies' policy needs: differences in agency size should matter more at the low end of the distribution than at the high end. For example, we would expect the real difference between a police department with 10 sworn officers and 100 sworn officers to be greater than the difference between a department with 1,000 officers and one with 1,090 officers.

Three variables are also included to account for circumstances in adminis-trators' personal lives that might affect their initiation of innovations. Agency heads who plan to retire in the near future are likely to perceive little benefit in honing a professional reputation pursuant to advancement and they have little reason to take up new policy initiatives. The model therefore includes a control for police chiefs who *plan to retire within five years*. The statistical model controls for respondents' family status, too. The direct costs and poten-tial risks of political action may be higher for *married* administrators and those with minor *children* than for those who are single or have no children. We might expect married chiefs of police and those with minor children might to be less likely to initiate CALEA accreditation.

Bureaucrats' gender, race, and ethnicity are potentially important vari-ables, too. Career concerns might affect administrators' political choices if a career opportunity structure is systematically biased in favor of or against a particular gender, certain races, and/or specific ethnicities. Individuals' per-ceptions of bias in a profession can affect their behavior, whether or not a systematic bias exists. Unfortunately, the data I use in this study are inade-quate to analyze the effects of gender, race, and ethnicity due to the very low frequency of women and racial/ethnic minorities in the sample of both police chiefs and utilities managers. Omission of these variables should not be inter-preted as ignorance or dismissal of them. On the contrary, I suspect that the very low frequency of women in the sample indicates that, as Nancy Burns has put it, "gender has already done much of its work" in the law-enforcement and utilities professions before bureaucrats ever advanced to a position where they might be studied (2002, 467). The same might be said of racial- and ethnic-minority administrators. An investigation of gender, race, and eth-nicity and their effects on bureaucratic ambition and political behavior are worthy of research, but lie beyond the data constraints of this study.

Results

Since the phenomenon of interest here is binary, I use a logistic regression model that predicts a chief's initiation of CALEA accreditation to test the

Table 4.1   Logistic models of police chief initiation of CALEA accreditation

Variable	Model P1 Coefficient (robust SE)	p*	Model P2 Coefficient (robust SE)	p*	Model P3 Coefficient (robust SE)	p*
Diagonal career path	2.84 (.88)	.00			3.00 (.95)	.00
Professional involvement			.03 (.09)	.73	−.07 (.11)	.50
Education			−.00 (.19)	.99	−.20 (.24)	.41
Married	−3.02 (1.18)	.01	−2.21 (1.11)	.05	−3.71 (1.39)	.01
Children	.13 (.95)	.90				
Plan to retire within five years	−1.06 (.90)	.24				
Log full-time sworn officers	.01 (.37)	.99	−.03 (.32)	.93	.24 (.37)	.52
Full-time elected officials	2.96 (1.45)	.04	1.59 (1.02)	.12	2.84 (1.13)	.01
City manager	−.30 (.89)	.73				
Intercept	.11 (1.38)		.93 (3.15)		3.06 (3.69)	
Log pseudolikelihood	−32.45		−39.88		−33.27	
Likelihood ratio χ^2	22.97		13.85		22.41	
$p > \chi^2$	.00		.05		.00	
McFadden's pseudo R^2	.26		.16		.26	
N	69		71		71	

Note: Cells contain coefficients, robust standard errors (SE), and p values generated by logistic models of police chiefs' initiation of CALEA accreditation. Model results reflect poststratification weighting to account for survey sample design.

*p-value generated by a two-tailed t test of significance.

relationship between career path and professional innovation. The coefficients, standard errors, and fit statistics generated by the model are reported as model P1 in table 4.1. Three variables generated substantively and statistically significant effects: *career path, marital status,* and the presence of *fulltime elected officials.* Somewhat surprisingly, responsibilities to minor *children* have a negligible effect on the likelihood of a chief of police initiating CALEA accreditation.[5] *Plans to retire within five years* reduced the likelihood that

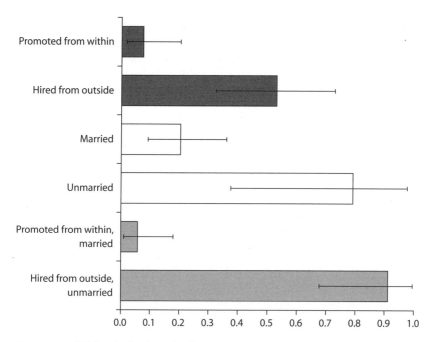

Figure 4.2 Likelihood of police chief initiating CALEA accreditation
Modeled likelihood that police chief initiates CALEA accreditation in his or
her current agency, with all other variables at their means. Thin bars depict
95 percent confidence intervals. Estimates based on model P1 (see table 4.1).

police chiefs initiated accreditation, but the effect is statistically dubious.
CALEA accreditation is correlated with agency size, but the effect of agency
size disappears when poststratification weights are applied. Council-manager
form of government has no appreciable effect on CALEA accreditation. However, police chiefs leading agencies with *full-time elected officials* are significantly more likely to initiate accreditation than those with part-time elected
officials.

The logistic regression generates log odds coefficients and standard errors
that are not easy to interpret intuitively. Moreover, the marginal effects of any
variable in a multivariate logistic model depend on the values of the other
variables in the model. So in order to interpret the model's results in an
intuitively meaningful way, figure 4.2 illustrates the model's estimated likelihoods of a chief of police initiating CALEA accreditation under different
conditions. Since career effects are of primary interest here, figure 4.2 shows
the effects of career path and marital status. All other variables are evaluated

at their means when illustrating the effects of specific variables. All estimated expected values are based on one thousand simulations drawn from a multivariate normal distribution using King, Tomz, and Wittenburg's (2000) CLARIFY procedure in Stata 10.1. This simulation procedure averages the model's predictions over the "fundamental variability arising from sheer randomness in the world"[6] (350).

As figure 4.2 shows, chiefs of police who were hired from outside their current agencies are much more likely to initiate CALEA accreditation than are chiefs who were promoted from within the agency. With other variables evaluated at their means, the model predicts a .53 likelihood of the chief of police initiating CALEA accreditation if arrived from outside the agency, compared with a .08 likelihood for a chief who climbed to the position from within the organization. As expected, married chiefs of police are significantly less likely to initiate CALEA accreditation than are unmarried chiefs: with other variables at their means, a married chief of police is .20 likely to initiate accreditation, an unmarried chief .79 likely. Combining career path and marital status underscores these effects: a married chief of police who was promoted from within is just .06 likely to initiate CALEA accreditation, while an unmarried chief who arrived from elsewhere is .91 likely to do so. These results are consistent with the view of professional innovation as a function of job mobility. Chiefs arriving from outside carry a reputation and mandate for professional innovation. Married administrators, for whom mobility might be more costly, are much less likely to seek accreditation for their agencies.

Conservation Water Rates and Utility Workforce Planning

U.S. municipal water utilities have no comprehensive accreditation regime comparable to CALEA's for law enforcement. So in order to evaluate the relationship between bureaucratic career path and professional innovation in local water utilities, I analyze agency heads' initiation of two policies favored by the profession: conservation-oriented water rates and workforce succession planning.

Conservation Rates

Virtually all municipal utilities in the United States collect fees, or rates, from their customers in exchange for water utility service. Utility rates collect revenue as necessary to meet a utility's operating and capital needs, but rates also can be designed to send signals to consumers about socially desirable use of a collective resource. Low prices can promote affordable water for basic sustenance (Hasson 2002) or signal a preference for more water use to encourage development, for example. Higher marginal prices can signal a desire to conserve water (Collinge 1996; Gaur 2007; Michelson, McGuckin, and Stumpf 1998).

Though American water utilities employ a wide variety of rate structures, they are easily categorized into five basic types:[7]

1. *Flat* rates, which charge all customers the same amount periodically, regardless of consumption
2. *Uniform* rates, which charge a single price for every unit of water consumed at any level of volume
3. *Declining block* rates, which charge higher per-unit prices for low volumes of water, but lower per-unit prices at higher volumes
4. *Inclining block* rates, which charge progressively higher per-unit prices for water at higher volumes
5. *Seasonal* rates, which charge higher per-unit prices during periods of peak demand or low resource availability and lower per-unit prices during periods of lower demand or higher resource availability

Seasonal rate variations may be used in conjunction with any of the other four.

At the most basic microeconomic level, principles of price elasticity imply that any rate structure imposing a marginal unit cost greater than zero encourages conservation. However, only structures 4 and 5, inclining block and seasonal rates, are generally considered conservation-oriented because these rate structures are designed with resource conservation in mind. Inclining block rates raise the marginal cost of water consumption at progressively higher volumes, while seasonal rates raise the marginal cost of water during periods of relative resource scarcity. Any rate structure can be designed to generate a desired level of revenue; the choice to increase or reduce total rate revenue is distinct from the choice of rate structure.

Water rates also can have important redistributional consequences because rate designs affect the allocation of costs and benefits among customers (Berry 1979; Mullin 2008; Teodoro 2005; Timmins 2002). Since virtually all people use public water utilities' services, rate design involves effective distributional decisions. Water utility services are heavily capital-intensive, and so the overwhelming majority of water utility costs are fixed. These fixed costs can be distributed across customers in an infinite variety of ways. High-volume customers, who pay more under conservation-rate structures, are unlikely to be scattered at random throughout a utility's service area; rather, they are likely to be geographically concentrated into specific neighborhoods. Geographically concentrated interests are likely to mobilize against threatening policies, which makes adjustment of water rates in ways that adversely affect high-volume water users "a political high-wire act," as Sandra Postel has observed (1999, 235). A conservation-oriented water rate structure is exactly the sort of risky, potentially controversial policy that a policy entrepreneur might be expected to champion.

A professional society, the American Water Works Association (AWWA), constitutes and governs the water utility management profession. AWWA establishes standards of practice, licensure, and ethics that carry the force of law in many states (Corssmit 2005). Dominant norms and values are not static in any profession, and in fact have changed significantly over time within the water utility profession. Water resource conservation generally, and conservation-oriented water rate structures particularly, have emerged and grown as AWWA priorities over the past three decades. AWWA's major conferences routinely feature numerous sessions on conservation, and for the past two decades AWWA has sponsored numerous conferences and publications devoted to conservation. The most recent edition of *Manual M1* devotes several chapters to conservation-oriented rate design and a further chapter on securing political support for new rates (AWWA 2000). Conservation-oriented rate structures are among the management practices now clearly favored by the water utility profession. This relatively coherent professional norm makes water rates a useful subject of study here.

Although water rate designs are adopted into law by elected officials, they are inescapably technical and are typically developed by and with professional utility managers (Dinar 2000; Timmins 2002). Berry's (1979) analysis of electricity rates demonstrates that bureaucratic professionalism can significantly affect utility rate design. Heavy administrative involvement in rate design, combined with high public salience, makes utility rates an excellent place to look for the influence of bureaucratic professionalism in policymaking. Indeed, rate setting is among the most visible, politically sensitive tasks that utility administrators must perform. While other actors are often involved in the rate design process (e.g., elected officials, lower-level staff members, consultants, and citizens), it is difficult to imagine a utility setting its rate structure without the significant involvement of its top administrator and its governing board (AWWA 2004; Dinar 2000).

Workforce Succession Planning

Recently, water industry leaders began to focus on the challenge of managing an enormous labor turnover expected in water utilities early in the twenty-first century as baby boomers reached retirement age. Beginning in the late 1990s and continuing into the 2000s, a series of studies funded by the American Water Works Association Research Foundation (AwwaRF) found that the U.S. water utility industry's workforce was graying faster than the American labor force as a whole (AwwaRF 2005). Estimates suggested that perhaps 40 percent of the water utility industry's labor force would retire within ten years (Frigo 2006). Meanwhile, the pool of available workers with adequate technical training in the industry was declining. These studies suggested that transferring systems knowledge to a new generation of utility operators and managers was critical to the future of the American water utilities industry and called for utilities to develop formal workforce succession plans.

In 2000, AWWA executive director Jack Hoffbuhr raised the issue in *Journal AWWA*, the industry's leading professional journal (Hoffbuhr 2000). In her opening address to the AWWA national conference in 2005, the AWWA president, Katie McCain, named workforce succession planning as one of the industry's three most pressing issues (McCain 2005). A 2006 AwwaRF report developed by a panel of water utility experts ranked the coming labor "crunch" as the second most important trend on its list of the industry's top ten, ahead of regulatory compliance, treatment technology, and finances; only inflation of energy costs was ranked ahead of workforce succession (AwwaRF 2006). The meteoric rise of workforce succession planning on the profession's agenda is evident in *Journal AWWA*'s coverage of the issue: from 1990 through 1999, the leading water utility professional journal published a total of four articles on workforce succession; from 2000 through 2009, it published thirty-eight articles on the topic. Clearly, workforce succession planning was "trendy" within the industry in the first decade of the new century.

The fashionability of workforce succession planning makes it an excellent subject for analysis of professional influences on local water utility policy. Recruiting and training new utility workers is costly in the short term, and the payoff to a utility from developing workforce succession plans comes only in the long term. Elected officials are unlikely to demand that utilities develop succession plans without prompting from administrators.

Analysis: Mobility, Conservation Rates, and Succession Planning

If job mobility encourages bureaucratic policy entrepreneurs to introduce professional innovations in their agencies, then we would expect governments that hire their utility managers from outside to adopt conservation rates and develop long-term workforce succession plans more often than those promoting bureaucrats from within. As with the analysis of police chiefs and CALEA accreditation, data from the survey described in chapter 3 are used in the analysis presented here. Water utility managers participating in the survey reported whether they had developed long-term workforce succession plans and also whether those plans were initiated under their leadership or by a previous manager. Respondents whose agencies had no workforce succession plans were asked if they planned to develop one in the future. Utility managers who personally initiated or planned to initiate a *workforce succession plan* were coded 1. Managers whose agencies had no workforce succession plan, who did not initiate a plan, and/or who did not expect to develop one in the future were coded 0.

To capture data on conservation water rates, I reviewed the current residential rate structure in place in each respondent's utility. Utilities with inclined block and seasonal rate structures were coded as having *conservation rate* structures. After adjusting for stratification, 26.6 percent of the surveyed utilities used some kind of conservation rate structure for residential customers. At the time of the survey, every participant's current utility rate ordinance or resolution had been adopted during the participant's tenure as head of the local utility. Independent review of each utility's rate resolution or ordinance verified that the current rates were adopted after each survey respondent began service as agency head.[8]

Just as with the police chiefs, utility managers were asked about their career paths. I coded a respondent as hired from outside *(diagonal career path)* if he arrived at his current position from a management job in another government; if he was promoted to his current position from within the government in which he currently works, I counted him as promoted from within. Sixty-one percent of water utility managers reported arriving at their current jobs from outside the agency; 39 percent were promoted from within.[9] As with police chiefs, the analysis of water utility managers included controls for the presence or absence of *full-time elected officials*, the presence or absence of a *city manager, plans to retire within five years*, and whether the respondent was married and/or had minor *children*. Conservation rate structures can carry significantly higher development and implementation costs than more traditional rate structures. Since we would expect that larger utilities are more likely to have the resources necessary to implement these policies, I control for agency size using the natural log of customer connections served by the respondent's utility.

Because the absolute need to conserve water varies widely across the United States, the model of conservation rate adoption also includes a control for water scarcity. Not surprisingly, Hewitt (2000) finds that utilities in hot, dry climates are more likely to adopt conservation rate structures than those in cool, moist climates. In the present study, I use the *Climatic Moisture* Index (I_m) developed by Willmott and Feddema (1992) as the main measure of water resource scarcity. As a metric of resource scarcity, the I_m has a number of advantages over simple climatic measures like precipitation, temperature, and sunlight because it integrates these variables with the land's water retention capacity and evapotranspiration potential.[10] In this way, the I_m "reflects the relationships between climate and the availability of moisture at the earth's surface" (Willmott and Feddema 1992, 84). A zero *Im* value reflects a climate where available water and climatic demand for water are exactly equal. Negative values of I_m indicate relatively little available moisture; positive values of I_m indicate relatively more available moisture. To put *Im* in more meaningful terms for readers familiar with American geography, the I_m value is .42 for Seattle, .32 for New York City, .13 for Omaha, −.08 for Dallas, and −.80 for Phoenix. The weighted mean I_m in the sample analyzed here is .21. Of course, the I_m does not account for every potentially relevant climatic condition, and short-term fluctuations in temperature or moisture conditions might cause localized or temporary drought conditions. Neither does the I_m account for water quality concerns that might drive water scarcity. However, the I_m is a valid metric used by atmospheric scientists and is a significant improvement over simple temperature and precipitation data as a measure of water scarcity.

The models in this study use the average annual *Moisture Index* values for each of the agencies' locations as calculated and published by Willmott and Feddema since 1992.[11]

Results

A pair of logistic models predicts a water utility manager's adoption of conservation rates and initiation of workforce succession planning to evaluate the relationship between career path and professional innovation. The coefficients, standard errors, and fit statistics generated by the model are reported as model WCR1 in table 4.2 and WSP1 in table 4.3. Not surprisingly, because water scarcity prompts governments to take conservation measures, *climatic moisture* is the strongest predictor of conservation rate adoption. As expected, managers with minor children were less likely to introduce these innovations. Utilities operated under a *council-manager form* of government were less likely to adopt both innovations, though the relationships are not quite statistically significant by conventional standards. *Full-time elected officials* have no effect on the likelihood of conservation rates, but they very strongly reduce the likelihood of workforce succession planning. As expected, *plans to retire within five years* reduce the likelihood of both innovations, though the effects are not statistically significant.

Most importantly for the theory of interest here, the models show that utilities with managers hired from outside are significantly more likely to adopt conservation rates and to develop workforce succession plans. Figures 4.3 and 4.4 show the models' estimated likelihoods of conservation rate adoption and workforce succession planning, respectively. All other continuous variables are evaluated at their means, and dummy variables are set at their modal values in these figures. The estimated expected values are based on one thousand simulations, using the King, Tomz, and Wittenburg's (2000) CLARIFY procedure in Stata 10.1. Figure 4.3 simultaneously illustrates the effects of climatic moisture and career path. As expected, the likelihood of conservation rates decreases as moisture increases. The disparity in the likelihood of conservation rates between utilities with agency heads hired from outside and those with agency heads promoted from within demonstrates that executive job mobility raises the likelihood of adopting this professional innovation. The differences are greatest under moderately dry to very dry climatic conditions. At the high ends of the moisture scale, the relative abundance of water attenuates the differences between agencies with executives

Table 4.2 Logistic models of water utility manager adoption of conservation rates

Variable	Model WCR1 Coefficient (robust SE)	p^*	Model WCR2 Coefficient (robust SE)	p^*	Model WCR3 Coefficient (robust SE)	p^*
Diagonal career path	3.36 (1.04)	.00			3.99 (1.18)	.00
Professional involvement			−.13 (.13)	.33	−.32 (.20)	.10
Education			.09 (.22)	.69	−.02 (.24)	.94
Children	−1.33 (.87)	.12	.97 (.99)	.33	−1.71 (1.02)	.10
Plan to retire within five years	−.16 (.89)	.86				
Full-time elected officials	−.04 (1.27)	.98				
Log customer connections	.98 (.41)	.02	.68 (.36)	.06	.85 (.45)	.06
City manager	−1.49 (.92)	.11	−2.29 (.81)	.01	−2.94 (1.18)	.01
Climatic moisture	−4.74 (2.28)	.04	−4.86 (1.11)	.00	−7.27 (2.26)	.00
Intercept	−9.95 (3.93)		−5.19 (4.81)		−6.08 (5.07)	
Log pseudolikelihood	−22.52		−25.08		−18.68	
Likelihood ratio χ^2	36.03		22.80		35.59	
$p < \chi^2$	.00		.00		.00	
McFadden's pseudo R^2	.44		.31		.49	
N	70		64		64	

Note: Cells contain coefficients, robust standard errors (SE), and p values generated by logistic models of conservation-rate adoption. Model results reflect poststratification weighting to account for survey sample design.

*p-value generated by a two-tailed t test of significance.

hired from within and those with executives hired from outside. These results suggest that, facing resource scarcity, mobile bureaucrats are more likely to respond with professionally sanctioned but politically risky policies than are their vertically promoted peers.

Figure 4.4 plots the relationship between utility size and the likelihood of an agency head initiating a workforce succession plan. As with conservation rates, utility managers hired from outside are more likely than those

Table 4.3   Logistic models of water utility manager initiation of workforce succession planning

Variable	Model WSP1 Coefficient (robust SE)	p^*	Model WSP2 Coefficient (robust SE)	p^*	Model WSP3 Coefficient (robust SE)	p^*
Diagonal career path	1.84 (.83)	.03			2.64 (.86)	.00
Professional involvement			.33 (.15)	.02	.34 (.13)	.01
Education			−.20 (.24)	.40	−.43 (.24)	.07
Married	1.84 (1.17)	.12	2.75 (.88)	.00	2.65 (.99)	.01
Children	−1.84 (1.05)	.08	−.98 (1.02)	.34	−1.82 (.97)	.06
Plan to retire within five years	−.96 (.92)	.30				
Full-time elected officials	−2.32 (1.40)	.10				
City manager	−.85 (.93)	.36				
Log customer connections	1.53 (.58)	.01	1.71 (.53)	.00	2.24 (.63)	.00
Intercept	−13.62 (4.15)		−14.88 (5.06)		−2.64 (1.30)	
Log pseudolikelihood	−27.74		−27.74		−22.46	
Likelihood ratio χ^2	22.54		26.95		37.51	
$p < \chi^2$	.00		.00		.00	
McFadden's pseudo R^2	.35		.33		.46	
N	62		60		60	

Note: Cells contain coefficients, robust standard errors (SE), and p values generated by logistic models of conservation rate adoption. Model results reflect poststratification weighting to account for survey sample design.
*p-value generated by a two-tailed *t* test of significance.

promoted from within to initiate succession plans. The effect of career path is strongest in small to medium-sized utilities. Larger utilities' greater staffing needs and organizational resources make workforce succession planning an easy decision. Adopting this particular professional innovation is relatively more costly for smaller utilities, and so the effect of executive mobility is stronger in them.

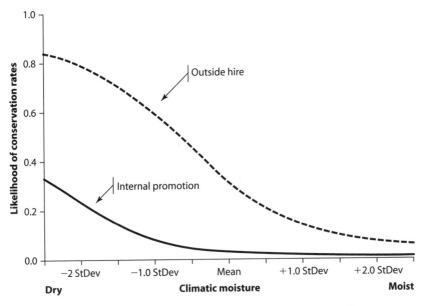

Figure 4.3 Effect of climatic moisture on conservation-rate adoption for managers promoted from within and hired from outside
Modeled likelihood that water utility applies conservation rates for residential customers. Other continuous variables set at their means; dummy variables are set at their modal values. Estimates based on model W1 (see table 4.2).

Professional Socialization?

What about professional identity? According to many theories of bureaucratic politics, the process of professional accreditation (through formal education, apprenticeship, and so forth) imbues individuals with the norms and values of their professions (Brehm and Gates 1997; Jones-Correa 2004; Lipsky 1980; Mosher 1968; Wilson 1989). Steeped in the cultures of their professions, administrators come to understand good and bad policy according to the conventions of their professional peers—so goes the argument. This socialization process causes bureaucrats to be "principled agents," as Brehm and Gates (1997) put it. In a professionalized bureaucracy, an administrator's preference for professional innovation may follow from his very identity as a professional gained through years of college, graduate school, and service in the ranks of his fellow professionals, not as a consequence of the bureaucratic labor market.

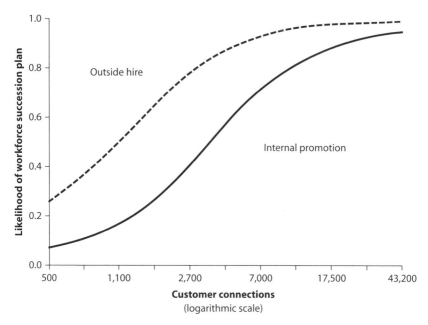

Figure 4.4 Effect of agency size on workforce succession planning for managers promoted from within and hired from outside
Estimated likelihood that a water utility manager initiated workforce succession plan. Other continuous variables set at their means; dummy variables are set at their modal values. Estimates based on model WSP1 (see table 4.3).

If professional socialization causes administrators to initiate professionally innovative policies, high levels of professional involvement would be associated with the introduction of professional innovations. The effects of career path might also be expected to diminish or disappear when indicators of professional identity are added to the analysis. I added comparative logistic models that included professional involvement and education to test the hypothesis that administrators' professional identities drive their professional innovation. Balla (2001) links participation in professional organizations with the diffusion of professionally sanctioned innovations, so I measured *professional involvement* by using number of professional meetings or conferences that the respondents participated in during the prior twelve months. This measurement approach is indirect, since it uses a behavioral metric (participation in conferences) to capture a social-psychological phenomenon (professional identity). It seems reasonable, however, to assume that those who identify strongly as professionals are relatively active in their professional communities and that such involvement builds and reinforces professional identity. I also include administrators' level of *education* in these models to capture its effect on professional identity. In order to make efficient use of the data, I excluded from these models all of the dummy variables that generated no statistically or substantively significant effects in models P1, WCR1, and WSP1.

Results

When analyzed without *diagonal career path, professional involvement* is a significant and positive predictor of bureaucrats' introductions of workforce succession planning in water utilities (model WSP2 in table 4.3). This result is consistent with professional socialization as a predictor of innovation. But *professional involvement* has no significant effect on the likelihood of conservation rates (model WCR2 in table 4.2), and water utility managers' level of *education* has a mildly negative (albeit statistically weak) effect on the likelihood of either innovation. Neither *professional involvement* nor *education* has a significant effect on police chiefs' initiation of CALEA accreditation. Meanwhile, the models with *professional involvement* and *education* are poorly fitted compared with the career path models. Taken together, these results indicate that professional socialization has little consistent, independent effect on professional innovation. Moreover, when *professional involvement* and *education* are included with *diagonal career path*, the strong effects of career path persist and improve the overall fits of the models (models P3, WCR3, WSP3).

That professional socialization alone fails to account for innovation is not surprising. In an era when virtually every public administration job is professional job, virtually every agency head is exposed to similar professional socialization experiences and shares most basic norms and values. It is not that professional socialization does not matter—the evidence here clearly shows that it does matter at some level and so is consistent with decades of research on professionalism in public administration. However, *accounting for variation in political behavior among professionals* requires recognizing that, in addition to socializing mechanisms, professions are labor-market phenomena. Many, most, or perhaps nearly all agency heads may think of themselves as professionals today, but job mobility creates marked incentives for bureaucrats to carry innovations from their professions to the governments that they serve. An agency head who is promoted from within does not necessarily identify as a professional any less than her peers hired from outside, but her professionalism is less likely to manifest itself as policy entrepreneurship.[12]

Mobility and Professions as Mechanisms of Innovation

The selection mechanisms at work in different opportunity structures affect the relationship between agency heads and the elected officials whom they serve. To a vertical climbing bureaucrat atop a career ladder, a local government's elected legislature or executive is "the boss." Securing and maintaining a top job in a vertical organization requires responsiveness to local preferences. To the diagonal climber, a local government is "the client." Securing a job via diagonal mobility requires honing a reputation for professionally sanctioned, innovative policy. Whether the bureaucrat considers the government he serves to be "the boss" or "the client" makes a significant difference in whether he introduces professional innovations to his agency. The analyses of professional innovation presented in this chapter demonstrate these patterns. Mobile bureaucrats are something like professional policy pollinators, bringing innovative policies to each stop on their diagonal career paths.

Policy entrepreneurship is risky for a professional bureaucrat. In the course of researching this book I interviewed a veteran executive who had recently taken a new job leading a large regional utility after being fired from his last post. Reflecting on his experiences, he mused:

> Leadership is a risky business. We desperately need leaders in government. But being a leader is risky business—it's personally risky and it's risky professionally. Leaders are often called upon to be change agents, something we desperately need them to be. But what happens to change agents? Everyone has heard the old adage "Jesus Christ was a change agent, and look what happened to him."

Policy entrepreneurship may be risky, but an established profession and a market full of other employers ensure that bureaucratic change agents in the United States fare considerably better in their conflicts with politicians than did Jesus of Nazareth. Diagonal career paths create an incentive for administrators to innovate despite the risks—because adherence to professional *principles* (that is, not only to elected *principals*) is part of what makes professional bureaucrats employable. In his landmark study on professions, Andrew Abbott (1988) observes:

> We have professionalism, in the first place, because our market-based occupational structure favors employment based on personally held resources, whether of knowledge or of wealth. *Such employment is more secure, more autonomous, and usually more remunerative, partly because it is organized in "careers,"* a strategy invented in the nineteenth century to permit a coherent individual life within a shifting marketplace. (324; italics added)

Professional identity may cause bureaucrats to *believe* more or less strongly that professional innovations are good, but career mobility offers an incentive to *act* professionally. Career mobility also offers an employment safety net for professionals who run afoul of their employers in pursuit of their profession's prized policies. Little wonder, then, that a diagonal career path is a robust predictor of professional innovation.

CHAPTER FIVE

The Psychology of Bureaucratic Entrepreneurship

Human Motivation and Political Advocacy

> He understood that the commissioner and the council have authority over him, so when we asked for information from him, he got it. He didn't stonewall, he didn't complain. He followed orders. He got things done. The downside was that if you didn't tell him to do something, he didn't do it. He never did anything in the way of reforms or initiatives or anything.
>
> A POLICE COMMISSIONER SPEAKING ABOUT
> A RETIRED FORMER CHIEF

> He just loves being a police chief. He didn't care what people said, he didn't care if people publicly challenged him. He didn't lose a minute's sleep over that stuff, because to him that's just part of being a police chief. He liked being a lightning rod. . . . He wanted you to know that he was taking on the tough, tough issues. He gave honest, informative, straightforward answers—sometimes very difficult answers. The media loved him.
>
> THE SAME POLICE COMMISSIONER SPEAKING ABOUT
> A SUBSEQUENT CHIEF, RECENTLY FIRED

Given identical professions, similar jobs, similar challenges, and similar opportunities, why are some bureaucrats more politically active than others? Why do some agency heads advocate vigorously for potentially incendiary policies—even launch quixotic crusades for them—while others are content to enjoy the perquisites of office and prestige of profession without inviting controversy?

When addressing the political dimensions of her job, a bureaucratic agency head must make two related decisions: which policies to pursue and how hard (if at all) she should try to change policy. Regarding the first decision, chapter 4 demonstrated that career path affects the diffusion of professional innovations: bureaucrats hired from outside are more likely to initiate professionally fashionable policy innovations than are those who were promoted to their posts from within their agencies. In this chapter, I address the second decision by exploring the psychological wellsprings of bureaucratic ambition. Specifically, I analyze the effects of achievement motivation (a concern for attaining a standard of excellence) and power motivation (a concern for having an impact on others) on agency heads' political advocacy.

My approach to measuring and allowing for variation in bureaucrats' motives distinguishes this study from other important works on bureaucratic political behavior in the public administration and political science traditions. Anthony Downs's *Inside Bureaucracy* (1967) suggests that administrators' motivations may vary, but simply offers a typology of bureaucratic motivations with no empirical grounding. Dewatripont, Jewett, and Tirole (1999a, 1999b) elaborate a theory of bureaucratic politics based on an assumption that all bureaucrats want to maximize their career advancement. Their model allows for variation in career ambition, but represents it mathematically simply as a discount rate in a cost-benefit analysis. That is, under Dewatripont, Jewett, and Tirole's theory, highly ambitious bureaucrats value future income highly, while less ambitious bureaucrats heavily discount anticipated future income. Consequently, highly ambitious bureaucrats act with an eye toward future career interests and their higher potential incomes, while less ambitious bureaucrats focus on their present jobs and disregard their future prospects. Dewatripont, Jewett, and Tirole's clever model provides a useful way to think about bureaucratic ambition, but unfortunately offers no means of distinguishing empirically between the ambitious administrator (who has a low discount rate) and the nonambitious (who has a high discount rate).

Some studies attribute differences in bureaucratic political advocacy to the personalities of agency executives (Loveridge 1971; Almy 1975; Wilson 1989), but without means of measuring personality independently such arguments amount to nontheory. In their foundational study of policy entrepreneurship, Schneider, Teske, and Mintrom concede that personalities are important determinants of the supply of entrepreneurs in a political system, but they dismiss personality as an object of research because they believe that psychological theories of entrepreneurship "do little to facilitate rigorous empirical testing" (1995, 71–74). In *Bureaucracy*, James Q. Wilson (1989) recognizes wide variation in administrators' motives, but ultimately despairs of finding a theory of bureaucratic motivation. In short, most political scientists and public administration researchers eschew theorizing about bureaucratic psychology, not because it is unimportant but because it is difficult to do so using their familiar theoretical frameworks and empirical methods.

But acknowledging a variable as important and then abandoning it as unknowable does not advance social science. Fortunately for students of the policy process, personality psychology offers a rich scientific literature on human motivation and its effects on organizational behavior. Contemporary research on motivational psychology applies rigorous, replicable empirical methods. In chapter 7, I discuss human motivation as a means of studying bureaucratic politics more generally, with special attention to the promises and perils of personality psychology for public administration research. In this chapter, I bring these methods to bear on the study of agency heads' political behavior.

Human Motivation

Motivation is a part of human personality. McClelland (1961, 1975) and Winter (1973, 1991, 2002a, 2002b) elaborate a theoretical framework and empirical methods for understanding human motivation. Motives are dimensions of personality that represent both conscious and unconscious goals that drive behavior in social, economic, and organizational settings (McClelland, Koestner, and Weinberger 1989; Winter 2002b). Motives represent both conscious and unconscious goals guiding behavior. While intelligence and skill provide mechanisms of behavior, motives are like fuel: they supply the energy that drives behavior in social settings. Different social situations can evoke different behavioral manifestations of motives.

In this study, I consider the three human motives of achievement, power, and affiliation, with special attention to the effects of achievement and power motivation on administrators' political advocacy. Achievement motivation is a concern for attaining a standard of excellence (McClelland 1961). Power motivation is a concern for impact on or influence over other people (Winter 1973). Affiliation motivation is a concern for establishing, maintaining, or restoring friendly relationships among people. These motives manifest themselves behaviorally, as Winter (2002b) explains them:

> The *achievement* motive is related to moderate risk-taking and using feedback to modify performance. Achievement-motivated people are rational negotiators, and seek information and help from technical experts. In contrast,

affiliation-motivated people are cooperative and friendly, but only when they feel secure and safe; under threat, they can become prickly and defensive, even hostile. They seek help and advice from friends and similar others. Finally, *power*-motivated people engage in a variety of "impact" and prestige-seeking behaviors. (26; italics in the original)

Table 5.1 summarizes the definitions and behavioral indicators of these three motives.

A substantial body of personality research has demonstrated that achievement motivation drives business entrepreneurship across time, gender, and culture.[1] Studies of business organizations show that entrepreneurs have higher levels of achievement motivation than do corporate managers (McClelland 1961; Wainer and Rubin 1969; Stewart and Roth 2007) and that achievement motivation affects individuals' choice of an entrepreneurial career (Lagan-Fox and Roth 1995; Sagie and Elizur 1999; Collins, Hanges, and Locke 2004). Achievement motivation is associated with attainment of objective organizational goals in business (Winter 1996; Spencer 2001). If *policy entrepreneurship* is a valid metaphor for individual action in the political arena—that is, if political actors behave in their "market" the same way that their commercial cousins do—then we would expect achievement motivation to predict efforts of administrators to advocate for innovations in their governments.

Power motivation is associated with success in hierarchical organizations and social settings that allow for one individual to direct the behavior of others. The power motive predicts performance and career success in hierarchical business organizations (Winter 1978; McClelland and Boyatzis 1982; Winter 1996), but not necessarily entrepreneurial business success (Winter 1973). Thus power motivation might fuel career ambition in hierarchical organizational careers. Representing a concern for impact or influence over others, power motivation would at first blush seem to be a wellspring of political action, too; in fact, power motivation is associated with aggression, military action, and "greatness" in politicians (Winter 2002b). However, in general, power motivation does not lead to greater levels of participation in democratic or pluralistic political processes (Browning and Jacob 1964; Winter 1973).

Reflecting a concern to connect and maintain close relationships with others, the affiliation motive is not specifically associated with either entrepre-

Table 5.1   The achievement, power, and affiliation motives

Motive	Definition and behavioral indicators
Achievement	Concern about a standard of excellence • Mentioning quality of performance • Success in competition • Unique, unprecedented accomplishment
Power	Concern about having impact, control, or influence on another person, group, or the world at large • Strong, forceful actions that have an impact on others • Controlling or regulating others • Trying to influence, persuade, convince, make a point, or argue • Unsolicited help or advice • Impressing others, prestige • Arousing strong emotions in another person
Affiliation	Concern about establishing, maintaining, or restoring friendly relations among persons or groups • Warm, positive, friendly feelings • Sadness about separation or disruption of a friendly relationship • Affiliative, companionate activities • Friendly, nurturing acts

Source: From Winter (2002a). Winter (1995), chapter 5, includes an extensive review of the empirical and theoretical literature on these three motives.

neurship or career advancement (McClelland 1975; McClelland and Boyatzis 1982). However, since affiliation motivation is part of a three-dimensional motive scheme, I analyze it alongside the achievement and power motives in this study.

Virtually no research to date has examined the effects of human motivation on public administrators' behavior. This dearth is unfortunate, since bureaucrats are, after all, human beings—Kafkaesque caricatures and social scientific models notwithstanding. If administrators' personalities affect their policymaking behavior in the ways that I hypothesized in chapter 3, we ought to find that administrators' achievement and/or power motives are directly related to their level of political activity. The affiliation motive ought to have no direct, significant effect on administrators' political activity.

Measuring Motives

Testing hypotheses about human motivation requires measurement of motives. For this study, data on administrators' motives were drawn from the interviews I conducted with police chiefs as part of the survey of agency administrators. The survey of police chiefs began with a Behavioral Event Interview (BEI), also known as a Critical Incident Interview. The BEI has been used successfully to gather data on organizational behavior across a variety of fields (Flanagan 1949; Winter 1991; Fountain 1999; Boyatzis 1998, 2005). In fact, the BEI has become something of a methodological staple in the study and development of business organizations and it is now widely employed by business firms in executive recruitment (Spencer and Spencer 1993; Fernández-Aráoz, Groysberg, and Nohria 2009). Following the standard BEI protocol, telephone surveys with police chiefs opened with two questions:

> Thinking back over your career in law enforcement, please describe a specific time in your career when you felt *effective* at work. Try to think of a particular event and be as specific as possible in describing what happened.

> Thinking back over your career in law enforcement, please describe a specific time in your career when you felt *ineffective* at work. Try to think of a particular event and be as specific as possible in describing what happened.

The wording of these questions was identical across all eighty-one interviews. Consistent with the BEI method, follow-up questions focus the respondent on behavior and avoid asking respondents directly about their attitudes or "philosophies" about politics, administration, or public policy. David McClelland (1998) has demonstrated that responses from the BEI can be coded to measure human motivation with results comparable to Thematic Apperception Tests (TAT) and other well-known psychological instruments (see also Gowing 2001).

The BEI method has a number of virtues, including the capacity to gather psychological and behavioral data in a consistent manner without "contaminating" respondents with theoretical cues. Under the BEI technique, respondents describe work incidents, their own behavior, the behavior of any other key players in the incident, and the outcome, all in their own words, with as little prompting as possible. The terms *effective* and *ineffective* in the two prompts are neutral, and are meant to evoke different responses from individuals with different motive profiles. The BEI technique contrasts with the stylized Rorschach "ink blot" test or TAT, which asks subjects to tell a story based on a picture. BEIs mesh seamlessly with ordinary substantive interview questions and so are not obtrusive or obviously psychological probes. These BEI items also yield more valid data than elite psychology data gathered "at a distance," since transcripts from the BEI responses are based on consistent prompts for all respondents. Generally, responses greater than 150 words can be validly and consistently coded for the achievement, power, and affiliation motives (Winter 2003). All of my interviews with police chiefs yielded responses greater than this minimum length.

Motive Coding

Transcribed answers to the two BEI questions allowed motive measurement according to the rules specified in Winter's *Manual for Scoring Motive Imagery in Running Text* (1994). Motive measurement involves scoring images in respondents' spoken answers that are consistent with the different motives in table 5.1. I scored the interview text for motives, and another scorer coded the text independently. The second scorer was trained prior to and independently from this project, had no instructions beyond the standard motive scoring protocols (Winter 1994), and had no information on the hypotheses being investigated. The category agreement for both sets of scores was .855.[2] Winter (1994) notes that intercoder category agreement greater than .850 is acceptable by prevailing norms of personality research. The analyses presented in this chapter use an average of the two scorers' motive scores for each respondent. This averaging of scores is intended to reduce coder error. To ensure that coder bias did not affect the substantive findings here, I repeated all analyses presented here using only the scores of the independent coder (thus excluding my own). The results were remarkably robust: in every case the direction of the effects for all variables were consistent, and the coefficients and standard errors (SE) for the theoretically important variables were very close.

Interview text was scored for *achievement* motive when respondents mentioned excellence—"good," "better," or "best" performance—or carrying out some special accomplishment or action. The following sentences include examples of achievement motive imagery captured from survey interviews with police chiefs:

> I excelled, I looked better than the average, and became a manager, and then a chief of police.
> I created a policy addressing that, and we reduced sick leave usage by more than sixty-five percent in one year.

We increased the minority recruitment by seven percent, which was the largest in the state.

I was trying to make progressive changes and implement new ideas to try to improve patrol.

We are recruiting better people and doing better background investigations.

Power-motive imagery was scored when respondents referred to one person or group having an impact on or influence over another person or group. Since the respondents in this study were seasoned law-enforcement officers, many of the power images in their responses are accounts of direct, physical impact of one individual over another. But answers that mentioned a concern for prestige, reputation, or fame also were coded for the power motive. The following sentences include examples of power imagery captured from my interviews with police chiefs:

Basically I had to kick him in the head until he quit fighting and I finally got the cuffs on him.

I was able to convince the city manager to give us the property.

The guy was a legend around here.

I directed him to sweep up all the trash, all the glass off the corner.

He had a knife in his hand, and the officer shot and killed him.

Affiliation-motive imagery was scored when respondents mentioned warm, close relationships among people, concern for disruption or absence of warm relationships, or nurturing acts that imply warm relations. The following sentences include examples of affiliation imagery captured from survey interviews with police chiefs:

I'm talking to him, consoling him, trying to make him as comfortable as possible until we get him to the hospital.

I was holding her hand as she was laying on the porch.

You pull everyone together and you go through that process together.

We got to know names, develop relationships.

I told him the kind of things that a friend should say to a friend.

For analytical purposes, motive images in running text were normalized to images per one thousand words in order to adjust for the length of respondents' answers. Table 5.2 summarizes the motive scoring results.

Table 5.2   Summary of police chiefs' motive scores

	Images per 1,000 words		
Mean of two scorers	Achievement	Power	Affiliation
Motive			
Mean	7.48	8.50	1.59
Standard deviation	4.47	4.45	2.30
Sample minimum	0.00	1.85	0.00
Sample maximum	21.43	24.00	9.16
Pearson correlations			
Achievement	1.00		
Power	−.18	1.00	
Affiliation	.06	.08	1.00
N = 81			

Note: Parameters reflect poststratification weighting.

Police chiefs' answers to the BEI questions varied widely in substance. In describing times when they felt effective, some police chiefs recounted classic "cop stories," with high-speed chases, gun battles with fugitives, and high-profile, high-pressure criminal investigations. Some talked about receiving acclaim for developing law-enforcement or crime prevention programs. Others talked about receiving high-fives from children, thank-you notes from recovering crime victims, or hugs from little old ladies. Three excerpts below reflect the diversity of substantive experiences that made chiefs of police feel "effective":

First the words of the chief of a large city in the West:

We applied for a multimillion-dollar grant that everybody in the country was going for. I put in for it, me and one other guy. Everybody was laughing at us. We ended up getting it. . . . We had a tremendous gang problem and a bunch of people had ideas about what they wanted to do. They turned it over to me since I was the one who got the money. I did exactly the opposite of what everyone else was going to do. I put together a high-speed, full-time, twenty-two-officer task force. We had the money to pay for it, and we figured out how to back-fill it over time and make it work. It ended up being the most successful program in the nation.

Next from the chief of a large midwestern city:

Someone had snuck out and called 911 and said that there was a disturbance at the bar. I pulled up around the back of the bar. One of them spotted me and took off running. The other guy tried to get out—I grabbed him at the door and took him down, handcuffed him, and the whole place got up and cheered. Apparently the two guys blocked the doors and were threatening people and creating quite a disturbance. . . . They never let me forget it, because they were so terrified. It made the papers and everything.

And third, the chief of a small Midwestern city:

We got to know names, develop relationships. And they would come up and tell us what was going on in town, or in their neighborhood anyway. If they had problems or concerns, just general issues with what was going on. They were just very open and friendly. There was very, very reduced agitation, I guess, from when you meet people you don't know that have a problem, and they immediately want to really be direct about their problem. It wasn't that way. It was more like talking to your brother or your best friend or whatever.

The three chiefs quoted scored among the top ten in the sample for the achievement, power, and affiliation motives, respectively.

Police chiefs' accounts of times when they felt ineffective were similarly diverse. Many told me about working hard at lengthy investigations and making arrests only to see their suspects acquitted or released on legal technicalities. Others spoke of failures to avert suicides or homicides. Several discussed operational or disciplinary frustrations with past supervisors or employees. Some identified frustrations in dealing with elected officials. Three excerpts below reflect the diversity of substantive experiences that made chiefs of police feel "ineffective."

First, a chief from a very large Midwestern city:

We put together this program because a lot of research from other departments and within our department. We drew from all the ranks within our department. Literally hundreds of years of police experience and managing police organizations. Then you have seven people whose expertise comes from the fact that they got elected to council dictating how a program's going to be designed and implemented. I found that completely frustrating, because I don't think it's in the best interests of the community or the police department.

The chief of a large southern city:

I've seen public officials involved in corruption—from police officers I've worked with to judges and others. It's sometimes like battling from within. I have fought corruption my whole career, and I've been in law enforcement more than forty years. I have arrested several of my partners I've worked closely with. . . . I've arrested people here in [he names the city] for public corruption. To me, I think, that's the worst thing you can do is betray the trust that people put in you when you put on the badge, by taking money and doing things you shouldn't do.

The chief of a large city in the West said:

I've done workshops on why we need to cooperate, why we need to forgive, how synergy can help us move beyond things that have happened in the past. Then I'll be in my office and somebody will make a comment that is—I'm sorry that the example I'm going to use is crude—but I'd never expect someone to be in my office and refer to a black person in a derogatory way. That should just not ever happen.

The above three chiefs, too, scored among the top ten in the sample for the achievement, power, and affiliation motives, respectively.

The diversity of answers to these questions is unsurprising. The terms *effective* and *ineffective* in the BEI prompts are meant to be neutral with respect to the variables of interest (in this case, the achievement, power, and affiliation motives), and hence to evoke different substantive responses from individuals with different motives. When conducting interviews, a few respondents responded to a BEI question by asking what I meant by *effective*. In keeping with the BEI technique, my answer was always: "Whatever *effective* means to you."

Motivation and Political Advocacy

If achievement and/or power motivation fuel bureaucratic ambition, then we would expect these motives to predict administrators' levels of political advocacy. I measure bureaucratic political advocacy as police chiefs' self-reported lobbying or political outreach activity related to an important policy issue. The survey questionnaire asked respondents to name the most important policy issue related to their agencies that their governments addressed in the past twelve months. Next the survey asked respondents to report their contact with various groups and individuals in their communities regarding that "most important policy issue." The survey questions about political advocacy were similar to those used in Jennings's (1963) study of public administrators' involvement in policymaking, the American State Administrators Project survey at the University of North Carolina (Bowling and Wright 1998), and the Texas Educational Excellence Project (Bohte and Meier 2001). Respondents were asked if they initiated contact with elected officials, community groups, and other agency officials regarding the issue the respondent identified. To the extent that survey items asked respondents to report past events, there is some risk of "telescoping"—that is, overreporting behavior by placing events that occurred in the distant past within the survey's timeframe. Fortunately, most local government administrators work on annual budget cycles and so have an easy cognitive device with which to place recent political issues in an annual timeframe. Moreover, the questions on past behavior focused on specific issues and so fixed the respondents' memory on a specific set of events (e.g., during the past twelve months, did you contact the mayor regarding—[naming a local policy issue]?), rather than asking more open-ended behavioral questions (e.g., how many times did you contact the mayor over the past year?). This approach helps to minimize potential overreporting due to telescopic responses.

Table 5.3 lists the thirteen individuals and groups included in the questionnaire and reports the percentage of police chiefs who reported initiating *contacts* with each. This measure of political advocacy captures breadth of advocacy, respondents who initiate contact with many different groups or individuals pursuant to a political issue being considered more politically active than those who contact fewer groups or individuals (however vigorously or half-heartedly). Initiating a broad set of contacts pursuant to some policy issue is the kind of costly behavior that we would associate with policy entrepreneurship. Measuring policy advocacy in this way also is consistent with a growing body of research on policy networks that associates policy innovation with individuals who develop multiple, broad social contacts (Mintrom and Vergari 1998; Lubell and Fulton 2008; Scholz, Berardo, and Kile 2008).

The phenomenon of interest here is the number of different political contacts that police chiefs initiated pursuant to their most important policy issues over the past twelve months, and so I use an ordinary least squares (OLS) model to assess the influence of motives on police chiefs' political advocacy. Of course, we would expect administrators' personal and institu-

Table 5.3   Self-initiated political contacts

Group or individual contacted	Percentage of police chiefs reporting self-initiated contact
City council	59.6
Neighborhood organizations	48.7
State or federal agencies or officials	43.7
City manager	39.7
Union or labor organizations	22.5
Political party officials	19.1
Racial or ethnic minority organizations	18.8
News media	17.8
Official citizen board	17.0
Mayor	15.7
Religious organizations	14.2
Developers	13.7
Businesses	4.7
Summary of total self-initiated contacts	
Mean	3.5
Standard deviation	2.3
Sample minimum	0.0
Sample maximum	9.0
$N = 81$	

Note: Table reports total self-reported contacts that respondents initiated related to their agencies' most important policy issue with the listed groups and individuals over the past twelve months. Parameters and percentages reflect poststratification weighting.

tional situations to affect their levels of political advocacy, too. The embittered writer of the letter quoted at the top of chapter 3 noted the direct costs and risks to their families' welfare that public administrators accept when they pursue policy innovation; hence, this analysis controls for police chiefs' *age*, whether they were *married*, and parenting responsibility for minor *children*. Variations in governance institutions (e.g., council-manager vs. mayor-council structure, full-time vs. part-time elected officials, etc.) also might be expected to affect administrators' opportunities to advocate for policies. However, analyses of bureaucratic political advocacy indicated no substantively or statistically significant effect for institutional structure and they are excluded from the analyses presented here.[3]

The OLS model estimates self-initiated contacts that police chiefs initiated with different groups and individuals. Table 5.4 reports the coefficients, robust

Table 5.4   OLS model of self-initiated political contacts

Variable	Coefficient (robust SE)	Standardized coefficient	$p*$
Achievement motivation	.20	.37	.00
	(.05)		
Power motivation	−.06	−.12	.37
	(.07)		
Affiliation motivation	.02	.02	.87
	(.14)		
Married	−3.37	−.45	.01
	(1.28)		
Children	−1.60	−.34	.03
	(.70)		
Age	−.01	−.04	.78
	(.04)		
Log full-time sworn officers	.13	.06	.51
	(.20)		
Intercept	6.41		
	(2.77)		
R^2	.50		
Adjusted R^2	.44		
N	69		

Note: Cells contain coefficients, robust standard errors (SE), standardized coefficients, and p values generated by ordinary least squares model of political contacts. Model results reflect poststratification weighting to account for survey sample design.
    *p-value generated by a two-tailed t test of significance.

standard errors, and standardized coefficients generated by the model.[4] The standardized coefficients represent the marginal effect that a one standard-deviation increase in the value of an independent variable has on the number of policy-related contacts that a police chief makes, with all else equal. I report standardized coefficients because the measures of motivation used here (images per thousand words in interview transcripts) are not intuitively meaningful. It is unusual for studies in political science and public administration publications to report standardized coefficients for OLS models. In most cases, the political scientist's more common practice of reporting unstandardized coefficients is sensible since most variables of interest to political scientists (e.g., agency size, age, marital status) are intuitively meaningful and so can be translated into marginal effects intuitively. By contrast, many important metrics used in psychological studies are quite abstract and have little intuitive meaning (what does it mean to be "one unit more achievement-motivated"?). Consequently, psychology publications typically report OLS results with standardized coefficients that offer a sense of the relationships between variables. I report both types of coefficients in the hope of communicating effectively with readers across disciplines.

Marital status and parenting responsibilities have their expected effects on political advocacy in this model, because *married* police chiefs and those with minor *children* are significantly less politically active than their peers who are unmarried and/or have no children. These findings reflect the direct cost of policy advocacy: time spent on politics is time spent away from a family. The effects of marriage and children also might indicate the job risks associated with policy entrepreneurship.

Achievement Motivation

As expected, the OLS model demonstrates that *achievement* motivation has a substantively and statistically significant positive effect on political advocacy. Just as a need for achievement fuels business entrepreneurs to invest energy and resources in pursuit of profits, achievement motivation evidently drives police chiefs to advocate for policies that are important to them.

I also used a logistic regression to model the effects of *achievement* motivation on the likelihood of a police chief engaging in a kind of political advocacy typical of bureaucratic policy entrepreneurship: contact with the media. Initiating contact with the news media regarding a policy issue is a decision to appeal to the public independently from and possibly "over the heads" of elected officials. Aggressive media contacts also figure prominently in the account of Chief Calvin Jensen's leadership in Greenport as related in chapter 2. Such media appeals by agency heads can be effective, but they are also markedly risky, as the commissioner quoted at the head of this chapter observed. Initiating contact with the news media is a favorite tactic of O'Leary's "guerrilla bureaucrats" (2005). In other words, initiating media contact on a policy issue is exactly the kind of risky, costly political behavior that we would expect from a policy entrepreneur. Figure 5.1 depicts the effect of *achievement* motivation on the likelihood, *ceteris paribus*, of a police chief initiating contact with the media. The strong upward sloping line in figure 5.1 illustrates the strong effect of achievement motivation on police chiefs' likelihood of initiating media contact, especially for chiefs with very strong achievement motivation.[5]

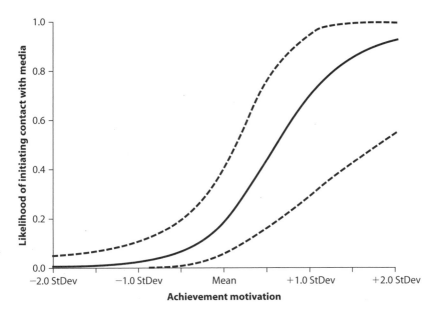

Figure 5.1 Likelihood of initiating contact with news media
Solid line represents the estimated likelihood that a police chief with varying levels of achievement motivation initiated contact with the news media regarding his agency's most important policy issue. Dash lines depict a 95 percent confidence interval.

Data on police chiefs' political contacts were collected through an Internet-based questionnaire; but here, the motive scores are based on the BEI questions asked at the beginning of a telephone interview conducted separately. In other words, data on the dependent and independent variables were here gathered independently from one another. For every one of the police chiefs who completed the online questionnaire, the policy issue addressed in the questionnaire was unrelated to the stories related in their BEI responses. That the motives revealed by the latter probe are consistent with political behavior reported on the former is potent evidence that the achievement motive drives political action.

Power Motivation

Somewhat surprisingly, the power motive shows a negligible effect on political advocacy.[6] This result contrasts with several other studies' findings that associate the power motive with organizational leadership. If power

motivation is a psychological driver of ambition, it evidently does not manifest itself in greater political advocacy among chiefs of police. Winter observed a similarly ambiguous relationship between power motivation and
participation in the political process in *The Power Motive* (1973), although he
found strong evidence that power motivation is a strong predictor of behavior
in many other areas of social life.

Since the power motive represents a concern for influence over others,
why is the power motive not associated with political advocacy? The answer
to this apparent paradox might be simply that the democratic political process
is a difficult place for a public administrator to satisfy his need for power,
especially in the law-enforcement profession. City agency heads approach
policymaking from a position of weakness relative to elected officials and
even many community groups. Public administrators may face direct challenges to their authority when they engage in the policymaking process, as the
cases in chapter 2 show. Any positive effect that power motivation might have
on a bureaucrat's political advocacy would thus be blunted by the frustration
that she might experience when challenged by organizational superiors or
citizens in the community at large.

By contrast, most law-enforcement executives have ample opportunities to
satisfy a need for power simply by working within their own agencies. Unlike
most civilian public agencies, police departments are paramilitary organizations with strong hierarchical structures. Sitting atop these organizations,
chiefs of police receive frequent and consistent reminders of their authority.
Unlike other agency heads, who are simply Mr., Ms., or Dr., chiefs of police
are addressed as Chief, which is an open reference to their positions of authority. Military-style police uniforms provide visible marks of rank. In some
larger departments, lower-ranking officers must stand and salute the chief
when he or she enters a room. As serving, sworn officers, most chiefs of police
carry a gun when working. Lines of authority, accountability, and discipline
are more clearly and strongly enforced within police departments than in
most other city agencies. Moreover, the very nature of law-enforcement work
involves projection of physical force by officers over other individuals. It is
possible that this very desire for immediate, interpersonal impact is what
draws many people to the law-enforcement profession. A veteran police commander explained to me why he had served for more than twenty years in a
large city that suffered from high crime rates: "When you're a fireman, you
want to fight fires. If I want to be a policeman, I don't want to go answer

barking dog calls. I want to close cases, catch bad guys, and put them in jail. That's why I work here."

The strength of a motive's influence on behavior usually is a function of the length of time since it was last satisfied, for "no matter how good my appetite generally is, I am unlikely to eat right after a big meal" (Winter 1996, 25). The usual patterns of personal interaction in hierarchical, paramilitary organizations are likely to satisfy police chiefs' power motives, just as they do in hierarchical business organizations (Andrews 1967: Wainer and Rubin 1969; Winter 1973). Because police chiefs may satisfy their need for power through day-to-day work, they may not necessarily need to participate in policymaking to satisfy the power motive. These are speculative, post hoc explanations, to be sure. But the finding that the power motive is not associated with political advocacy among police chiefs is consistent with psychological research on business organizations.

Affiliation Motivation

As expected, *affiliation* motivation is not significantly related to political advocacy. However, the scoring protocol used in this study requires coding the three motives simultaneously; also, the coding rules make one motive's score dependent in part on the coding of the other two motives. I therefore include *affiliation* motive in the models despite their negligible effects in the models.

Declining Benefit

As a manifestation of achievement motivation, bureaucratic ambition is meaningful only if there are higher-status jobs available. Administrators who hold low-status jobs but enjoy a measure of career mobility have many potential paths to advancement. Administrators holding high-status jobs have fewer potential job destinations that offer higher status. As a public administrator's career progresses, there are fewer and fewer advancement alternatives available to her. Thus for the ambitious, the greatest potential payoff from policy entrepreneurship is to be found in low-status jobs, and the career incentives for political advocacy fall as a bureaucrat's job status increases. As agency heads secure progressively higher-status jobs, they reach a point of declining career benefit from political action. We would therefore expect the effect of a bureaucrat's achievement motivation on her level of political advocacy to depend on her current job's status. Though the direct effect of achievement

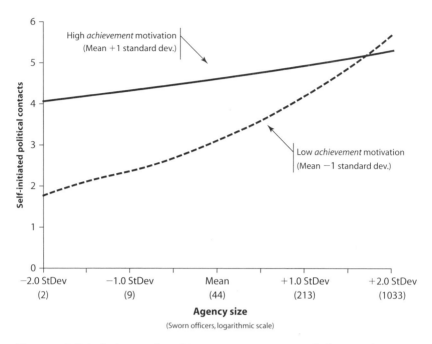

Figure 5.2 Political advocacy by achievement motivation, with direct and motive-status interactions
Lines represent the estimated number of political contacts made by high- and low-*achievement*-motivated police chiefs over the past twelve months. Other continuous variables set at their means and dummy variables set at their modal values. Agency size is plotted on a logarithmic scale with labels transformed to integers. Estimates based on negative binomial regression count model (see table B2).

motivation is to increase political activity, its effect, interacted with agency size, would be negative if bureaucrats perceived declining benefits to political action as they ascended to progressively higher-status jobs. In fact, adding an achievement motive–agency size multiplicative interaction term to a model of police chiefs' political advocacy demonstrates such diminishing marginal returns from policy entrepreneurship, as figure 5.2 illustrates.[7]

The two lines in figure 5.2, generated by a negative binomial regression model, show estimated political contacts for police chiefs with high *achievement* motivation (one standard deviation above the mean) and low *achievement* motivation (one standard deviation below the mean), evaluated at various agency sizes.[8] Higher *achievement* motivation is associated with higher levels of political activity across nearly the entire range of agency sizes. Political activity also increases as agency size increases for both the high- and low-achievement-motivated administrator, which probably reflects the greater political duties that leading a large agency requires. Most remarkable in figure 5.2 is the shrinking disparity between the individual with high achievement motivation and the individual with low achievement motivation as agency size increases. The influence of the *achievement* motive is most pronounced in low-status positions, where police chiefs with very high achievement motivation are very active political advocates. But as agency size (and therefore job status) increases, the *achievement* motivation has less influence on political advocacy. In fact, in the very-highest-status jobs, the influence of the *achievement* motive on political activity disappears entirely: estimated self-initiated political contacts for bureaucrats from across the achievement-motive distribution converge at about five contacts. This result affirms the achievement motive as a source of diagonal career ambition: its effect is strongest where advancement opportunities are the greatest, and its effect declines as advancement opportunities decline.

The Psychology of Bureaucratic Policy Entrepreneurship

Theorists from John Stuart Mill (1848) to Joseph Schumpeter (1989) have recognized that entrepreneurship is essential to generating business profits, comparative advantage, and growth in a capitalist economy. But entrepreneurs are by definition exceptional individuals. It should come as no great surprise, then, that a great deal of research on business organizations has focused on identifying the psychological causes of entrepreneurship. To understand the motivations that drive entrepreneurs is to hold the key to profits and the wealth that they generate. The value that business firms place on identifying and nurturing entrepreneurial personality is evident in the money that they spend on services offered by specialized management psychology firms. The Hay Group, for example, is a management consulting firm that uses social psychology to improve business organizations. The Hay Group runs the McClelland Center for Research and Innovation, and in its work with corporate clients the Hay Group uses the McClelland/Winter three-dimensional motive theory and the BEI technique (along with many others). Founded in

1943, the enterprise has evidently been fruitful: by 2010 the Hay Group boasted more than 2,600 employees in forty-seven countries and generated hundreds of millions of dollars in annual revenue. A persistent finding in studies of entrepreneurial personality is that achievement motivation drives innovation and entrepreneurship in business enterprises.

The finding that achievement motivation also fuels political advocacy among public agency heads is important for students of the policy process on at least three levels. First, the achievement motivation's affect on policy entrepreneurship evidently is consistent with its affect on business entrepreneurship. This finding affirms the policy entrepreneur as a theoretical construct. With this finding, *bureaucratic policy entrepreneur* becomes a predictive theory, not just a post hoc description. Second, revealing the motivational psychology behind bureaucratic policy entrepreneurship fills an important theoretical void that political scientists had previously abandoned as intractable (Wilson 1989; Schneider, Teske, and Mintrom 1995). Finally, the declining influence of achievement motivation on political advocacy as job status increases demonstrates a link between achievement motivation and diagonal career ambition among public administrators.

The power motive, representing a concern for impact or influence over others, would at first blush seem to be a likely driver of political advocacy, too. That power motivation does not drive political advocacy among police chiefs may be due to the peculiarities of the law-enforcement profession. But this apparent incongruity may also reveal another important parallel between policy entrepreneurship and business entrepreneurship. Research on business firms shows that individuals with strong power motivation tend to succeed in large, hierarchical organizations but not in entrepreneurial enterprises. Although they are concerned with making an impact on others, power-motivated individuals are uncomfortable with the uncertainties that necessarily accompany entrepreneurship and engagement in the oft-messy process of policymaking in a pluralistic democracy. Since policy entrepreneurship is inherently risky and its rewards uncertain, it follows that power motivation would not drive political advocacy among bureaucratic agency heads. Sitting atop hierarchical organizations, public agency heads are likely to have ample opportunities to satisfy their psychological needs for power without stepping into the political arena.

In chapter 3, I defined ambition as the manifestation of human motivation in an institutional context: ambition is where the motivational rubber meets the opportunity road. Taken together, the findings in chapters 4 and 5 affirm this metaphor. Chapter 4 shows that differences in career paths lead to varying degrees of policy innovation; this chapter shows that differences in achievement motivation lead to varying levels of political advocacy. The achievement motive determines how fast a bureaucrat's political wheels spin, while the career path determines the direction in which they go.

CHAPTER SIX

Ramps and Ladders

How Career Systems Foster or Inhibit Bureaucratic Entrepreneurship

> We're getting the same kind of people over and over. In today's system, to
> get to the top, you follow the same kind of pattern.
>
> SERGEANT DON BLACK, TWENTY-NINE-YEAR VETERAN
> OF THE AURORA, COLORADO, POLICE DEPARTMENT
> ON THE SELECTION OF A NEW APD CHIEF

Chutes and Ladders is a popular children's board game sold in the United
States by the Milton Bradley Company. The game is an adaptation of the
English board game Snakes and Ladders, which is itself an adaptation of the
traditional Hindu game Leela.[1] Chutes and Ladders is played on a square
board marked out into one hundred smaller, numbered squares. Players place
tokens on the board and seek to be the first to advance from square one to
square one hundred. Players take turns using a spinner to determine how far
they may move on each turn. Along the route, players may encounter "ladders" and "chutes" on the board. When a player lands on a square at the
bottom of a ladder, she moves her token to the square at the top of the ladder,
skipping several, sometimes many, squares in the process. Just so, when a
player lands on a square at the top of a chute, she slides her token back down
to the square at the bottom of the chute.

Chutes and Ladders is at once a pleasant diversion and a mild morality
lesson, for each ladder and chute includes cartoon depictions of good or bad
child behavior and their related consequences. Squares that show good conduct move players up ladders to squares that show positive outcomes; square

nine, for example, shows that a child who mows the lawn will climb up to square thirty-one, where he will get to play at a carnival. Just so, squares that show bad conduct send players down chutes to unhappy cartoons; the child who rides her bicycle recklessly in square sixty-four slides back to square sixty, where she suffers a broken arm. The lesson seems clear enough; good behavior moves players ahead and bad behavior sets players back. However, Chutes and Ladders is an ironic illustration of the consequences of good and bad choices, because players' choices have no bearing whatsoever on the outcome of the game. The spinner, not a player's decision, determines how far a player progresses. There are no tactical or strategic elements to Chutes and Ladders, and at the beginning of the game each player has an equal probability of winning. While the board is littered with good and bad behaviors and their results, as a game Chutes and Ladders generates purely stochastic outcomes (Althoen, King, and Schilling 1993).

A Different Kind of Game

A similar sense of randomness has bedeviled research on innovation in the bureaucracy, as entrepreneurial public administrators seem to appear by chance, like winners in Chutes and Ladders. We have seen that career mobility creates incentives and opportunities for bureaucrats to innovate; we have seen that bureaucrats' psychological motivations are measurable and linked to their political advocacy. Taken together, these findings show that bureaucratic ambition creates (or inhibits) policy entrepreneurship among public administrators. But the usefulness of bureaucratic ambition as a theory of policy change or as a theory of management is limited indeed if administrators with entrepreneurial personalities simply emerge at random from the executive ranks of the public service. A satisfying theory of bureaucratic policy entrepreneurship must offer some explanation for why they appear at some times and not at others, for a theory that predicts unpredictability is no theory at all. Administrators "who create [innovation] are willing to run greater than ordinary risks," a despondent James Q. Wilson observed in *Bureaucracy* (1989). "Predicting who they will be is not easy; so far it has turned out to be impossible" (1989, 227).

But what if bureaucratic policy entrepreneurship is not merely random? Or to put things in Wilson's terms, what if the emergence of a "change-oriented personality" is not the result of "chance appearance"?[2] This chapter marries career path to motivation and shows how the ladders and ramps by which bureaucrats advance or fail to advance create conditions more or less amenable to policy entrepreneurship. The picture that emerges is of public administration career systems in which individuals' strategic choices matter a great deal and that are more or less likely to produce bureaucratic policy entrepreneurs. Bureaucratic success at career advancement via ramps and ladders is fundamentally different from a game of Chutes and Ladders.

Random Careers?

In a seminal 1977 article, "Almost Random Careers," James C. March and James G. March argue that public administration careers are, in fact, stochastic processes. March and March argue that job matches occur when individual bureaucrats and governments find each other mutually attractive and end when other matches appear more favorable to one or both. In order to maximize their likelihoods of finding good matches, both buyers and sellers of labor try to conform to the standard expectations of the market. For this reason, buyers of professional labor will tend to offer similar salaries, benefits, and work conditions. Similarly, sellers of professional labor will tend to exhibit similar qualifications. Individuals whose characteristics deviate substantially from the system's dominant favored characteristics will advance slowly and will eventually be eliminated from the system. For example, if governments that employ a public health director tend to prefer candidates with a master's degree in public health (MPH), then an individual with an MPH may find he has several head job opportunities; one without an MPH probably will not advance quickly, or may simply leave the profession. As individual actors, bureaucrats are more capable of learning and adaptation to perceived system demands than are the governments for which they work. Moreover, individual bureaucrats more easily enter and exit the market than do governments. Thus, individuals with long careers in a public administration profession will adapt through a series of jobs and will be relatively homogenous in job-relevant characteristics, especially late in their careers. This ability to adapt to dominant market demands tends to reduce heterogeneity across bureaucrats over time.

To test their theory, March and March track individual superintendents in Wisconsin school districts, including their movement into the profession, between districts, and out of the profession. March and March then compare the observed mobility among superintendents against Markov models that assume stochastic job changes across the market with fixed probability. Comparing actual career patterns against the stochastic models' predicted patterns reveals a remarkable consistency: the superintendents March and March study apparently experience "almost random careers." The theoretical implication is that, collectively, career outcomes for top bureaucrats and the governments that they serve seem to be governed by essentially stochastic conditions.

The practical consequence of the theory that March and March lay out is that contenders for government executive jobs have remarkably similar resumes. Observing only school superintendents' ages, education, number of jobs, and tenure in jobs, March and March see a basically homogeneous set of professional careers with individuals distributed to governments "almost randomly." Administrators seem to move from government to government with little to distinguish one from another. In this model, public administration careers are little more than vast, complicated games of Chutes and Ladders: advancements and setbacks happen by chance, and what appear to be behavioral causes and consequences are only coincidences, like so many cartoons on a game board. Indeed, the Markov chain and microsimulation model that March and March use to analyze public administration careers is astonishingly similar to the models that Althoen, King, and Schilling (1993) use to predict outcomes of Chutes and Ladders games. Any exceptional qualities that an administrator might exhibit—an entrepreneurial streak, for example—are merely consequences of an irreducible stochastic element in a professional job market tuned for equilibrium, argue March and March.

If public administration job markets generate almost random careers, it follows that administrators' personalities would be distributed almost randomly and that bureaucratic policy entrepreneurship would be similarly random. If so, then Wilson's despair of finding a theory of bureaucratic entrepreneurship would be justified. Yet the career system model that March and March depict is not so much random as it is probabilistic: superintendents advance through their profession with a fairly fixed probability, depending on their experience, education, and so forth. Further, the causal mechanisms at the root of March and March's theory are strategic choices made by employers and employees. The professional marketplace as a whole determines the standards by which individuals are deemed qualified, but those standards arise out of the cumulative choices of school district boards when making hiring decisions and candidates making labor decisions. Career advancement may seem "almost random" from outside the professional labor market, since the qualified candidates for the superintendent post may seem strikingly similar, exhibiting only the most minor differences. But from the perspective of the professionals and school boards engaged in the labor market, securing a superintendent's job is hardly accidental. To an ambitious professional, attaining a top administrative job is the result of specific choices: to secure educational credentials, maintain good professional standing, gain specific kinds of experience, and cultivate a reputation. To elected officials buying professional labor, making a hire also is the result of specific choices: the studying and weighing of candidates' credentials, references, experiences, and reputations. In this respect, "almost random careers" is an unfortunate moniker for the phenomenon that March and March observe since the process of career development is actually anything but random. The patterns that they find are not due to the turns of a spinner but rather reflect the cumulative rational decisions of many professionals and governments. Processes of selection and adaptation effectively "filter out" of the profession those bureaucrats who lack the requisite qualifications for advancement and who choose not to obtain them.

I argue that a similar probabilistic pattern affects the distribution of agency heads' personalities. Just as the hiring and promotional practices of a profession systematically promote school administrators who are active in the American Association of School Administrators and stymie those without doctoral degrees, job market decisions methodically promote or eliminate those with certain motive profiles. Studies of business organizations have found that individuals with strong achievement motivation advance rapidly in creative and entrepreneurial business environments due to the evaluative standards applied in such settings (McClelland 1961; Andrews 1967; Wainer and Rubin 1969; Stewart and Roth 2007). Individuals with strong power motivation thrive in hierarchical organizations, where advancement involves effectively directing other individuals to perform their appointed tasks (Andrews 1967; Winter 1978; McClelland and Boyatzis 1982; Winter 1996). Other research indicates that achievement and power motivation also affect individuals' choice to pursue careers that are likely to satisfy these motives (McClelland 1961; Winter 1973; Lagan-Fox and Roth 1995; Sagie and Elizur 1999; Collins, Hange, and Locke 2004). In other words, careers can progress along diagonal *ramps* and/or vertical *ladders*, but different kinds of individuals are likely to advance on each path. If professional administration job markets operate similarly, then the emergence of bureaucratic policy entrepreneurs is not random but rather a predictable consequence of the market for professional administrative labor.

Keys to Advancement

For any bureaucrat, advancement from one administrative post to another requires two decisions: (1) a government's decision to offer a job to an individual; and (2) an individual's decision to accept the job. Employers and employees bring different expectations to the relationship, and each seek matches that they expect will satisfy their needs. The processes that create, sustain, and/or end these matches determine how professional public administrators move through a career system.

Qualifications

Naturally, local governments hiring top administrators for their agencies look at job candidates' qualifications. Larger agencies generally offer their agency heads higher salaries, more perquisites, and greater prestige than smaller agencies; hence, as in chapter 5, I use *agency size* to measure a job's status. If larger governments prefer candidates with higher levels of education and if bureaucrats cultivate their resumes in pursuit of career advancement, we would expect to see agency heads' levels of *education* increase with agency size. Moreover, measurements of dispersion for education should decrease with agency size, since administrators ascending to high-status positions will have adapted to market expectations for academic credentialing. In other words, the agency heads should be more similar and less diverse in their job qualifications as their status increases. Finally, if professional credentialing is more important as a selection criterion for agencies hiring from outside, as I argued in chapter 4, then level of education should be higher among diagonal climbers than among vertical climbers.

Figure 6.1 shows mean education by agency size quartile for police chiefs and water utility managers. In both professions, *education* increases from the first quartile (the smallest 25% of the sampled agencies) to the fourth quartile (the largest 25%).[3] Crucially, the diversity of these qualifications shrinks at higher strata of each of the professions. Figure 6.2 shows the standard deviations of education for each profession by quartile. Standard deviations for education fall significantly from the first to the fourth quartile for both

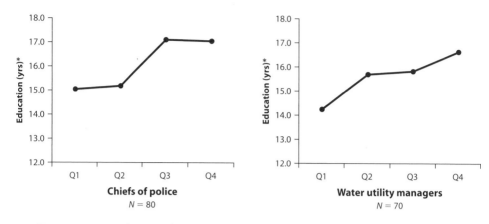

Figure 6.1 Mean education by quartile
*Education is the highest level of education completed in years.

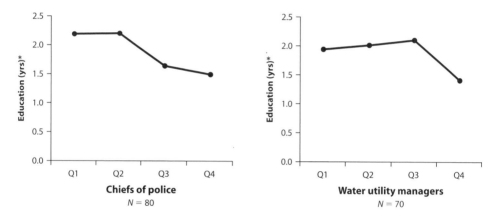

Figure 6.2 Standard deviation of education by quartile
*Education is the highest level of education completed in years.

professions.[4] Increasing levels of education coupled with falling measures of dispersion reflect professional career systems that systematically promote individuals with higher academic qualifications to higher posts. To the ambitious administrator, the patterns seen in figures 6.1 and 6.2 demonstrate effective adaptive strategies to increase his probability of advancement through the profession. Individuals observe and imitate these strategies and then obtain the educational credentials that they believe will increase their probabilities of advancement. From outside the professional labor market,

Table 6.1   Mean education and agency size for vertical and diagonal climbers

	Promoted from within	Hired from outside	*p**
Chiefs of police			
Education (years)**	15.86	16.54	.08
Log agency size	3.97	3.82	.65
(sworn officers)			
N = 75			
Water utility managers			
Education (years)**	15.00	16.11	.01
Log agency size	9.25	9.36	.36
(customer connections)			
N = 70			

*p-value generated by a one-tailed difference-in-means t test.
**Number of years of education completed.

there appears to be little difference between candidates, especially at progressively larger, higher-status agencies: contenders for agency head jobs in large governments are all likely to have advanced degrees. The result is that agency heads' resumes look more and more alike as they reach higher-status jobs.

An ambitious individual will only pursue such an adaptive strategy toward career advancement if she perceives that her probability of advancement will increase significantly by attainment of an advanced academic degree. For those who advance to top administrative positions vertically, the probability of advancement may be as much or more a function of length of tenure or adherence to organizational norms as it is to attainment of academic credentials. If ambitious professionals are strategically adaptive, then we would expect to see lower overall levels of educational attainment among administrators who were promoted from within than among those who were hired from outside.

Data from both professions bear out this expectation. As shown in table 6.1, police chiefs and water utility managers who advance to their current positions diagonally—that is, those who left administrative posts in other agencies before taking their current jobs—are, on average, more highly educated than those who advance vertically.[5] These differences might simply reflect differences in agency size if diagonal climbers generally serve larger, higher-status agencies on average. However, there is no meaningful correlation between agency size and career path, and there is no significant difference in mean log agency size between vertical and diagonal climbers (see table 6.1).

These patterns reflect the processes of employer selection and employee adaptation working in parallel. Education is not an innate characteristic but rather a credential gained deliberately and voluntarily. Knowing that agencies hiring water utility directors from outside will be looking for academic credentials, an ambitious utility manager looking to move to another agency will seek an advanced engineering or administration degree. If an administrator is not ambitious, if he perceives no opportunities outside his current organization, or if advancement within his organization is not dependent on educational attainment, there is less incentive for him to acquire higher education.

The Nature of the Job

Day-to-day work in public administration jobs can be quite different in top positions of an organization from work at what Michael Lipsky (1980) has called the "street level." In archetypal professions like medicine, law, and architecture, the substance of the job changes relatively little as careers progress: most top surgeons still perform or direct surgery, top lawyers still practice law, and top architects still design buildings. Though advancement in these fields often requires increased attention to administrative matters, doctors, lawyers, and architects may reach the upper echelons of their professions by continuing to practice medicine, law, and architecture. The shift to full-time administration is optional for advancement in these fields. By contrast, the "nature of the job" changes with increasing job status in most public administration jobs. As professional careers progress, the shift from "doing" to "managing" is much more pronounced in public agencies than in architecture firms, for example. As police officers and utility engineers advance in job status, they spend increasing amounts of time on administrative and policymaking duties. In medium to large organizations, decision making, as opposed to service delivery, becomes the task of import as bureaucratic professionals advance through their careers (Simon 1997). Consequently, the street-level bureaucrat's work is much different from the mezzo-level bureaucrat's. A police chief's typical workday is quite different from a patrol officer's, and a utility director's is quite different from a treatment plant operator's. These differences are more pronounced in larger agencies. A chief of police in a small department may continue to drive a patrol car and investigate crimes; the manager of a small utility may continue to operate water treatment and distribution facilities. But department heads in medium or large agencies spend virtually no time on such tasks, instead devoting their time to management and policymaking.

In police organizations, many of which exhibit predominantly vertical advancement, effective patrol officers and detectives must abandon patrol and investigation for management and policymaking if they wish to advance in rank, status, and pay. Both tradition and pension systems can create size-able disincentives for mobility among midlevel police administrators. As one chief told me: "In law enforcement, you tend to only have movement at the top. There's not much movement at the middle ranks. We bring people in at the bottom, we keep them here forever." Individuals who become chief of police in such organizations may have chosen to take the chief's job be-cause they relish the opportunity to lead an organization and work with elected officials to craft policy. It is just as possible, however, that an officer in a vertical organization becomes chief because there are few other quali-fied candidates within the agency and there is no other way for him to ad-vance. In 2010, the mayor of Utica, New York, named Mark Williams as his city's new chief of police. A twenty-two-year veteran of the Utica Police De-partment, Williams rose through the ranks in a department with a standing tradition of promoting its chief from within. But even as he was promoted, Chief Williams was nostalgic about his days on patrol: "I love the street action, but I guess I'm too old to do that now. It's what stinks about these promotions is you become more administrative and you miss the street" (Miner 2010, 1A).

By contrast, individuals do not advance diagonally by default. Rather, pub-lic administrators advance diagonally because they actively seek or have been recruited for posts that require administrative and policymaking work. If behavior reveals preferences, we might infer that individuals who seek diago-nal advancement to top administrative jobs enjoy the managerial and policy-making responsibilities that these jobs require, or at least do not mind them as much as those who advance vertically. Put another way, administrators who advance diagonally probably like being mezzo-level bureaucrats (as opposed to street-level bureaucrats) more than those who advance vertically.

My interviews with police chiefs confirmed this pattern. The two Be-havioral Event Interview (BEI) questions that opened my interviews asked police chiefs to discuss one positive and one negative work experience:

Thinking back over your career in law enforcement, please describe a specific time in your career when you felt *effective* at work.

Thinking back over your career in law enforcement, please describe a specific time in your career when you felt *ineffective* at work.

In chapter 5 and later in this chapter, I use responses to these questions to capture data on human motivation. However, content analysis of responses to the BEI prompts can also be used to gather attitudinal and behavioral data (Anderson and Nilsson 1964; Borman and Dunette 1975; Anderson and Wilson 1997; Fountain 1999). When I reviewed and categorized all of the BEI responses, four types of stories emerged:

Policy-and-politics stories—about challenges and/or triumphs in the policymaking arena

Management stories—accounts of difficulties and/or successes within an organizational work setting

Cops-and-robbers stories—about investigations, arrests, pursuits, or violent encounters

Human-interaction stories—about specific personal interactions, both positive and negative

Just a handful of stories did not fit easily into one of these four broad categories. Table 6.2 offers illustrative excerpts from BEI interview responses of each type. The first two types of responses—*policy and politics* and *management*—refer to "decisional" dimensions work (Simon 1997). The second two types—*cops* and *robbers* and *human interaction*—deal with operational aspects of organizational work. Categorized in this way, the responses to the BEI prompts on incidents that made respondents feel "effective" and "ineffective" give a sense of what aspects of work "turn-on" or "turn-off" police chiefs. Comparing these substantive responses from chiefs who were promoted from within against those from chiefs who arrived from outside reveals a distinct difference in what makes the two groups of chiefs feel effective. Figure 6.3 summarizes chiefs' responses to the first BEI question ("when you felt *effective*"). Responses to the second BEI question ("when you felt *ineffective*") are summarized by type in figure 6.4.

Experiences that make chiefs of police feel effective differ significantly between those promoted to the chief's position from within an agency and those who advanced from another agency. When talking about incidents that

Table 6.2   Example excerpts from critical incident interview responses, by type

	"Felt effective"	"Felt ineffective"
Policy and politics	When I was a planning officer I proposed a division to address juvenile issues. This was back in the 1980s. The idea was one-stop—take care of everything from school resource officers, to gang unit, child abuse, sexual assault. I proposed the division. The next year it was put into the budget and adopted and ultimately established in the [other city] police department, too.	I've been trying to convince the city manager and the current mayor that we need to be a little more aggressive or attentive to updating the city's overall emergency plan. Particularly, the portion that applies to the police department and what the police department would do in some kind of major situation. I kind of got it going, but I couldn't keep it moving. I couldn't keep people interested in it.
Management	They decided they were going to host the [major international event] here. I was part of that. . . . What I had to do was restructure my whole police department. I made two out of the three sergeants lieutenants, and one of the sergeants was made deputy chief. I had to take all of my patrolmen and make them sergeants. We hired eighty state police officers and they all came here and they stayed at the high school in the gym. They rotated twelve-hour shifts.	I was a lieutenant at this department and I was in charge of training and working for a deputy chief at the time. This person was extremely negative, extremely focused on small details that didn't matter. No matter how thoroughly things were addressed or approached, there was always one more question. This guy used to write questions on the tiniest of Post-it notes, and he'd use both sides of the note—I swear to God! I still remember saying, "Man, I can't get anything through this guy."
Cops and robbers	The guy jumped out, and he had a Marine Corps coat—an overcoat. He opened it up, pulled a handgun from his left side. We both exchanged rounds. Then what happened, I got all four individuals down on the ground. Two of my other cars came up at that time and I called out, "Watch out! They have guns."	I pull him over and charge him, take him to court. We convict him, but he takes it all the way to circuit court. I have a witness there, who was a mom leaving the school. And he's found not guilty. That would be the most frustrating time. It's like, "This isn't worth it. You catch somebody red-handed, you've got an eye-witness, and the court just lets him go."
Human interaction	Then he turns around, sticks his hand out to me, shook my hand, and says, "I just want to thank you for treating me like a human being. You're the first police officer I've ever dealt with who's treated me decently."	I'm talking to him, he's looking at me kind of in a daze, not knowing what's going on. I'm talking to him, consoling him, trying to make him as comfortable as possible until we get him to the hospital. The next day they call up and say the kid died. And I mean, that just floored me.

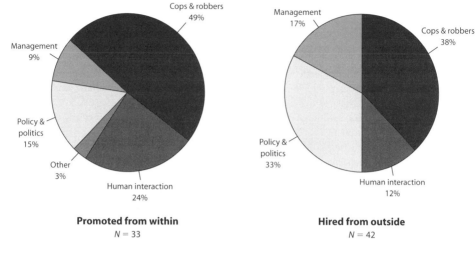

Promoted from within
N = 33

Hired from outside
N = 42

Figure 6.3 Turn-ons for vertical and diagonal climbers
Police chiefs' responses to "effective" Behavioral Event interview prompts.

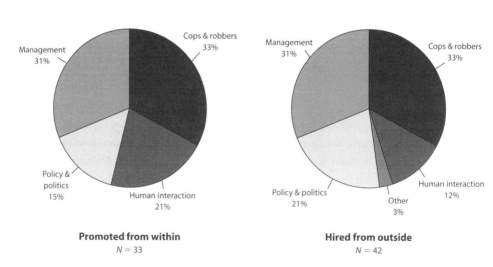

Promoted from within
N = 33

Hired from outside
N = 42

Figure 6.4 Turn-offs for vertical and diagonal climbers
Police chiefs' responses to "ineffective" Behavioral Event interview prompts.

made them feel effective, a large majority (72.7%) of vertical climbers cite operational aspects of work, while just 24.3 percent talk about decisional aspects of their jobs. Diagonal climbers are split evenly, with exactly one-half citing operational and one-half citing decisional aspects of work when asked what made them feel effective.[6] Police chiefs who advance diagonally are, on average, more likely to feel effective in the decisional dimensions of their jobs than their vertical-climbing counterparts, who are more likely to feel effective in the operational aspects of their jobs. Differences in what makes the two groups of chiefs feel ineffective are less pronounced. So while the lows of a police chief's work are similar across career paths, the highs are different for vertical and diagonal climbers.

These differences were especially apparent in my interviews with two particular police chiefs. The first was a twenty-one-year veteran of a large, Midwestern police department who ascended vertically through the ranks to become chief of police in a department that historically has always promoted its chief from within. When I asked him about his policy priorities for the coming year, he spoke of ongoing budgetary struggles and the difficulty of getting his city manager and elected officials to fund his agency:

> It's frustrating when the city manager comes to you and says, "what can you do with one position less? Or two positions less? Can you get a little more money through forfeiture or something?" It's frustrating. We're at the point now that we're reducing staff through attrition. It's gotten to the point where, whenever somebody in the department is looking at retirement or thinking of moving to another agency, I'm practically begging them to stay because I know I won't get their position back. We suck it up and try to get things done as best we can. That's decision making. It's what a manager is supposed to do, I guess.

This chief was downcast throughout the interview, particularly as discussion turned to administrative or policymaking matters. Just as Utica's Chief Williams expressed nostalgia for street-level policing, this Midwestern chief indicated discomfort about working with politicians and expressed a longing for more tangible police work: "It's sad in a way, but probably the time when I felt most effective was when I was out pushing a patrol car—you know, driving, enforcing the law, writing violations and arresting people, training the new guys." This chief's despondency over administrative matters was palpable in our conversation; I couldn't help feeling sympathy for this experienced and decorated police officer who found himself trapped and miserable in an unwanted policymaking role. But the career opportunity structure available to him was vertical, giving him no other perceived avenue for advancement. When I asked him why he took the chief's job, he told me: "I was deputy chief, and so I was next in line." Though he was only in his mid-forties at the time of the interview, he indicated that he planned to retire from law enforcement within five years.

Not all police chiefs disdain their policymaking duties, however. A chief of a large southern department facing similar budgetary pressures described his political efforts to win support for funding in the coming year. During his interview, he mentioned without prompting that it was an election year in his city. I asked whether elections made his job easier or more difficult. His response is worth quoting at length:

> Election years are much better in many respects, especially for the leaders of the police department. That's because you'll get all kinds of promises. Now we haven't had a raise in three years, but this is an election year and we've already been promised a raise next month. I don't anticipate another raise for another three years, until the next election. That's just the way it is. I understand, as a police chief, that you have to take advantage—you have to recognize that every fourth year is an opportunity for us. . . .
>
> Once you're around long enough you kind of read the system and you know when to get active and start to ask for things and you know when not to ask for things. This year we have people running for city council, and I've met with those candidates privately. I've had private meetings with the state attorney general. I've already had private meetings with a candidate for governor, and I've given my two cents' to all of them. Four years ago I had a meeting with the guy who's governor now. . . . They've promised me that if they're elected they'll come through with what I need.
>
> Now, any other time—I mean, if this were the year after the election—I probably couldn't get a meeting with them. To talk to a governor? Or a candidate for governor? With the state attorney general? Hah! Right now, they'll call me and want to talk. But next year they won't want to talk with me. They probably wouldn't even return my phone call.
>
> A police chief can be, I don't want to say a "kingmaker," but he can make a difference in an election. In many communities a police chief carries a lot of

weight and can swing a lot of votes. Just think about how many people are police officers—it's almost always the biggest department in a city. And they all have families and friends, and these people vote. . . .

There are times when you know you have some leverage to push, with your support and the votes you can send their way, so you get out and do it. And I do it. I go out and give talks at [he names two organizations] and I mention their names. Now, I don't tell anybody, "Go and vote for so-and-so." But you can pretty clearly make it known who is taking care of law enforcement.

His tone of voice and frequent chuckles revealed an administrator who not only tolerated but relished the strategic, political aspects of his job. A typical diagonal "ramp climber," this chief had led two smaller departments before reaching his current post. He told me with a laugh: "It doesn't make any difference the size of the department—the small ones and the large ones, the politics are all the same." In his early sixties, this chief planned to serve for at least five more years.

Both of these chiefs of police served large departments facing financial difficulties, but there was a stark difference between their responses to my questions about policy plans. To the vertical-climbing midwestern chief, budgetary constraints were set by the city manager and elected officials; he was to make do with the resources given to the police department. He discussed the budgetary and policymaking aspects of his job with resignation, as if they were to be endured out of a sense of duty. The ramp-climbing southern chief approached his department's financial difficulties as a political game to be won strategically. Rather than accepting priorities and directives from elected officials, he sought to shift political conditions in his city, thereby reshaping his putative principals' policy preferences. The southern chief was successful in extracting promises of support from politicians for his preferred policies in exchange for his support in the electoral arena.

These differences in political behavior are in part due to the two chiefs' markedly different attitudes toward policymaking and political work, evident in both the tone and the substance of their stories. The midwestern chief sat uncomfortably behind the chief's desk, wistfully recalling his days on patrol and looking forward to early retirement. The southern chief evidently enjoyed the politics of his job enough to climb ramp after ramp on his way to the large department he now leads.

Opportunity Structures as Personality Filters

So far this chapter has examined educational attainment and bureaucrats' attraction to or repulsion from policymaking work in vertical and diagonal career paths. What these variables hold in common is that they result from the conscious, deliberate choices of buyers and sellers of bureaucratic labor. For governments, the choice is to hire individuals with higher or lower levels of education for positions at the head of agencies. For individuals, the choice is to seek an advanced degree and/or to take an executive job in a government agency. Selection and adaptation are at work overtly here. Professionals observe their peers' behavior and intentionally select strategies that will improve their probabilities of advancement. The decision to seek advancement via movement to a different agency is similarly purposive and calculated: an individual who is attracted to decisional tasks will seek administrative agency head jobs where they are found, while one who eschews decisional work will take such a job only when it is the sole path to advancement.

But unlike a college degree or a past career path, motives are stable elements of personality; they are not deliberately selected nor chosen adaptively. If different motives are associated with advancement in different opportunity structures, it is not due to adaptive learning but because motives drive behaviors that lead to success or failure in career advancement. Whether individuals can or cannot intentionally alter their own personalities is an ongoing question in psychology. Timothy Wilson (2002) mounts an impressive case that individuals can consciously change their unconscious personalities with sustained effort over time. In any case, choosing to pursue an advanced degree, take a job, or run for office in a professional society are discrete decisions that are quickly realized, unlike choosing to change one's motivations. Moreover, unlike education and career path, motives do not appear on professional resumes. Chapter 5 demonstrated that achievement motivation is associated with political advocacy. If individuals with high achievement motivation advance with varying probability along different career paths, then we may infer that political advocacy is rewarded by some career opportunity structures and punished by others.

Winning Personalities

I use an ordinary least squares regression model to test the effects of human motivation on police chiefs' advancement in different opportunity structures. Recall that the sample used here is stratified by agency size. However, unlike the statistical analyses in chapters 4 and 5, the models reported in table 6.3 are not poststratification weighted because the dependent variable in these models is *agency size*. The model shows the direct effects of *achievement* and power *motivation* on job status, as well as interaction terms, to test the effects of these motives as conditioned by opportunity structure. *Diagonal agencies* are police departments that "always," "usually," or "sometimes" hire the chief from outside, which comprise 48 percent of the sample. As in chapter 5, log agency size is my measure of job status. We have seen that level of education is positively correlated with agency size, so I include a control for *education*. I also include a control for *career length* (in years) since individuals who have been in the profession for many years are more likely to have advanced to high-status positions than those who have been in the profession for less time. Table 6.3 reports the results of the regression model.

As expected, *career length* and *education* have strong positive effects on career advancement in both models. More importantly for the present analysis, the interactive results indicate that the motives leading to career advancement in vertical opportunity structures are quite different from those in diagonal structures. *Achievement* motivation has little effect in vertical agencies, but a strong, positive effect on job status in *diagonal agencies*. Meanwhile, *power* motivation has a similarly strong, positive effect on job status in vertical agencies, but it apparently bears little on advancement in diagonal agencies. In fact, there is a startling symmetry in the effects of *achievement* and *power* motivation in diagonal and vertical agencies, respectively: their effects are nearly exactly opposite in both magnitude and statistical significance. These models reveal the "winning personalities" in each opportunity structure: achievement motivation fuels career advancement along diagonal ramps, while power motivation fuels advancement via vertical ladders.

If administrators' political behavior flows from their motives, and if career opportunity structures reward specific kinds of political behavior with advancement, it follows that an administrator's motive profile will partly determine his probability of advancement in a given opportunity structure. In chapter 5, I showed that an administrator's political advocacy increases with his achievement motivation. That individuals with stronger achievement motives tend to advance in diagonal opportunity structures demonstrates that policy entrepreneurship is an important determinant of advancement on a diagonal career path. The power motive's positive effect on advancement in

Table 6.3   Police chief job status by motive in vertical
and diagonal opportunity structures

	Log agency size (full-time sworn officers)		
OLS linear regression	Coefficient (standard error)	Standardized coefficient	p^*
Variable			
Achievement motivation	−.05	−.13	.37
	(.06)		
Power motivation	.15	.37	.05
	(.07)		
Affiliation motivation	.03	.05	.66
	(.07)		
Achievement × diagonal agency	.15	.45	.06
	(.08)		
Power × diagonal agency	−.10	−.33	.28
	(.09)		
Diagonal agency	−.73	−.22	.50
	(1.09)		
Education (years)	.32	.40	.00
	(.08)		
Career length (years)	.05	.27	.01
	(.02)		
Intercept	−3.32		.03
	(1.53)		
R^2	.40		
Adjusted R^2	.32		
N	73		

Note: Cells contain coefficients, standard errors (SE), standardized coefficients, and p values generated by ordinary least squares model of log agency size, measured in number of full-time sworn officers. Diagonal agencies (coded 1 in the model) "always," "usually," or "sometimes" hire the chief of police from outside. Vertical agencies (coded 0) "always" or "usually" promote the chief of police from within the agency.
    $^*p$-value generated by a two-tailed t test of significance.

the vertical opportunity structures suggests that policy entrepreneurship is not so important for advancement where chiefs of police are promoted from within. Coupled with earlier studies of power motivation in organizations, this finding suggests that vertical organizations tend to select individuals who adhere to and are comfortable in hierarchical social structures. Just as educational credentials affect the probability of advancement, so does personality.

But as noted earlier, an important difference between motives and other qualifications is that motives are not consequences of individuals' deliberate decisions. If an individual with a certain motive profile faces different probabilities of career advancement within different opportunity structures, it is not due to her conscious, adaptive behavior but to some bias within the opportunity structure. Career-opportunity structures appear to act as "filters," systematically allowing some kinds of personalities to advance to high-status positions and stymieing others.

To illustrate these results in more intuitively meaningful terms, consider two imaginary police officers, Andy and Bob, each with a master's degree and seeking in their careers to advance diagonally (that is, by moving from one agency to another). Suppose that Andy's achievement motivation is one standard deviation above the mean (11.95) and Bob's is one standard deviation below the mean (3.01), but that they each have average power motivation. According to the March and March (1977) "almost random careers" model, Andy and Bob face a virtually identical probability of advancement since each has adaptively attained the market's preferred qualifications observable by potential employers on a resume. If so, Andy and Bob will advance (or fail to advance) largely according to chance, like players in Chutes and Ladders. But according to my theory of bureaucratic ambition, the diagonal, "ramped" opportunity structure in which they seek to advance favors policy entrepreneurship. Therefore, Andy is likely to attain a substantially higher-status job by the end of his career due to his strong achievement motivation. The model shown in table 6.3 yields the following estimates of the two chiefs' destinations after forty-year professional careers:[7]

Andy would be chief of police in an agency with approximately 254 full-time sworn officers, such as the Chandler, Arizona (population 177,000), police department

   Bob would be chief of police in an agency with approximately 107 full-time sworn officers, such as the Des Plaines, Illinois (population 59,000), police department.

Achievement motivation makes a substantial difference in career outcomes in these two cases, with Andy's higher achievement motivation leading to a much-higher-status job by retirement for him than for Bob.

Crafting illustrative hypothetical scenarios for comparative career destinations in vertical opportunity structures requires a different approach because we must assume that candidates for chief of police must have begun their careers in the agencies that they aim to lead. Consider two more police officers, Carla and Diane, who also have master's degrees. Suppose that Carla's power motivation is one standard deviation higher than the mean (12.95) and Diane's power motivation is one standard deviation below the mean (4.05), but that they each have average achievement motivation. Because advancement to police chief in a vertical agency requires progressing within a single organization, the probability of Carla or Diane becoming chief of police depends on the size of the agency in which she begins her police administration career. The opportunity structures in which they seek to advance favor individuals who thrive in hierarchical organizations, so we would expect Carla to be more successful than Diane in advancing to the chief's desk in a large vertical organization. Again applying the OLS equation from table 6.3, we have the following estimate for these two professionals after forty years:[8]

> Carla might expect to advance vertically to the position of chief of police in an agency with up to 639 sworn officers, similar in size to the Sacramento, California (population 407,000), police department.
>
> Diane might expect to advance vertically to the position of chief of police in an agency with up to 187 sworn officers, such as the Ann Arbor, Michigan (population 114,000), police department.

Here power motivation has a dramatic effect on the two imaginary officers' career prospects. With her strong power motivation, Carla has a good chance of reaching the chief's office by retirement if she seeks career advancement in a very large vertical agency. With a weaker power motivation, Diane is unlikely to advance to chief in a very large vertical agency. Diane's best chance of becoming chief of police through vertical advancement by retirement is in a small or medium-sized agency.

Ramps and Ladders

Administrators who become agency heads by climbing vertical organizational ladders are evidently quite different from those who arrive on the job diagonally via ramps from other agencies. It comes as no surprise that diagonal climbers are, on average, better educated than vertical climbers and that the diversity of bureaucrats' qualifications becomes attenuated at higher strata of the profession. These findings basically reaffirm the March and March (1977) career-systems theory: ambitious, adaptive individuals in a career system observe and mimic the qualities of others who have succeeded. The

differences in education between vertical and diagonal climbers reflect deliberate decisions of individuals to adapt to their respective career-opportunity
structures. Little wonder, then, that candidates for high-status agency heads
have remarkably similar resumes.

But differences in attitude toward the job and in career advancement by
motive profile argue for an important revision to the March and March model
of "almost random careers." For the chiefs of police studied here, the probability of advancement to high-status positions is not only a function of deliberate, adaptive behavior but also of personality. Achievement motivation is
associated with successful career advancement for police chiefs on diagonal
career paths. Power motivation is a similarly important determinant of advancement for chiefs of police promoted vertically from within their agencies. These differences in career advancement for individuals with similar
motive profiles in different opportunity structures indicate that the professional labor market itself is biased in ways that filter out individuals whose
motives do not drive behaviors favored by the opportunity structure.

Unlike items on a resume, motives are not directly observable by employers. I showed in chapter 4 that job mobility creates incentives for administrators to introduce professional innovations. In chapter 5, I showed that
administrators' political advocacy increases as their achievement motivation
increases. We may infer, then, that greater innovation and political advocacy
—or policy entrepreneurship—are rewarded with improved probability of
advancement for administrators in diagonal opportunity structures. Similarly,
maintenance of and adherence to organizational hierarchy is rewarded with
improved probability of advancement for administrators in vertical opportunity structures.

Not-So-Random Careers

On one level, these findings are consistent with March and March (1977):
The differences in probability of advancement for similarly motivated people
in different opportunity structures reflect systemic biases in bureaucratic
career-opportunity structures. Looking across a market full of homogenously
qualified bureaucrats, March and March modeled bureaucratic careers as simple Markov processes—like games of Chutes and Ladders—and concluded
that the substantive policy decisions that administrators make are irrelevant
to their career advancement. They complain that school boards evaluate, hire,
and fire superintendents based on factors that are "not necessarily relevant,

but controllable factors" like "style of dress, time allocation, and official sex education" (1977, 407). March and March go so far as to disparage accounts of career success and failure resting on differences in behavior as mere "fictions intended to reassure us about justice and encourage the young," just like the moralistic cartoons on a Chutes and Ladders game board (408).

Yet the evidence I have presented in this chapter suggests that bureaucrats' political choices actually matter a great deal in determining their career advancement. Significantly, while March and March model career *movement* (changing jobs) as a stochastic process, they do not attempt to fit career *advancement* (moving from lower-status to higher-status jobs) to a stochastic model. In fact, they note—but do not model—a pronounced pattern of movement by superintendents from smaller, rural districts to larger, urban districts. That March and March include time allocation and sex education in their list of irrelevant factors in administrative careers betrays a theoretical gap in their article. Choosing fashionable clothes may or may not be important for determining job advancement, but choosing and advocating for professionally fashionable policies surely is. A bureaucrat's political behavior contributes to a "track record" that future employers can observe and that affects the probability that she will advance in her career. Differences in motivation among bureaucrats cause differences in political behavior, which in turn change their probabilities of advancement in different opportunity structures. Unlike a game of Chutes and Ladders, the political choices that administrators make and the consequences of those choices for their career advancement along ramps and ladders are not merely coincidental fictions. When we consider differences in motivation between those who advance in a profession and those who do not, it becomes evident that public administration careers are not as random, nor bureaucrats as indistinguishable, nor their political choices as inconsequential as March and March assert.

Careers, Motivation, and the Origins of Entrepreneurial Bureaucrats

Dependent as it is on executive personality, the "supply side" of bureaucratic policy entrepreneurship has been difficult for political scientists to explain. In his landmark *Bureaucracy*, James Q. Wilson (1989) glumly concluded that bureaucratic policy entrepreneurship defied theoretical explanation precisely because it was so dependent on the chance appearance of "a change-oriented personality" (227). But as I have shown, career-opportunity structures affect the probability of such personalities emerging in the leadership ranks of an organization. Diagonal advancement opportunities provide fertile soil for achievement-motivated administrators seeking to grow careers. Vertical career structures are less likely to produce risk-taking, politically active personalities at the executive level. However, vertical career structures are likely to attract and promote power-motivated administrators who will maintain and adhere to organizational hierarchies. Ramps and ladders each provide paths to advancement, but the administrators who scaled ladders are a psychologically different lot from those who clambered up ramps.

So while Wilson was correct in emphasizing the importance of executive personality in driving policy innovation, he was mistaken in characterizing the emergence of such personalities as simply serendipitous. Ironically, two pages after he despairs of finding a theory of executive personality, Wilson (1989), citing Carlson (1961), notes that in local school districts

> one important reason [for policy innovation] is the way in which school executives are recruited. Those brought in from outside the system proposed more changes than those who were promoted from within. The reason seems clear: the outsiders got many of their rewards from their professional peers elsewhere in the country, whereas the insiders (who had spent their whole lives in the system they now administered) got their rewards from the job itself. The outsiders were often chosen because of the high opinion other outsiders had of them, even if they failed in their new job, they might expect to go on to even better jobs elsewhere, provided that they failed for the right reason—that is, failed while striving to attain some goal that was approved of by their profession. (229)

We have seen that a market full of potential clients creates diagonal advancement opportunities and attendant incentives for bureaucratic policy entrepreneurship. Over time, then, such diagonal career opportunities tend to favor achievement-motivated individuals, who Wilson might say have "change-oriented personalities."

That opportunity structures so affect the psychological composition of governments' executive ranks implies that the emergence of bureaucratic policy entrepreneurs is partly a consequence of institutional design, for career-opportunity structures are not organic phenomena but rather are consequences of synthetic rules and customs. In other words, through government agency design, hiring, and promotional policies, it is possible to exert some control over the supply of bureaucratic policy entrepreneurs.

CHAPTER SEVEN

What Bureaucratic Ambition
Means for Democracy

Ambition is a good servant, but a bad master.   LAURA INGALLS WILDER

Unhappy with the condition of his police department, Mayor Jerry Abramson of Louisville, Kentucky, went shopping for a new chief and found one in Robert C. White.[1] On arriving in Louisville, Chief White introduced a series of reorganizations and disciplinary policies to change a department with a disturbing record of violence and adversarial relationship with several community groups. He reached out to the media and neighborhood groups, publicized an anonymous tip line to encourage cooperation by crime witnesses, and initiated controversial meetings with the city's gang leaders. Chief White simultaneously launched a "violent offenders task force" that "went after the worst of the worst" Louisville criminals (Salvato 2005). Many of Chief White's innovations drew the ire of Louisville's Fraternal Order of Police and some city council members, but he earned the loyalty of his mayor and the guarded respect of many community leaders.

Chief White's efforts also earned him attention from outside Louisville. Late in 2007, Chicago's mayor, Richard Daley, began searching for a new leader for his city's police department, hiring a national search firm and expressing a desire for an outsider to help the troubled agency. Though Mayor

Daley ultimately hired another candidate, Chief White was a finalist for the Chicago job (Rozas and Ciokajlo 2007). Meanwhile, back in Louisville, Mayor Abramson announced that he would not seek reelection, and White's controversial leadership of the police department emerged as a significant issue in the ensuing mayoral campaign. Chief White has made no secret of his ambition, and Louisville likely will not be his last stop: "A police department should have new energy, new ideas coming in," he said. "I'm not a guy who believes a police chief should stay around for ten or eleven years."[2]

Policy entrepreneurship born of bureaucratic ambition is evident in Chief White's path to Louisville and in his potential path away from it. Also evident are the tensions and dilemmas of accountability that bureaucratic ambition can create. In this book I have shown that professional innovation occurs when a demand for innovation meets a supply of mobile, ambitious professionals. I have shown that public administrators' personalities—achievement motivation, in particular—fuels their political advocacy. I have also shown that entrepreneurial (that is, achievement-motivated) bureaucrats do not emerge randomly but rather are predictable consequences of career-opportunity structures.

To this point, I have largely left aside the normative implications of bureaucratic ambition in a democratic state. The normative implications are significant, however, because bureaucratic ambition necessarily divides an administrator's loyalty between the organization that he serves at present and the universe of organizations that he might serve in the future. To the extent that he is ambitious, a bureaucrat will tend to value the latter over the former. For administrators whose careers proceed entirely within a single agency, the present and future employers are one and the same. For professions with significant job mobility, responsiveness to the market means adherence to professional norms and values. Both organizational loyalty and professional norms and values condition a bureaucrat's political behavior: ambition helps determine their relative strength. As a mobile, ambitious agency head, Chief White is likely to make political decisions with Louisville's elected officials in mind, but also with an eye toward appealing to the thirty or so U.S. cities larger than Louisville, including Chicago. To the extent that Chief White's professional imperatives align with his elected officials' priorities, this client-professional relationship is likely to be happy. Problems of democratic accountability and governance may arise, however, when professions and elected officials understand "good policy" in markedly different ways.

In this concluding chapter, I put the study's findings into the context of ongoing research on public administration and bureaucratic politics, while also noting important limitations and directions for future research on bureaucratic ambition. I end by considering the ways in which bureaucratic ambition bears on the perennial practical and normative problems of agency accountability in an age of professional public administration. The result is, I hope, a provocative and useful discussion for researchers and practitioners alike.

Bureaucratic Professions as Markets for Policy Innovation

Public administration scholars have long pondered the effects of professional norms on bureaucratic behavior in an age of professionalized public agencies. For the most part, studies of bureaucratic professionalism have cast professions as socializing forces that cause administrators to form norms and values, which are then carried into action within public agencies. In their review of research on bureaucracy and democratic governance, Meier and O'Toole (2006) grumble that too many political scientists—particularly those advancing principal-agent models—neglect administrators' values in their models of bureaucratic politics. Stripped of these professional values, the administrators that populate many political scientists' models are "automatons or kleptocrats," as Daniel Carpenter (2006) has called them, mindlessly responding to organizational incentives put before them by elected officials or greedily maximizing their reward with minimal effort. Carpenter complains that such models dangerously oversimplify the realities of agency politics. He calls for models of bureaucracy to "be more *psychologically realistic*, incorporate the complexity of politics and policymaking . . . and all the while still maintain a degree of goal pursuit and rationality" (42; italics added).

The trouble comes in explaining variation in bureaucratic political behavior when virtually all administrators identify as "professionals," undergo similar professional socialization, and espouse similar values. In this study I have tried to take bureaucrats' professional values seriously, but in a way that also accounts for variation in the political choices that they make. My findings that career path is a strong predictor of innovation and that professional involvement is not indicate that professionalism is as much a labor-market phenomenon as a cultural one. In other words, professional values matter in public administration because professionalism is a necessary condition for career advancement. This finding resonates with preeminent sociological theories of professions and professionalism (e.g., Larson 1977; Brint 1994; Abbot 1988), which stress the economic, institutional, and functional dimensions of professions and place comparatively little emphasis on professional socialization. Professions create and sustain markets for bureaucratic labor. My claim is not that bureaucrats' professional values do not matter, but rather that *when* and *how much* they matter depends a great deal on the job markets in which they work. Bureaucratic ambition allows us to make theoretically grounded predictions about whether bureaucrats are more or less likely to pursue professional innovations.

The Market for Bureaucratic Policy Entrepreneurs

I have argued that elected officials and their bureaucratic agency heads form both principal-agent and client-professional relationships. Elected official and administrator alike bring expectations of a client-professional relationship to their interactions when the administrator is recruited from elsewhere. Theoretically, the key difference between the two is that the client-professional framework recognizes the possibility of voluntary exit from the relationship by the bureaucrat and so introduces a markedly different set of incentives from those typically depicted in a principal-agent framework. A principal-agent relationship and is more likely to hold where agency heads are promoted from within. Bureaucratic ambition tends to strengthen the client-professional relationship and contravene the principal-agent relationship where job mobility exists because ambitious administrators are likely to drive innovation proactively, rather than simply implement policies received from elected officials. The client-professional framework, then, is a complement to the principal-agent framework as a tool for students of bureaucratic politics. Career-opportunity structure and bureaucratic ambition give us a reasonable means of supposing which of the two frameworks is likely to apply in a given government and at a given time.

Recognizing bureaucratic job mobility as a political force also requires a modest but important revision of the received wisdom about efficiency in government agencies. An enduring verdict in the study of government bureaucracies is that they are, in general, less efficient than are private organizations. James Q. Wilson's (1989) seminal treatise *Bureaucracy* identifies several reasons why government organizations are less efficient than their private-sector counterparts, including an observation that inefficient or ineffective public agencies are not eliminated from the market naturally and that "public executives have weaker incentives than do private executives to *find* an efficient course of action" (349; italics in original). Without market competition to reward successful organizations and eliminate unsuccessful ones, governments are doomed to endure inefficiency from their bureaucracies, concludes Wilson.

This book provides an important amendment to Wilson's arguments, and perhaps conventional wisdom, about bureaucratic (in)efficiency. Public administration career-opportunity structures can provide tremendous incentives for bureaucrats to perform. Market competition may have little impact on a *bureau's* performance, but labor markets can shape an individual *bureaucrat's* performance in profound ways.[3] Career opportunity structures inhibit or encourage policy entrepreneurship. They systematically block some individuals from and channel others to the top posts where they can have the greatest policy influence. In this way, professional job mobility provides something like the market-clearing mechanism for administrators that Wilson sensed was missing in public agencies. The kinds of individuals, political activity, and policies "cleared" by a public administration labor market depends on the mechanics of that market. Diagonal opportunity structures cultivate client-professional relationships between elected officials and bureaucrats, and so reward innovation; vertical opportunity structures foster principal-agent relationships, and so reward anticipation of, compliance with, and acquiescence to elected officials' preferences. Bureaucratic ambition thus offers some traction on the supply side of the policy entrepreneurship model, at least for one class of policy entrepreneurs.

Personality and Bureaucratic Politics

On launching this study I did not anticipate breaking any epistemological ground, but by commingling personality and institutions in a single theory I seem to have done so, after a fashion. This book attempts to reintroduce personality psychology to political science research on elite political behavior. Personality theory has an important history in political science, but studies of elite personality have of late fallen out of favor in the discipline. Some prominent studies of elite political psychology applied Freudian frameworks that are now generally debunked (e.g., Lasswell 1934). More crucially, much of the past research on elite psychology is difficult or impossible to falsify or replicate in a systematic fashion (e.g., Barber 1992). Political science as a discipline has largely abandoned elite psychology as a subject of study in recent years. Ironically, this disappearance has occurred at a time when applications of psychological theory and methods have increased rapidly in political scientists' studies of public opinion and behavior (Monroe et al. 2009).

Fortunately, social psychologists and organization theorists continued to study personality after most political scientists abandoned it. The theory of human motivation that I employ in this book generates falsifiable hypotheses and has been successfully applied in other contexts. My research design is replicable, and my empirical methods have been tested and refined by prior research. Personality psychology as a subfield has progressed considerably over the past several decades, and despite occasional suggestions that advances in neuroscience have rendered personality research obsolete, it is unlikely to disappear any time soon. In fact, recent neuroscience research has affirmed and extended personality psychologists' studies of human motivation.[4] For example, recent experimental research has linked endocrine production to human motivation. Schultheiss, Campbell, and McClelland (1999) find that power motivation conditions the effect of testosterone on competitiveness in men. Schultheiss, Wirth, and Stanton (2004) find that affiliation motivation affects the production of progesterone in response to social stimulation and that the effects of power motivation on testosterone is different for men and women. Tiwari et al. (1996) link childhood nutrition to the development of both cognitive ability and achievement motivation. With the emergence of "behavioral economics," some economists have begun developing ways to build personality psychology into their models. Borghans et al. (2008) see great promise in the combination of personality psychology and economic models and lay out an ambitious research agenda for both disciplines. These developments are exciting since they hold out the possibility of integrating theory and methods from social psychology, neuroscience, and economics into more robust and valid models of human behavior. Political scientists and public administration researchers have been slow to recognize these advances and apply them.

At the same time, this study's integration of institutional and psychological mechanisms lends a political scientist's institutional sensibilities to the body of research on human motivation. Most research on human motivation in politics is essentially noninstitutional; that is, individuals' motives are shown to cause behavior, but without consideration of environmental conditions (e.g., finances, legal strictures). This book is one of very few studies that put human motivation in an institutional context, and the only study of human motivation I am aware of that considers the effect of institutional constraints on political behavior. I hope that this book helps reintroduce motive theory and personality psychology more generally to the study of political organizations.

Rationality—Bounded and Otherwise

The theory of bureaucratic ambition advanced in this book rests within the rational-choice tradition: its central claims are about individual decisions to maximize utility given the conditions and constraints of an institutional framework. According to Weingast (2002), "Rational-choice approaches begin with a set of individuals, assumed to have a well-defined set of preferences . . . institutions constrain individual choices, how individuals interact, their information and beliefs, and their payoffs" (662). The career path elements of my bureaucratic ambition theory clearly fit this definition of "rational-choice institutionalism." However, one might fairly question how "well-defined" preferences are under the theory that I have advanced. Certainly preferences are less-well-defined when human motivation is a measured variable than when it is an assumed constant; measurement of personality (or anything else, for that matter) inevitably exposes a study to a multitude of methodological hazards. For this reason, I suspect that some doctrinaire rational-choice theorists—especially those who prefer formal principal-agent models—might be uncomfortable with my claim to the rational-choice franchise. But in exploring elite psychology, I seek to extend and refine rational-choice theories built upon assumed goals, not to refute them. Preferences are perhaps more empirically valid and practically useful when they are measured, even if they are not as crisply defined as when they are assumed.

Herbert Simon recognized in a 1985 article some ways that psychological theories might enhance rational-choice models. Human behavior is rational, argued Simon, but only within limits inherent to the human condition. According to Simon, a comprehensive rational-choice theory must account for

1. The decision maker's goals, or utility function
2. The information that the decision maker has about his situation and the consequences of the choices available to him
3. The decision maker's ability to draw inferences from the information that he has

Simon complains that most political scientists' rational-choice models address only number 2 on the list and simply make assumptions about numbers 1 and 3. He urges political scientists to use cognitive psychology to account for individuals' varying abilities to process and use information (no. 3). Recent works that integrate cognitive models into studies of public opinion and participation suggest that political scientists are heeding Simon's call.[5] In the same article, Simon sees little hope finding a scientifically tractable means of assessing individuals' utility functions (no. 1), since they lie beyond the conscious self and so "we can't report them, no matter how much we wish to cooperate with the researcher" (1985, 301).

Surely Simon's skepticism about a person's ability to report his utility function accurately and honestly was well founded. He may have been too quick to despair, however. Motivation theory and methods offer potent, if necessarily incomplete, means of addressing the utility quandary. Assessments of motivation provide a look at the unconscious, psychological "wellsprings of action," as Simon put it, even if they do not yield precise polynomial utility functions. Bureaucratic ambition addresses the first two of Simon's three requirements for rational-choice models (goals and institutional conditions); ongoing research on cognitive psychology holds out tantalizing possibilities for addressing the third.

Directions for Further Study

As with any modestly fruitful scientific inquiry, the answers that this study produces generate more questions. The measurement and sampling methods applied in this book offer a high degree of confidence, but ultimately the quantitative empirical analyses presented here are based on a sample of 153 agency heads serving two professions during one year in the early twenty-first century. It is facile, perhaps, to call for further empirical research on an empirical study. Nonetheless, more data on bureaucrats' career paths, innovations, and personalities are needed. I hope that this book will prompt others to expand and improve upon my theory of bureaucratic ambition. Here I discuss some promising directions for future research.

Politics and Bureaucratic Careers over Time

The cross-sectional data used in chapters 4, 5, and 6 limit this book's analysis to the innovations that were professionally fashionable at the time of the survey and to bureaucratic political behavior proximate to the time of the survey. The limitations of cross-sectional research design on studies of policy diffusion are well understood (Berry and Berry 1990). This study's use of cross-section data avoids some potential pitfalls because the data are behavioral and refer to specific decisions (e.g., political contacts made on a specific issue within the twelve months prior to the survey). Studies of administrative careers over time would further enhance our understanding of the relationships between bureaucratic career paths and political action. Researchers might trace administrators' career paths over time, observing their innovations and advocacy in each of their posts. A carefully crafted longitudinal study would provide more direct evidence of the effects of bureaucratic ambition on innovation and bureaucratic policy entrepreneurship. The story of Chief White cited at the beginning of this chapter and the illustrative cases offered in chapter 2 provide this kind information for a handful of administrators. Future studies might seek to develop similar career and policymaking histories for many more administrators.

Other Professions, People, Places

This book investigates bureaucratic ambition for just two public administration professions: law enforcement and water utility management. These professions were selected mainly for their substantive diversity and their ubiquity in the United States. That the hypotheses tested for both professions generally hold true is encouraging. But of course, law enforcement and water utilities are only two of many distinct public administration professions in the United States (to say nothing of the world). Does bureaucratic ambition apply in the same way to other professions in other public agencies? One clear avenue for future research is to investigate bureaucratic ambition in other public administration professions using similar empirical methods.

Studies of other professions might illuminate the ways that race, ethnicity, and gender play out in opportunity structures and how these variables condition bureaucratic ambition. The professions studied in this book are, in the United States, all overwhelmingly white and male. It seems likely that gender, race, and/or ethnicity might affect public administration job markets in ways that condition bureaucratic ambition. Do men and women perceive different job opportunities? Do bureaucrats' ethnic identities affect their choices of policy innovations? Are the costs of political advocacy different for whites and nonwhites? If so, what are the implications of these systemic biases for policy entrepreneurship and the innovations that emerge from public agencies? Studies of more diverse public service professions could offer traction on these questions.[6]

The need for replication in other professions is especially evident for the elements of this study that deal with human motivation. The data collected for this study allowed motive analysis only for chiefs of police; whether the motivational patterns of political activity and career advancement observed among police chiefs hold true for other public administration professions is not known. Law enforcement is one of very few domestic public service professions in the United States that employs a hierarchical, paramilitary organizational form, and law enforcement is unique insofar as it involves the potential intentional projection of deadly force on a daily basis. A study of motives in a profession that does not typically involve projection of force or a paramilitary organizational form, such as education, utilities, parks management, social work, or public finance, would offer additional leverage on the role of the power motive in bureaucratic political behavior.

Similarly, a broader set of professions might shed light on what role, if any, affiliation motivation might play in agency heads' behavior. Since ambition is my main psychological interest in this book, the motivational analyses of police chiefs in this study focus on achievement and power motivation. The affiliation motive demonstrates no appreciable effects in the study's quantitative analyses and receives scant attention compared with the other two motives. It is reasonable to suppose that the affiliation motive might not affect political behavior among police chiefs in the same way that it might for administrators in other professions. Individuals who desire warm relationships with others might respond to organizational and professional conditions in different ways. As I note in chapter 3, affiliation motivation might cause some bureaucrats to forego innovation in order to maintain harmonious relationships in their agencies and communities. Conversely, if an administrator strongly values his personal relationships with his professional peers, he might pursue a professional policy agenda in order to strengthen those relationships. In this way, the affiliation motive might be a psychological predictor of an individual's relative preference for social, or solidary, benefits (Olson 1965).

Studies of human motivation across several professions, both public and private, could offer valuable insight on why individuals are drawn to specific professions. Conventional wisdom suggests that individuals select professions because they are somehow drawn to the substantive work of a profession: a lawyer might enjoy rhetoric and argument, a physician might like working with patients, and an engineer might get pleasure from solving practical, physical problems. Studies of motivation and career advancement in other public administration professions might help show whether and why differently motivated individuals seek out or avoid different professions, as they appear to do in the private sector (McClelland 1961; Winter 1973; Lagan-Fox and Roth 1995; Sagie and Elizur 1999; Collins, Hange, and Locke 2004). If the findings of chapter 5 apply to other public administration professions, we might expect achievement-motivated individuals naturally to seek professions with diagonal opportunity structures and power-motivated individuals to seek professions with vertical opportunity structures.

Finally, studying bureaucratic ambition in other professions might also offer clues as to why career opportunities vary so widely across professions. Why is career advancement in U.S. military bureaucracies purely vertical? Why is advancement in school superintendency mostly diagonal? In the past, advancement in police administration has generally been vertical, but according to many of the chiefs I talked with, police administration has become increasingly diagonal in recent decades. If this perceived trend is true, why has it occurred? Public administration career paths may evolve as institutions according to historical chance in some path-dependent way. Alternatively, form may follow function: a profession's substantive task may lead it to evolve one or another opportunity structure. In his classic *The Forest Ranger*, first published in 1960, Herbert Kaufman (2006) describes in great detail the personnel policies that define forest rangers' vertical career-opportunity structures in the United States Forest Service (USFS). Kaufman argues that the USFS recruitment, job assignment, training, and promotional policies encourage compliance with and discourage dissent from central USFS policies and protocols. Some of these personnel policies were designed intentionally to strengthen organizational compliance, while others had the same effect by accident, argues Kaufman. Several researchers have followed Kaufman with updates on the USFS (e.g., Tipple and Wellman 1991; Koontz 2007) and similar examinations of career paths in several other professions and organizations (Green 1989; McCabe et al. 2008; Tilson and Gebbie 2001; Thacker, Koo, and Delany 2008; Björk, Glass, and Brunner 2005). This research remains fragmented across subjects and disciplines, however. Badly needed are general theories that explain the development of public-sector career systems across professions, functions, and levels of government. Do vertical opportunity structures somehow inherently complement military and/or law-enforcement organizations? Is there something about school administration and city management in the United States that causes diagonal opportunity structures to predominate in those professions? If career-opportunity structures evolve according to function, then changing government needs might drive new kinds of career paths. For example, Chu and White (2001) argue for significant changes to U.S. military career systems to accommodate changes in American cultural, political, demographic, and economic conditions. Theory and methods from history, sociology, economics, and organizational studies ought to bear on these important questions.

The administration of U.S. local government is organized in ways that are not applicable to some other governments. How does bureaucratic ambition play out in centralized state or national systems where advancement occurs only vertically? What about governments where bureaucratic executives are not *specialized professionals* (e.g., civil engineers, public health officers, educators, etc.) but rather *professional administrators* with generalized skills and experiences, as in the archetypal Whitehall model? Studies of bureaucratic motivation and career opportunity structures in other, radically different systems might generate different and interesting results.

The patterns of agency heads' political behavior observed in this book might apply similarly to business corporations, nonprofit groups, churches, academic institutions, and international organizations. Stripped to its basic elements, the theory of bureaucratic ambition advanced in this book might well apply to any organization or group of organizations that employs professional labor. Studies similar to this one in a wide variety of organizations might yield important lessons on how human motivation and career opportunities affect the workplace decisions of executives in all sectors of the labor market.

Bureaucratic Ambition and Democratic Governance

The problem of bureaucratic accountability in a democratic state has been perhaps the most vexing normative issue in public administration since its genesis as a field of study. Efficient and effective government requires a degree of administrative discretion and professional expertise, but democratic governance requires limiting the administrative power of the state and ensuring its accountability to the citizens that it serves. Complicating matters is the pervasive and enduring involvement of expert bureaucrats in every phase of the policymaking process: professional bureaucrats initiate policy proposals, set legislative agendas, implement programs, and evaluate policy outcomes. How, then, can democratic governments maintain bureaucratic accountability in an era when effective administration requires a breadth of knowledge and depth of expertise beyond what any elected representative could hope to have?

Political scientists Carl Friedrich and Herman Finer took up this question in a celebrated debate conducted through a series of papers published in the 1930s and 1940s. Friedrich and Finer both recognized that the scale and scope of administration in the modern state required a degree of technical acumen far beyond the understanding of any body of elected officials. In a discussion that presaged generations of scholarship on bureaucratic professionalism and principal-agent models, Friedrich and Finer agreed that administrators' command over expertise presented at least a potential threat to democratic governance.

In the face of that threat, Friedrich (1935, 1940) argued that no procedural or rule-based system could ensure bureaucratic accountability to the voting public in any government agency that required specialized administration. Legislatures might proscribe certain bureaucratic behaviors, but effective government inevitably requires that administrators are empowered to make many, perhaps most, important policy decisions. So long as there is any possibility of disagreement between principal and agent over the proper ends and means of government policy, rule-based systems will ultimately fail to guard against bureaucratic misbehavior. Rather, *professionalism* was the key to responsible and responsive government, Friedrich argued. A bureaucrat who is imbued with "the standards and ideals of his profession" has a positive force driving him to perform in the public interest and also an "inner check" on temptations to shirk or abuse his position (Friedrich 1940, 13). Besides their consciences, Friedrich argued that professional bureaucrats also would be subject to "thorough scrutiny by their colleagues in what is known as the 'fellowship of science'" (1935, 38). Professional norms enforced by social institutions would constrain abuses of administrative power where the rule of law could not.

A skeptical Finer (1936, 1941) doubted that professionalism could be a meaningful check on bureaucratic mischief. If responsibility to a professional community is at least potentially inconsistent with responsibility to popularly elected politicians, then professionals must be made subordinate to elected officials and not to professional peers. Finer questioned whether any community of administrators could be truly objective and scientific, despite professionals' claims and solemn oaths. "Political responsibility alone is 'objective,'" argued Finer, "because it is to a body external to the one who is responsible, its standards may be stated with finality and exactitude, and its rewards and punishments made peremptory" (1936, 582). The rule of law and clear hierarchical institutions are essential to bureaucratic accountability, and so Finer called for formal institutional arrangements to strengthen politicians' direct control over the bureaucracy. Finer singled out the British parliamentary cabinet system for special praise because it puts majority members of parliament directly in charge of the government's administrative agencies.[7] Professional sentiments and ideals in the bureaucracy are well and good, argued Finer, but "the first commandment is, Subservience! [*sic*]" (1936, 582).

The echoes of Friedrich and Finer resound not only in the seven decades or so of scholarship since their debate, but also in countless real-world initiatives to strengthen professionalism and/or hierarchical accountability in the bureaucracy.[8] Friedrich's call for administrative professionalism is evident in efforts to build professional identity through specialized education, symbolism, rituals, and other mechanisms of socialization. Graduate schools of public administration, public policy, education, forestry, public health, social work, criminal justice, and other public-sector professions have proliferated steadily since the early twentieth century. Carl Friedrich himself was an original faculty member of Harvard's Graduate School of Public Administration (now the Kennedy School of Government). Scores of public-sector professional societies hold conferences, grant certifications, honor their outstanding members with awards, and otherwise promote professionalism. For example, the National Board for Professional Teaching Standards (NBPTS) offers teachers a voluntary "board certification" of their compliance with "the nation's highest advanced teaching standards." The NBPTS certification process is entirely voluntary and is not required by any state licensure regime, but it offers its certified teachers a strong sense of professionalism and a potentially valuable credential.[9] Recent research indicates that agency accreditation by the Commission on the Accreditation of Law Enforcement Agencies (CALEA, discussed and analyzed in chapter 4) heightens rank-and-file officers' personal sense of professionalism (Hughes 2010). Together, these kinds of institutions and traditions are meant to endow administrators with the "ideals of profession" that Friedrich hailed.

At the same time, Finer's call for strict, democratic accountability of administrators to their elected masters reverberates in bureaucratic reforms that are meant to increase transparency, reward compliance with directives from elected officials, and punish deviance from those same directives.[10] The most notable of these reforms in the past century (in the United States, anyway) came in the Reorganization Act of 1939, which consolidated several U.S. federal government executive functions under the Executive Office of the President in an effort to strengthen bureaucratic accountability to the president in classic principal-agent style. More recently, Finer's concern for democratic accountability has manifested itself in a hodge-podge of related reforms that can be labeled loosely as the New Public Management (NPM). The precise meaning of NPM remains a matter of debate among scholars and practitioners, but NPM generally involves using microeconomic, quasi-market mechanisms to improve government efficiency, effectiveness, and accountability (Hood 1991). Toward that end, NPM-driven reforms have sought to empower administrators by decentralizing policymaking and reducing "red tape," while simultaneously setting and demanding attainment of explicit performance metrics. The idea is that public managers can be most effective when liberated from cumbersome guidelines and regulations. In turn, administrators are supposed to be responsible for meeting specific standards. In some cases, the NPM has taken the form of privatization or contracting of government functions, from municipal water service to security in war zones to private-sector providers. In other cases, NPM initiatives set forth quantitative performance guidelines for public agencies, with specific rewards and sanctions for managers and agencies based on their performance. Perhaps the most famous example of NPM-driven reform is the federal 2002 No Child Left Behind Act, which requires local school districts to conduct standardized academic testing and specifies consequences for poorly performing schools.[11] While the mechanisms that follow from principal-agent theory and NPM are quite different, they share common roots in Finer's concern for bureaucratic subservience to elected officials.[12]

In his 2008 John Gaus lecture to the American Political Science Association, Donald Kettl used the Friedrich-Finer debate to frame the history of thought on professionalism and accountability in the bureaucracy and sought to unite the two traditions in what he called *blended accountability*.

With blended accountability, procedures, monitoring, and rule-of-law provide bureaucratic accountability to the extent practicable, with professional
norms and values offering a behavioral backstop against administrative abuses
or flouting of the public will (Kettl 2009). Unfortunately, Kettl observes,
blended accountability founders under the staggering complexity of governing in the twenty-first century:

> When the forces shaping public policy cross so many boundaries, and when
> private forces so powerful shape public decisions, hierarchy breaks down. So,
> too, do professional norms, when the interacting forces involve such different
> professions, organizations, and sectors. The challenge is aligning such dispa-
> rate action into a pattern of results that fits the public interest. . . . What layer of
> accountability can we add to help plug the gaps that existing authority- and
> norm-based systems leave? The honest answer is that no one knows for sure.
> (2009, 16)

In the end, then, Kettl arrives more or less in the same place where Friedrich
and Finer began seven decades earlier: daunted by the complexity of public
administration in the modern era and groping for an institution (or "layer of
accountability") to ensure that bureaucracies operate in the public interest.
Notably, Kettl's treatment of bureaucratic accountability leaves aside the possibility of significant disagreement between professions and elected officials
over the meaning of "the public interest"—a possibility that clearly troubled
both professors Friedrich and Finer. Professional values and elected officials'
values do not necessarily diverge, but neither do they necessarily coincide.
The case studies in chapter 2 provide vivid reminders that bureaucrats' loyalties to professional principles can cause them to run afoul of their elected
principals at times. If a bureaucrat's elected officials call for one policy and her
professional norms point to another, to whom or what should she be responsive? Who or what, if anyone or anything, will hold her accountable?

Administrative Job Markets as Political Institutions

Most studies of bureaucratic politics and public administration follow Friedrich in pointing to administrators' socialization through education and organizational experiences as the source of professional values. However, in this
study we have seen that career path drives professionalism as much or more
than socialization does. Ironically, this finding is consistent with preeminent
sociological works on professionalism, which highlight the economic and

functional dimensions of professions and place comparatively little emphasis on the processes of socialization (Larson 1977; DiMaggio and Powell 1983; Abbot 1988).

If professions are primarily labor-market phenomena, then it follows that professional values are market values, representing the predominant values of buyers in the market for professional labor. For public administrators, professional values are those of the government agencies, especially the agencies that offer the highest-status jobs in the profession. These prestigious posts are the jobs to which ambitious professionals aspire. Since these desirable jobs are in larger cities, professions are likely to promote policies with broad appeal to large constituencies, especially in professions that feature substantial job mobility. Like an ambitious U.S. senator who seeks to build a national constituency through involvement in foreign affairs or national tax reform, an ambitious bureaucrat will build a policy reputation befitting the job to which he aspires.

Steven Brint (1994) argues that, as professions mature and establish competitive labor markets, scientific rationality gradually gives way to popular sensibility as the root of professional principles. Professional norms, however rational or scientific, cannot deviate too greatly from popular preferences since a profession must build and maintain a clientele that is willing to pay for its services. Consequently, as professionals become ubiquitous, competition for jobs and integration of professionals into the broader society narrow the gap between professional values and mainstream American values. Though professions are responsible to no specific body of elected officials, their values come to approximate those of the nation at large. In this sense, bureaucratic professionalism is a kind of check on the majority (or perhaps a powerful minority) in a government, especially a local government. If the framers of the U.S. Constitution were wary of a tyrannical bureaucracy, they were no less wary of tyrannical elected legislatures and executives.[13] In *Federalist 10*, James Madison argues that the government of a nation with more numerous factions is less likely to abuse its minorities than are governments of small communities. With fewer—but perhaps more deeply divided—factions, a smaller state is prone to abuse of minorities by tyrannical majorities. In professions with significant career mobility, professional success requires pursuing the values of the market at large, rather than any specific client's values. For the physician, pursuing the values of the market at large means prescribing the treatments that are held up as legitimate and appropriate by the profession, even when a patient prefers a novel or obsolete regimen. For professional public administrators, career advancement in a mobile job market means pursuit of the policies held up as laudable by the profession, rather than serving immediate organizational superiors. Professions are thus centripetal political forces, causing administrators, especially ambitious ones on diagonal career paths, to converge toward widely accepted policies that reflect broad political values.

In light of this quasi-representative role, a neutral bureaucracy that dutifully and accurately implements elected officials' policy directions may be as undesirable as it is chimerical.[14] Frederick Wirt (1985) noted this normative ambiguity over bureaucratic professionalism in local government:

> The professional executive officer is the invisible actor in urban decision making, recalling Shelley: "the awful shadow of some unseen Power floats, though unseen, among us." The professional's "shadow" may be "awful" to those who see in it insensitivity and obstruction of local values and control. But it is difficult to escape the impression that many benefits arrived on the local scene in the briefcases and journals of the professional executive officer. (106)

As an agent to his elected principal, an administrator is bound to follow orders. At the same time, as a professional to his elected client, an administrator is bound by professional standards of practice. Neither ethic is necessarily imperative, and both forces act simultaneously to condition the bureaucrat's political behavior. Bureaucratic ambition determines the strength of each force, as the availability of administrative job opportunities gives relative weight to one or the other.

As I have observed throughout this book, public administration professions are institutions; they are collections of synthetic rules and customs. That opportunity structures systematically affect the diffusion of innovations and the psychological composition of governments' executive ranks implies that bureaucratic professionalism and policy entrepreneurship are consequences of institutional design. Through education, accreditation, hiring practices, and promotional policies, it is possible to exert some control over the character of policies and vigor of political advocacy that emerge from the executive ranks of public agencies. In other words, it is possible to regulate the supply of bureaucratic policy entrepreneurs.

More crucially, professional public administration career systems can help provide an "accountability layer" that Kettl (2009) sensed was necessary to reconcile Friedrich's prescription for a responsible bureaucracy (professional norms) with Finer's (rule of law). Strikingly, in the essay that launched his debate with Friedrich, Herman Finer argued that strong, hierarchical rule of law was necessary to ensure sound administration, not so much because professional norms were somehow bad but because bureaucrats lacked market incentives to reward "virtuous but impecunious" behavior (1936, 583). Critically, neither Friedrich's appeal to professionalism nor Finer's appeal to political responsibility seems to have anticipated substantial bureaucratic career mobility within a single profession. As participants in a competitive labor market, bureaucrats are simply loyal neither to their professional norms nor to their hierarchical superiors. Rather, administrators are most loyal to their professional norms when employment conditions give them political license to practice as professionals. Just as the degree of job mobility available to a bureaucrat enhances or erodes his incentive to innovate, a bureaucrat's degree of job mobility helps determine the extent to which he sees his elected officials as "the boss" or "the client." Job mobility gives a professional a reason to take risks and bear personal costs in the name of professionalism. Job mobility provides elected officials with access to a market for innovation and lends potency to the rewards and sanctions that they set out for their administrators. Bureaucratic ambition thus mediates the conflict between professionalism and democratic accountability, and across thousands of government agencies in the United States, perhaps, balances these oft-conflicting values.

Good Servant or Bad Master?

Inevitably, an ambitious bureaucrat's actions pursuant to a professional career align more closely with some interests than others. Whether one perceives the ambitious professional bureaucrat as a hero or as a villain in any particular case likely depends on whether professional values align with one's own, as the pseudonymous cases from chapter 2 illustrate. In San Alonso Carmen Osborne's ill-fated decision to retire the Los Rios reservoirs aligned with the interests of the city's engineering contractors and against the interests of Los Rios area homeowners. An intense, vocal group of San Alonso citizens undermined Osborne's efforts in the end. Whether Osborne's policy would have best served the interests of the majority of San Alonso citizens remains an open question. The clash between Osborne and the Los Rios Alliance was not as simple as "citizens versus suits," for the professionals in the Water Department represented citizen interests, too. Certainly Osborne and her staff considered themselves to be representatives of a quiet constituency of San Alonso residents who would have preferred a secure water system to a historical curiosity.

Calvin Jensen's tumultuous service as chief of police in Greenport also reflects a clash of values. Ramp-climbing Jensen built a career in law-enforcement administration as a reformer, bringing professional innovations to the police departments that he led. As in his prior jobs, Jensen approached Greenport as a professional providing a client with specialized, expert service. True to his reputation, Jensen made swift and sweeping changes to department policies, angering many but retaining the mayor's endorsement. When Jensen clashed with the mayor over an investigation, the mayor quickly asserted his control of the police department by firing one of Jensen's key deputies. The move signaled a change in the relationship between the mayor and Jensen from client-professional to principal-agent. Jensen resigned from Greenport shortly thereafter and took a head job in an agency elsewhere. He was replaced by a chief promoted from within who willingly (if unhappily) shielded the mayor from an emerging scandal. On one level, the mayor's assertion of authority over these police chiefs affirmed the principal-agent relationship between elected official and bureaucrat. On another level, it marked a triumph for the police union over supporters of police reform. In his pursuit of professionalism, Jensen represented the values of an important minority (perhaps even a majority) of Greenport citizens.

It is more difficult to identify winners and losers from Jude Alesky's superintendency of Mount Brantley School District, since stability, not innovation, was the hallmark of his tenure. Changes forced by the No Child Left Behind Act significantly improved the achievement standards, assessment techniques, and teacher-evaluation methods applied in Mount Brantley schools, as Alesky enthusiastically acknowledged. That exogenous force was necessary to prompt these improvements suggests that the "winners" in Mount Brantley were the families whose students have been well educated by Mount Brantley schools, while the "losers" were those whose education has suffered over the years from less-than-optimal achievement standards, assessment techniques, and evaluative methods. As a preserver of the status quo and cautious innovator, Alesky's superintendency served best those who were satisfied with the district.

The blessings of bureaucratic ambition and professional public administration are thus mixed. At their worst, bureaucrats' professional sensibilities may drive them to disregard or even flout their elected officials' instructions and their communities' preferences. The ambitious bureaucrat may impose a faddish managerial scheme or introduce innovations that are ill-suited to her agency's needs. Utility managers may build costly state-of-the-art, reverse-osmosis treatment plants that land them on the cover of *Engineering News Review* when simpler and cheaper technologies might be adequate. Police chiefs may devote time and resources to interagency disaster planning and counterterrorism when the city council might prefer neighborhood traffic enforcement.

But at their best, professional public administrators stand for broad, pluralistic values that would otherwise have few champions in the policy process. The ambitious bureaucrat may bring her agency state-of-the art technology from the pages of her professional journals or advocate for policies that serve people who lack effective elected representation. For utility managers, professionalism in policymaking means promoting water conservation pricing when the city council would rather keep water rates flat and low. For police chiefs, professionalism means community policing and nonlethal weapons when the mayor might prefer racial profiling and drug seizures.

This study has taken a small step toward understanding how institutions channel professional public administrators' career ambition into political behavior. By accident or by design, government hiring and promotional practices help determine the strength of professional influence over bureaucrats' political decisions. Bureaucratic professions are political institutions, and like elections, parties, and legislatures they are capable of reinforcing or undermining pluralistic democracy. Because bureaucratic policy entrepreneurs are born of public-administration career systems, these systems are important to those who study public organizations and the policy process. Bureaucratic career systems are even more important to those who would create and control public agencies, for the institutions that define public administration careers determine whether bureaucratic ambition is a good servant or a bad master.

Appendix A: *Survey Methodology*

This appendix details the survey sampling and administrative procedures that I used to gather the data on police chiefs and water utility managers.

Sampling Frame

The survey sampling frame includes municipal police chiefs and water utility managers serving local governments in the United States. The frame was defined for each profession using U.S. federal government catalogues of local government agencies.

Police agencies listed in the U.S. Justice Department's Bureau of Justice Statistics 2000 Census of State and Local Law Enforcement Agencies (CSLLEA) composed the police frame (U.S. Dept. of Justice 2003).[1] The CSLLEA includes all public law enforcement agencies in the United States that employ at least one sworn officer. All agencies coded as "municipal police" departments serving cities, towns, villages, or townships were included in the frame. State, county, and university law enforcement agencies were excluded from the frame, as were agencies serving U.S. territories.

Water utilities owned by local governments and listed in the U.S. Environmental Protection Agency's (EPA) 2004 Safe Drinking Water Information System (SDWIS) composed the water utility frame.[2] Systems owned by general purpose municipal governments and special districts were included in the frame. Water systems serving U.S. territories were eliminated from the frame.

The CSLLEA and SDWIS include size categories for police departments and water utilities, respectively. Very small police departments (with fewer than three full-time sworn officers) were excluded from the frame. Small and very small water utilities (serving populations below 3,300) were excluded, too. While these small and very small agencies compose a substantial share of the total agencies in each profession, collectively they serve a very low proportion of the total U.S. population. Moreover, many very small water utilities are nonprofessional, in some cases operated entirely by volunteers. Heads of such agencies have very limited administrative and policy-making responsibilities. The final sampling frame included 9,784 police agencies and 15,973 water utilities. Tables A1 and A2 summarize the sampling frame by agency size.

Table A1   Police agency survey sampling frame

Size group (number of sworn officers)	Municipal police agencies		Population served	
	Agencies	%	Population	%
Very small (<3)*	2,623	21.1	3,021,801	1.6
Small (3–12)	5,192	41.8	19,522,896	10.4
Medium (13–50)	3,347	27.0	43,553,511	23.3
Large (51–250)	1,086	8.8	56,350,888	30.1
Very large (>250)	159	1.3	64,500,809	34.5
Total	12,407	100.0	186,949,905	100.0

Source: U.S. Justice Department, Bureau of Justice Statistics 2000 Census of State and Local Law Enforcement Agencies (CSLLEA).
*Very small police agencies (fewer than three sworn officers) excluded from the frame.

Table A2   Water utility survey sampling frame

Size group (population served)	Utilities		Population served	
	Utilities	%	Utilities	%
Very small (<500)*	6,515	29.0	1,557,568	0.7
Small (501–3,300)*	9,270	41.2	13,701,774	6.4
Medium (3,301–10,000)	3,603	16.0	21,051,511	9.8
Large (10,001–100,000)	2,795	12.4	79,078,796	36.8
Very large (>100,000)	305	1.4	99,310,124	46.3
Total	22,488	100.0	214,699,773	100.0

Source: U.S. Environmental Protection Agency, 2004 Safe Drinking Water Information System (SDWIS).
*Very small and small water utilities (serving fewer than 3,300 pop.) excluded from the frame.

Sample

Once the frame was established, I employed a stratified sampling method to draw representative data from agencies of many sizes. As seen in tables A1 and A2, great majority of agencies are very small and serve small proportions of the total U.S. population. For this reason, a simple random sample would likely offer little data on large and medium-sized governments. Since large and medium-sized governments serve the majority of the U.S. population, stratifying to ensure their inclusion in the sample is important for drawing conclusions about the nation as a whole

(Dziegielewski and Opitz 2004). Stratification also ensured that data are gathered from agencies occupying every stratum of these professions, which is important since career progression is an important element of this study.

A random sample of agencies within each size stratum shown in tables A2 and A3 composed the final survey sample: thirty-eight per stratum for police and fifty per stratum for water utilities. Two police agencies were eliminated at random to result in exactly 150 sampled agencies for each kind of agency. A few selected governments were removed from the sample. In two cases the top administrative positions were vacant in the governments selected for the sample. One police agency drawn from the frame was removed from the sample because its government had been dissolved since the 2000 CSLLEA. Contact information in the databases for a handful of agencies proved to be inaccurate.

Administration

To gain maximum generalizability with limited resources this survey emphasized careful instrument design and response rate rather than a large sample size. To encourage their participation, sampled administrators received an introductory mailing on official University of Michigan stationery to introduce the study and warn them of the survey's impending arrival. Experimental research demonstrates that these notification letters can generate higher response rates than studies without advance letters (Traugott, Groves, and Lepkowski 1987), especially when the notification letters use a university letterhead (Brunner and Carroll 1969; Fox, Crask, and Kim 1988). Notification letters appealed to issue interest and respondents' sense of professional duty (Sheehan and McMillan 1999). Advance notification letters were sent to respondents at their agency addresses two weeks prior to telephone contact or email invitation. The email invitation included a link to the survey web site. Water utility managers were offered a $10 Visa gift card upon completion of the survey as an incentive to participate. Police chiefs were not offered this incentive because they were all contacted directly by telephone, and most agreed to complete the survey questionnaire at the end of the interview.

Approximately ten to fifteen days after sending the advance introductory letters via postal mail, water utility managers were sent email invitations containing hyperlinks to the web-based survey instrument. Nonrespondents to the initial email were sent reminder messages after five days, and again after ten and fifteen days.

Because the police chief survey required a brief telephone interview, I telephoned respondents ten to fifteen days after sending the advance introductory letters. Generally interviews with chiefs were arranged by appointment, though in several cases my phone call was connected directly to the chief for an immediate interview. Telephone interviews ranged from six to twenty-two minutes in duration, though most lasted about ten minutes. These interviews were tape-recorded the respondent's permission and transcribed following the interview. All transcripts were stripped of identifying information and tape recordings were destroyed upon the project's completion, as

Table A3   Summary of survey response

	Police chiefs	Water utility managers	Total
Initial sample	150	150	300
Invalid cases			
Bad frame information	3	9	12
Post vacant	6	2	8
Other	3	0	3
Net valid cases	138	139	277
Responses			
Initial invitation	14	32	46
Second invitation	39	20	59
Third invitation	19	10	29
Fourth invitation	10	8	18
Total responses	81	70	151
Refusals	8	1	9
Nonresponses	49	69	118
Response rate, % of all cases	54.0	46.7	50.3
Response rate, % of valid cases	58.7	50.4	54.5

required by the University of Michigan Institutional Review Board. At the conclusion of each interview, I asked the respondent to fill out the Internet-based questionnaire as a follow-up. Over a seven-week period, I conducted a total of eighty-one interviews with chiefs of police as part of the survey.

Gaining access to the chiefs for interviews proved challenging in many cases. I made repeated telephone calls and/or e-mail invitations to several respondents before gaining access to them. A number of individuals refused participation at the outset. During the telephone survey period I called each sampled chief of police at least four times before abandoning him or her as a nonrespondent, except when met with outright refusals, for a total of more than three hundred telephone calls. An average of 2.3 telephone calls were required for each respondent. Table A3 summarizes the survey responses.

Once I gained access to the selected chiefs of police, however, I found them to be forthcoming and cooperative, by and large. A few police chiefs were reluctant to discuss details of their experiences at first, and the telephone medium limited my ability to develop a rapport with them. But with few exceptions, police chiefs were eager to help. At the end of each interview, I asked police chiefs to complete the Internet-based questionnaire at their convenience. Participation in the online questionnaire was very good among those who were interviewed, with seventy-one out of eighty-one police chiefs completing the questionnaire. While data on degree of political participation was impossible to gather for questionnaire nonrespondents, some data on policy variables were available from public sources. For example, police agencies' accreditation status and participation in the Commission on Accreditation for Law Enforcement Agencies (CALEA) and Global Justice database are available publicly. Some agencies also had career histories, educational credentials, and personal profiles of their executives posted on their public Web sites. I recorded these data myself for nonrespondents when they were available independently.

Appendix B: Supplementary Regression Analysis Results

This appendix shows the results of the negative binomial regression analyses used to develop figures 5.1 and 5.2 in chapter 5. The rest of the book's regression results are reported in chapters 4, 5, and 6.

Table B1   Logistic model of police chief initiation of contact with news media (used to generate figure 5.1)

Variable	Coefficient (robust SE)	p*
Achievement motivation	.58	.00
	(.19)	
Power motivation	.11	.31
	(.10)	
Affiliation motivation	.25	.25
	(.22)	
Married	−2.59	.01
	(.99)	
Children	−2.42	.10
	(1.47)	
Age	.04	.31
	(.04)	
Log full-time sworn officers	−.61	.20
	(.48)	
Intercept	4.86	
	(2.60)	
Log pseudolikelihood	−14.64	
Wald χ^2	15.30	
$p > \chi^2$	.03	
McFadden's pseudo R^2	.55	
N	59	

Note: Model results reflect poststratification weighting to account for survey sample design.
*p-value generated by a two-tailed t test of significance.

Table B2   Negative binomial model of self-initiated political contacts
(used to generate figure 5.2)

Variable	Coefficient (robust SE)	p^*
Achievement motivation	.10	.01
	(.04)	
Power motivation	−.01	.70
	(.02)	
Affiliation motivation	.02	.49
	(.03)	
Achievement × log full-time sworn officers	−.02	.10
	(.01)	
Married	−.73	.00
	(.22)	
Children	−.22	.13
	(.15)	
Age	−.01	.62
	(.01)	
Log full-time sworn officers	.23	.02
	(.09)	
Intercept	1.14	
	(.64)	
Log likelihood	−136.46	
Wald χ^2	28.44	
$p > \chi^2$	.00	
McFadden's pseudo R^2	.09	
N	69	

*p-value generated by a two-tailed t test of significance.

Notes

CHAPTER 1: Principles, Principals, and Ambition

Epigraph. Wilson (1989), 227.

1. For an excellent review of scholarship on policy entrepreneurship, see Mintrom and Norman (2009).

2. Salvato (2005), "In Louisville, a Measured Police Response," *New York Times*, September 27, A12.

3. Donald Kettl (2002) observes that Wilson's (1887) division of public administration and politics into separate provinces has caused scholars in both fields to be provincial. "If public administrationists used Wilson's article as a manifesto to define the field, many political scientists seized on it as a justification for dismissing it" (2002, 41).

4. Wilson's 1887 article is so widely and frequently cited that scholars often credit it with setting the intellectual agenda for the study of public administration in the United States over the past 120 years. Van Riper (1983) puts the birth of the politics–administration dichotomy much earlier, and observes that Wilson's 1887 article actually received relatively scant attention until it was "rediscovered" by the discipline after 1950.

5. For an excellent review of the evolution and growth of principal-agent models in political science, see Miller (2005).

6. O'Leary (2005) devotes an entire book to accounts of those who intentionally contravene their organizational superiors' wishes. O'Leary argues that some of these "guerrilla bureaucrats" are driven by their professional sensibilities about good policy, though others simply act out of spite.

7. Kaufman ([1960] 2006) and Meier and O'Toole (2006) are notable exceptions. Brehm and Gates (2008), *Teaching, Tasks, and Trust*, also examine the processes by which individuals within bureaucratic organizations develop their task preferences, in part to address this lacuna in their 1997 book, *Working, Shirking, and Sabotage*. Brehm and Gates (2008) do not take up professionalism, however, since its focus is solely within an agency and so does not address the influences of an external peer community.

8. Similarly, Gailmard and Patty (2007) develop a principal-agent model of agency expertise built on a pair of assumed bureaucratic types: "zealots," whose goal is

implementation of favored policies, and "slackers," who seek to shirk their duties in more familiar principal-agent fashion.

9. This understanding of the terms *profession, professional,* and *professionalism* is a compilation of theories of professionalism from Carr-Saunders (1936), Polanyi (1957), Wilensky (1964), Larson (1977), and Abbott (1988).

10. Maestas, Fulton, Maisel, and Stone (2006) develop an ambition theory to model state legislators' decisions to run for Congress. Unlike other studies of ambition in legislators, their inquiry surveys legislators directly about their reasons for running (or not running) for office. However, their empirical method relies on the legislator answering honestly and accurately on his or her reasons for making past political decisions.

11. Meier and O'Toole complain that political scientists' studies of bureaucracy generally have been either institutional or behavioral and that "only modest intertribal communication occurs between these two [literatures]" (2006, 23). *Bureaucratic Ambition* aims to communicate with both tribes.

12. Dr. Nicholas Garrigan, the main character in Giles Foden's (1998) novel *The Last King of Scotland* (and the 2006 film of the same name), finds himself in just this position as personal physician to Ugandan president Idi Amin.

CHAPTER 2: Glorious Heroes, Tragic Heroes, Antiheroes

1. The verb *to satisfice,* a term from organizational theory, was coined by Herbert Simon. A combination of *satisfy* and *suffice,* it means to have mere adequacy as one's goal, rather than excellence. A typical analytical assumption is that people try to maximize their performance. Simon observed that often people in organizations don't try to be excellent; rather, they try to be sufficient.

2. Scholars of literature may not be as interested in this last question.

3. Paul Manna (2006) argues that policy entrepreneurs require "license" (strength of argument and legitimacy) and "capacity" (strength of resources and organizational capability) to win significant policy changes (14–15). According to Manna, when policy entrepreneurs working in America's federal system lack either license or capacity at their own level of government, they seek to "borrow strength" from other levels of government. Chief Jensen arrived in Greenport when a U.S. Justice Department investigation of the city's police department was in progress. Jensen turned an aggravating DOJ investigation into leverage for his own policy agenda, while simultaneously maintaining a public face of defiance against federal intrusion. In this way, Jensen "borrowed strength" from the federal government in support of a local policy initiative.

4. Osborne's attempt to use EPA rulemaking to drive a local policy innovation also fits Manna's model of policy entrepreneurship admirably (see chapter 2, note 3). The San Alonso utility department had sufficient "capacity" to carry out their plans for Los Rios, but lacked sufficient "license" to gain approval for them. By working directly with EPA regulators, Osborne and her staff sought to borrow strength (in this case, "license") from the federal government.

5. The public meetings sponsored by the utilities department were held in September, October, and November 2002. I do not mean to suggest that the department intentionally scheduled the public meetings to coincide with the first September 11 anniversary. However, holding the meetings during a period of national reflection on terrorism and its consequences can only have helped the department's efforts to frame the Los Rios project as a security issue.

6. Recently, economists have developed a few formal models that consider the possibility of bureaucratic exit from the principal-agent relationship (Dewatripont, Jewitt, and Tirole 1999a, 1999b; Prendergast 2007; Kaarbøe and Olsen 2003).

CHAPTER 3: A Theory of Bureaucratic Ambition

Epigraph. From an unpublished letter to a major daily newspaper in the city where the letter's author worked. I received a copy of this letter directly from its author and quote it here on condition of anonymity.

1. As Walker defines it in his seminal article on policy diffusion across states, an innovation is "a program or policy which is new to the state adopting it, no matter how old the program may be or how many other states have adopted it" (1969, 881).

2. See, for example, Kingdon (1984), Schneider, Teske, and Mintrom (1995), Mintrom and Vergari (1998), Mintrom (2000), Rabe (2004), Manna (2006), and Minrom and Norman (2009).

3. See chapter 7 for a discussion on how this theory is (or is not) a "rational choice" theory.

4. The Soil and Water Conservation Society (SWCS), established in 1943, is the leading organization of soil and water conservation professionals. The SWCS has more than five thousand members and seventy-five local chapters in North America. The SWCS Web site maintains an online database for professionals and soil conservation agencies looking for job matches.

5. Agency size is by far the strongest predictor of executive salary in Meier and O'Toole's (2002) study of Texas school districts.

6. The 1986 Goldwater-Nichols Act has created a modicum of lateral movement between armed services, but these "joint service" officers remain employees of their home, or primary service, effectively "on loan" to another service (Snider 2003). Snider argues that the "borrowing" of officers across armed services has not led to a true joint officer profession. Significantly, Snider uses the term *profession* to describe the officer corps of each branch of the U.S. armed services separately: the navy is one profession, the army another; the air force, the Marine Corps, and the Coast Guard are likewise distinct professions, according to Snider. He calls for the creation of a "new joint warfare profession" to help achieve the goal of Goldwater-Nichols to improve integration and joint planning in the United States armed services. Provisions for career advancement are central to Snider's proposal for a joint profession.

7. There are exceptions, however. For example, city attorneys rely on close familiarity with a state's municipal governance statutes and licensing to practice within a

state, so for many municipal attorneys, the job market may be effectively limited to a single state.

8. In chapter 7, I raise specific questions about the variation in career opportunity structures across professions and discuss possible directions for future research on this issue.

9. Physicians who serve wealthy or celebrity patients sometimes put principal before principle. In an essay in *Slate*, Dr. Kent Sepkowitz (2009) describes the temptation to become a "groupie-like" physician to high-profile patients. Sepkowitz argues that the disregard of professional ethics in pursuit of money and celebrity relationships led physicians to overprescribe drugs that caused the deaths of Michael Jackson, Elvis Presley, Anna Nicole Smith, and other celebrities.

10. *Henry VIII*, act 3, scene 2.

11. Surveys of public administrators focused on attitudes about the nature and role of public administration (or "role orientation") have long been a staple of empirical research on bureaucrats' political behavior in the public administration literature (e.g., Almy 1975; Hogan 1976; Green 1989; Dunn and Legge 2000).

12. Introductory mailings, phone calls, and e-mail invitations all prominently identified this research as originating from the University of Michigan. Regional familiarity with the university may have increased the probability of participation for Midwestern administrators.

CHAPTER 4: The Market for Bureaucratic Entrepreneurs

1. Ironically, while researching this book, I was contacted by a search consultant who wanted to know whether I would be interested in taking an agency executive position with the municipal government he was working for. After politely declining to apply for the post, I seized the opportunity for an impromptu interview and spent about twenty minutes asking the consultant about his own career and approach to executive recruitment.

2. See chapter 3 for a brief outline of the survey methodology used in this study. Appendix A offers additional details on survey methodology.

3. Based on CALEA's online database, www.calea.org/agcysearch/agencysearch .cfm (accessed May 20, 2009).

4. These percentages reflect poststratification weighting. The raw percentages are 56 percent hired from outside, 44 percent promoted from within.

5. The models in this chapter may understate the effect of parenting responsibilities, since the survey question on which it was based asks about children under eighteen years old and so does not capture ongoing responsibilities for college-aged children. Parenting responsibilities do not necessarily end on a child's eighteenth birthday, as many parents of college-aged students would attest.

6. See Michael Tomz, Jason Wittenberg, and Gary King, CLARIFY: Software for Interpreting and Presenting Statistical Results. Version 2.0, Cambridge, MA: Harvard University, June 1, 2001.

7. A sixth structure, sometimes called "water budgets," or "individualized rates," has emerged in recent years. These rate structures impose different inclined block price schedules on each customer, based on individual factors like number of rooms, household size, lot size, and vegetation (Chesnutt and Pekelney 2002; Gaur 2007). While individualized rates are clearly oriented toward conservation, only a handful of utilities in the United States (and none in the surveyed utilities) had adopted such rate structures at the time of the survey.

8. In two cases, conservation rates structures had been adopted before the survey respondent began service as agency head, but were adjusted during the respondent's tenure (e.g., shift from two-tier inclining block to three-tier inclining block).

9. These percentages reflect poststratification weighting. The raw percentages are 60 percent hired from outside, 40 percent promoted from within.

10. Water scarcity (or abundance) is a consequence of the interactions between precipitation, soil absorption, evapotranspiration, and temperature. Failure to account for those interactions may explain why Mullin (2008) found a modest positive relationship between temperature and the inclined block rates, but no effect for precipitation.

11. An archive of the Willmott-Feddema Climatic Moisture Index (1992) is available from the Center for Climatic Research at the University of Delaware: http://climate.geog.udel.edu/~climate/.

12. LeRoux and Pandey's (2008) study of city managers finds a similar link between ambition and policy choices and finds little evidence that professional values or altruism drives policy entrepreneurship.

CHAPTER 5: The Psychology of Bureaucratic Entrepreneurship

Epigraphs. Interview with a police commissioner from a very large city, quoted on condition of anonymity, April 2005.

1. For foundational works on achievement motivation, see McClelland (1961) and Wainer and Rubin (1969). Winter (1996) and Stewart and Roth (2007) offer reviews of more recent related studies.

2. The more familiar intercoder Pearson correlations were .828 for *achievement*, .804 for *power*, and .844 for *affiliation*. In training for motive scoring, the other scorer and I both had demonstrated category agreement of .850 or above with calibration materials prescored by experts as specified in Winter (1994).

3. The effects of motivation in models that included governance institution variables were essentially the same as those without governance institutions. Further, models that included governance institutions offered very little improvement in fit or predictive value.

4. The OLS model results are remarkably robust. The effects of achievement and power motivation observed in table 5.4 were replicated in models specifying different collections of institutional and personal controls. The dependent variable of interest here is a discrete event count (number of different contacts initiated) and is naturally

limited to values between zero and thirteen. With its continuous linear form, the OLS model might theoretically yield nonsensical predictions (e.g., negative or fractional political contacts). However, substantively identical results were produced by similarly specified, bounded Tobit regression models and Poisson and negative binomial event-count models. I report the OLS model results because more readers are likely to be familiar with OLS than its more exotic cousins.

5. The coefficients, robust standard errors, and fit statistics generated by the logistic regression model that was used to generate figure 5.1 are reported in appendix B. All other continuous variables are evaluated at their means; dummy variables are evaluated at their modal values. All reported estimates are based on one thousand simulations drawn from a multivariate normal distribution using King, Tomz, and Wittenburg's "clarify" procedure in Stata 10.1. See Michael Tomz, Jason Wittenberg, and Gary King 2001, CLARIFY: Software for Interpreting and Presenting Statistical Results, Version 2.0, Cambridge, MA: Harvard University, June 1.

6. I also constructed a series of models that tested the interaction of the *power* and *achievement* motives, reasoning that the influence of the power motive on a police chief's political advocacy might be conditional on his or her achievement motive. In all these models, the interaction term generated coefficients and standard errors that were weaker, but consistent with those generated by the achievement and/or power motives directly. The *power* motive apparently is simply not a significant driver of political advocacy among chiefs of police, even when coupled with *achievement* motivation.

7. The coefficients, robust standard errors, and fit statistics generated by the negative binomial regression model that was used to generate figure 5.2 are reported in appendix B. All other continuous variables are evaluated at their means; dummies variables are evaluated at their modal values. All reported estimates are based on one thousand simulations drawn from a multivariate normal distribution using King, Tomz, and Wittenburg's "CLARIFY" procedure in Stata 10.1. Note that I used no poststratification weighting in this model because the sample's stratification based on agency size would attenuate the effects of agency size in the equation.

8. Alternative specifications using OLS and Tobit regressions generate similar results. I use a negative binomial event-count model to generate figure 5.2 because it generates more intuitively meaningful prediction estimates. Moreover, as a species of maximum-likelihood estimation, the negative binomial regression allows each variable's marginal effect vary according to the values of other variables in the model. This quality is useful in demonstrating the interactive effect seen in figure 5.2.

CHAPTER 6: Ramps and Ladders

Epigraph. BeDan (2005).

1. Harish Johari (1980) offers a monograph-length religious interpretation of Leela. Johari puts the origins of the game at around two thousand years ago and argues that the game offers its players not simply diversion and morality tales but also deeper spiritual understanding of existence. "Leela is a game of synchronicity," Johari

states. "And synchronicity simply means that all events in the phenomenal world are related—and can be understood in their proper relationship if only a proper link can be forged. The game is such a link" (14). Unfortunately, my analysis of bureaucratic career paths offers more limited enlightenment.

2. See the passage quoted from Wilson's *Bureaucracy* (1989) in the epigraph to chapter 1.

3. Tests of difference-in-mean education between the first and fourth quartiles show statistically significant differences for police chiefs ($t = 3.43$, $p < .01$) and water utility managers ($t = 4.12$, $p < .01$), with one-tailed tests of significance.

4. Tests of difference in standard deviation of education between the first and fourth quartiles are statistically significant for police chiefs ($t = 2.14$, $p = .05$) and water utility managers ($t = 1.90$, $p = .10$), with one-tailed tests of significance.

5. Recall that individuals are only counted as diagonal climbers if they were hired directly into their current agency head positions from outside the agency. Individuals who were originally hired from outside for lower-ranking positions and later promoted to agency head are coded as vertical climbers. See chapter 4 for a discussion of and rationale for this coding of career path.

6. Tests of difference in proportion of respondents who talked about decisional aspects of work (*policy, politics,* and *management*) between vertical and diagonal climbers is statistically significant ($p = .02$ with a two-tailed test of significance).

7. These are illustrative examples only. These cities are not necessarily included in the survey sample or any other portion of the study. Staff size and population data are from the U.S. Justice Department's Bureau of Justice Statistics 2000 Census of State and Local Law Enforcement Agencies (U.S. Dept. of Justice [2003]).

8. While it is most common for police officers in vertical advancement organizations to begin as patrol officers and remain in the same agency for their entire careers, mobility does sometimes occur in these organizations "at the bottom." Officers sometimes move laterally from one vertical agency to another at the patrol level. It is uncommon, however, for officers to move from a midlevel position in one agency with a tradition of vertical advancement to a similar job elsewhere once they begin to advance within an agency.

CHAPTER 7: What Bureacratic Ambition Means for Democracy

Epigraph. Wilder (2004), 98.

1. Robert C. White is the police chief with a diagonal career path and record of innovation mentioned in the opening pages of chapter 1.

2. Quotes excerpted from Gerth (2003).

3. For example, Meier and O'Toole (2002) show that a competitive labor market for school superintendents creates tangible individual incentives for managerial performance, with stronger performance leading to higher executive salaries.

4. See Hall, Stanton, and Schultheiss (2010) for an excellent review of biopsychological and neurological research on human motivation.

5. See Monroe et al. (2009) for an overview of recent trends in the study of political psychology.

6. I thank Jennifer Jensen for suggesting this idea.

7. Observers of British politics in the late twentieth and early twenty-first centuries may chuckle at Finer's (1936) praise for the political accountability of that country's bureaucracy. Decades of research on the relationships between bureaucrats and politicians under what has become known as the British "Whitehall model" have not been kind to Finer's claims. To cite just one example, Prime Minister Margaret Thatcher clashed famously and furiously with senior Whitehall bureaucrats who obstructed, delayed, weakened, and otherwise resisted Conservative Party initiatives in the 1980s (Cristoph 1992). During that era, the BBC aired a popular situation comedy titled *Yes, Minister,* which lampooned the frustrations of a fictional cabinet minister who struggled to govern effectively despite resistance of his staff of clever, recalcitrant Whitehall bureaucrats. Fittingly, *Yes, Minister* was a favorite of Thatcher's, and she even co-wrote and appeared on an episode of the program. Far from the model of strict political responsibility that Finer extolled, the very word *Whitehall* has come to symbolize a particular species of bureaucratic autonomy from politicians.

8. See table 1.1 and its accompanying discussion in chapter 1 for a brief summary of research on bureaucratic politics in the principal-agent and bureaucratic professionalism traditions.

9. The NBPTS Web site also notes that "Certification provides routes for NBCTs to advance as master teachers, school leaders and mentors," ts.org/become_a_candidate/the_benefits (accessed June 2010).

10. For a litany of twentieth-century federal bureaucratic reform efforts and an excellent theoretical discussion thereof, see March and Olson (1983).

11. See the case of Mt. Brantley School Superintendent Jude Alesky in chapter 2 for an example of the impact of NCLB on one administrator's management of his school district.

12. See Meier and O'Toole (2006) for an interesting discussion of the ways that principal-agent theory and NPM complement and contradict one another (141–45).

13. The will of a legislature and the will of the people are not one in the same, Norton Long (1952) reminds us; executives, courts, and bureaucracies also may make legitimate claims to represent the "will of the people." Bureaucrats are more numerous than elected officials in all but the smallest towns, and bureaucracies frequently are more economically, racially, and socially diverse than the elected officials that they serve and the elites in their communities (Jennings 1963). Several studies indicate that diverse bureaus respond to diverse populations, providing a kind of representation through administrative discretion (Krislov 1974; Meier and Stewart 1992; Meier and Bohte 2001). A burgeoning literature on "representative bureaucracy" continues to explore bureaucrats as political representatives.

14. Building on Holstrom's (1982) impossibility theorem, Gary Miller (2000) proves that moral hazard—including the principal's—is inevitable in any budget constrained organization. No system of bureaucratic political control that relies on

sanction or procedural constraint is adequate to overcome this moral hazard. Miller argues that the solution to this dilemma is to constrain the principal from involvement in administration and strengthen bureaucratic professionalism. Miller's study is notable because it advances a game-theoretical formal challenge to principal-agent theory, and because it arrives at the startling conclusion that elected officials are best served when bureaucrats disregard their political masters and instead act according to their professional norms. Reviewing the Friedrich-Finer debate, Miller puts himself squarely in Friedrich's camp.

APPENDIX A: Survey Methodology

1. Data from the CSLLEA were drawn from the National Archive of Criminal Justice Data, hosted by the Inter-university Consortium for Political and Social Research (ICPSR), Ann Arbor, Michigan. Data from the CSLLEA are posted online at http://webapp.icpsr.umich.edu/cocoon/NACJD-STUDY/03484.xml.

2. Designed as a regulatory database, the SDWIS included data on 159,796 water systems in 2004. The vast majority of these systems are very small, privately owned systems that serve only a handful of customers each. The 2004 SDWIS included data on 32,148 systems owned by local governments. In many cases, a single local government operates many water systems listed in the SDWIS database. Data from the SDWIS were drawn from the EPA's Office of Ground Water and Drinking Water, Washington, DC. The SDWIS data are posted at www.epa.gov/safewater/sdwisfed/sdwis.htm.

References

Abbott, Andrew. 1988. *The System of Professions*. Chicago: University of Chicago Press.

Aberbach, Joel D., Robert D. Putnam, and Bert A. Rockman. 1981. *Bureaucrats and Politicians in Western Democracies*. Cambridge, MA: Harvard University Press.

Alford, Robert. 1969. *Bureaucracy and Participation*. Chicago: Rand McNally.

Almy, Timothy. 1975. "Local-Cosmopolitanism and U.S. City Managers." *Urban Affairs Quarterly* 10 (3): 243–72.

Alpert, Geoffrey P., and John M. MacDonald. 2001. "Police Use of Force: An Analysis of Organizational Characteristics." *Justice Quarterly* 18 (2): 393–409.

Althoen, S. C., L. King, and K. Schilling. 1993. "How Long Is a Game of Snakes and Ladders?" *Mathematical Gazette* 77 (478): 71–76.

American Water Works Association (AWWA). 1972. *Manual M1: Principles of Water Rates, Fees, and Charges*. 2nd ed. Denver, CO: American Water Works Association.

———. 2000. *Manual M1: Principles of Water Rates, Fees, and Charges*. 5th ed. Denver, CO: American Water Works Association.

———. 2004. *Avoiding Rate Shock: Making the Case for Water Rates*. Denver, CO: American Water Works Association.

American Water Works Research Foundation (AwwaRF). 2005. *Succession Planning for a Vital Workforce in the Information Age*. Denver, CO: AwwaRF.

———. 2006. *A Strategic Assessment of the Future of Water Utilities*. Denver, CO: AwwaRF.

Ammons, David N., and James J. Glass. 1988. "Headhunters in Local Government: Use of Executive Search Firms in Managerial Selection." *Public Administration Review* 48 (3): 687–93.

Anderson, Lance, and Sandra Wilson. 1997. "The Critical Incident Technique." In *Applied Measurement Methods in Industrial Psychology*, ed. D. Whetzel and G. Wheaton, 89–112. Palo Alto, CA: Davies-Black Publishing.

Andersson, Bengt-Erik, and Stan-Goran Nilsson. 1964. "Studies in the Reliability and Validity of the Critical Incident Technique." *Journal of Applied Psychology* 48 (6): 398–403.

Andrews, John D. W. 1967. "The Achievement Motive and Advancement in Two Types of Organizations." *Journal of Personality and Social Psychology* 6 (2): 163–68.

Balla, Steven J. 2001. "Interstate Professional Associations and the Diffusion of Policy Innovations." *American Politics Research* 29 (3): 221–45.

Barber, James David. 1992. *Presidential Character: Predicting Performance in the White House*. Englewood Cliffs, NJ: Prentice Hall.

BeDan, Michael. 2005. "City Officials, Lawmakers, Citizens All Impressed by Three Chief Hopefuls." *Aurora Sentinel and Daily Sun*, September 14, sec. A.

Bendor, Jonathan, Serge Taylor, and Ronald Van Gaalen. 1987. "Stacking the Deck: Bureaucratic Missions and Policy Design." *American Political Science Review* 81 (3): 873–96.

Berry, Frances Stokes, and William D. Berry. 1990. "State Lottery Adoptions as Policy Innovations: An Event History Analysis." *American Political Science Review* 84 (2): 395–415.

Berry, William D. 1979. "Utility Regulation in the States: The Policy Effects of Professionalism and Salience to the Consumer." *American Journal of Political Science* 23 (2): 263–77.

Birkland, Thomas A. 1997. *After Disaster: Agenda Setting, Public Policy, and Focusing Events*. Washington, DC: Georgetown University Press.

Björk, Lars G., Thomas E. Glass, and C. Cryss Brunner. 2005. "Characteristics of American School Superintendents." In *The Contemporary Superintendent*, ed. Lars G. Björk and Theodore J. Kkowalski, 19–44. Thousand Oaks, CA: Corwin Press.

Bohte, John, and Kenneth J. Meier. 2001. "Structure and the Performance of Public Organizations: Task Difficulty and Span of Control." *Public Organization Review* 1 (3): 341–54.

Borghans, Lex, Angela Lee Duckworth, James J. Heckman, and Bas der Weel. 2008. "The Economics and Psychology of Personality Traits." *Journal of Human Resources* 43 (4): 972–1059.

Borman, Walter, and Marvin Dunnette. 1975. "Behavior-Based versus Trait-Oriented Performance Ratings: An Empirical Study." *Journal of Applied Psychology* 60 (5): 561–65.

Bowling, Cynthia J., and Deil S. Wright. 1998. "Change and Continuity in State Administration: Administrative Leadership across Four Decades." *Public Administration Review* 58 (5): 429–44.

Boyatzis, Richard E. 1998. *Transforming Qualitative Information: Thematic Analysis and Code Development*. Thousand Oaks, CA: Sage.

———. 2006. "Core Competencies in Coaching Others to Overcome Dysfunctional Behavior." In *Linking Emotional Intelligence and Performance at Work*, ed. Vanessa Druskat, Gerald Mount, and Fabio Sala, 81–96. Mahwah, NJ: Lawrence Erlbaum Associates.

Brehm, John, and Scott Gates. 1997. *Working, Shirking, and Sabotage: Bureaucratic Response to a Democratic Public*. Ann Arbor: University of Michigan Press.

———. 2008. *Teaching, Tasks, and Trust*. New York: Russell Sage.

Brint, Steven. 1994. *In an Age of Experts*. Princeton, NJ: Princeton University Press.

Browning, Rufus P., and Herbert Jacob. 1964. "Power Motivation and the Political Personality." *Public Opinion Quarterly* 28 (1): 75–90.

Brunner, G. Allen, and Stephen J. Carroll Jr. 1969. "Weekday Evening Interviews of Employed Persons Are Better." *Public Opinion Quarterly* 33 (2): 265–67.

Burlingame, David, and Agnes L. Baro. 2005. "Women's Representation in Law En-forcement: Does CALEA Involvement Matter?" *Criminal Justice Policy Review* 16 (4): 391–411.

Burns, Nancy. 1994. *The Formation of American Local Governments: Private Values in Public Institutions.* New York: Oxford University Press.

———. 2002. "Gender: Public Opinion and Political Action." In *Political Science: State of the Discipline,* ed. Ira Katznelson and Helen V. Milner, 462–87. New York: W. W. Norton.

Campbell, Colin, S.J., and Donald Naulls. 1991. "The Limits of the Budget-Maximizing Theory: Some Evidence from Officials' Views of Their Roles and Careers." In *The Budget-Maximizing Bureaucrat: Appraisals and Evidence,* ed. Andre Blais and Stephanie Dion, 85–118. Pittsburgh, PA: University of Pittsburgh Press.

Carlson, Richard O. 1961. "Succession and Performance among School Superintendents." *Administrative Science Quarterly* 6 (2): 210–27.

Carpenter, Daniel. 2001. *The Forging of Bureaucratic Autonomy.* Princeton, NJ: Princeton University Press.

———. 2006. "Reputation and the Regulator." Paper presented at the University of Bath Center for Regulated Industries Conference on Frontiers of Regulation— "Assessing Scholarly Debates and Policy Challenges," Bath, U.K.

Carr-Saunders, Alexander M. 1936. *The Professions.* Oxford: Clarendon Press.

Carter, David L., and Allen D. Sapp. 1994. "Issues and Perspectives of Law Enforcement Accreditation: A National Study of Police Chiefs." *Journal of Criminal Justice* 22 (3): 195–204.

Chesnutt, Thomas W., and David M. Pekelney. 2002. "A Primer on Individualized Water Rates: Designing and Implementing Water Budget-Based Rates." Presented at the Water Sources Conference of the American Water Works Association, Las Vegas, NV.

Christoph, James B. 1992. "The Remaking of British Administrative Culture." *Administration and Society* 24 (2): 163–81.

Chu, David S. C., and John P. White. 2001. "Ensuring Quality People in Defense." In *Keeping the Edge: Managing Defense for the Future,* ed. Ashton B. Carter and John P. White, 203–34. Cambridge, MA: MIT Press.

Clingermayer, James C., and Richard C. Feiock. 1997. "Leadership Turnover, Transaction Costs, and External City Service Delivery." *Public Administration Review* 57 (3): 231–39.

Collinge, Robert A. 1996. "Conservation Feebates." *Journal AWWA* 88 (1): 70–78.

Collins, Christopher J., Paul J. Hanges, and Edwin A. Locke. 2004. "The Relationship of Achievement Motivation to Entrepreneurial Behavior: A Meta-analysis." *Human Performance* 17 (1): 95–117.

Commission on Accreditation for Law Enforcement Agencies (CALEA). 2006a. "About CALEA," www.calea.org/newweb/AboutUs/Aboutus.htm.

———. 2006b. *Standards for Law Enforcement Agencies,* 5th ed. Fairfax, VA: CALEA.

Corssmit, C. W. 2005. *Water Rates, Fees, and the Legal Environment*. Denver, CO: American Water Works Association.

Crewson, Philip E. 1997. "Public Service Motivation: Building Empirical Evidence of Incidence and Effect." *Journal of Public Administration Research and Theory* 7 (4): 499–518.

Dahl, Robert A. 1961. *Who Governs?* New Haven, CT: Yale University Press.

Datta, Lois-ellin. 1990. *Case Study Evaluations*. Washington, DC: U.S. General Accounting Office.

Dewatripont, Mathaias, Ian Jewitt, and Jean Tirole. 1999a. "The Economics of Career Concerns, Part I: Comparing Information Structures." *Review of Economic Studies* 66 (1): 183–198.

———. 1999b. "The Economics of Career Concerns, Part II: Applications to Missions and Accountability of Government Agencies." *Review of Economic Studies* 66 (1): 199–217.

DiMaggio, Paul J., and Walter W. Powell. 1983. "The Iron Cage Revisited: Institutional Isomorphism and Collective Rationality in Organizational Fields." *American Sociological Review* 48 (2): 147–60.

Dinar, Ariel. 2000. *The Political Economy of Water Pricing Reforms*. Washington, DC: Oxford University Press.

Downs, Anthony. 1957. *An Economic Theory of Democracy*. New York: Harper.

———. 1967. *Inside Bureaucracy*. Boston: Little, Brown.

Dunn, Delmer, and Jerome Legge Jr. 2000. "U.S. Local Government Managers and the Complexity of Responsibility and Accountability in Democratic Governance." *Journal of Public Administration and Theory* 11 (1): 73–88.

Dziegielewski, Benedykt, and Eve Opitz. 2004. "Water Demand Analysis." In *Urban Water Supply Management Tools*, ed. Larry W. Mays, 1.1–1.37. New York: McGraw-Hill.

Eulau, Heinz, and Kenneth Prewitt. 1973. *Labyrinths of Democracy*. New York: Bobbs-Merrill.

Fernández-Aráoz, Claudio, Boris Groysberg, and Nitin Nohria. 2009. "The Definitive Guide to Recruiting in Good Times and Bad." *Harvard Business Review* 87 (5): 74–84.

Finer, Herman. 1936. "Better Government Personnel." *Political Science Quarterly* 51 (4): 569–99.

———. 1941. "Administrative Responsibility in Democratic Government." *Public Administration Review* 1 (4): 355–50.

Flanagan, John C. 1949. "Critical Requirements: A New Approach to Employee Evaluation." *Personnel Psychology* 2: 419–25.

Fountain, Jane. 1999. "A Note on the Critical Incident Technique and Its Utility as a Tool of Public Management Research." Paper presented at the annual meeting of the Association of Public Policy and Management (APPAM), Washington, DC.

Fox, Richard J., Melvin R. Crask, and Jonghoon Kim. 1988. "Mail Survey Response Rate: A Meta-analysis of Selected Techniques for Inducing Response." *Public Opinion Quarterly* 52 (4): 467–91.

Frank, John. 2008. "Chief Seeks Agency Critique." *St. Petersburg Times*, January 8, 2008.

Friedrich, Carl J. 1935. *Problems of the American Public Service*. New York: McGraw-Hill.

———. 1940. "Public Policy and the Nature of Administrative Responsibility." In *Public Policy*, ed. Carl J. Friedrich and E. S. Mason, 3–24. Cambridge, MA: Harvard University Press.

Frigo, Mark. 2006. "Knowledge Retention: A Guide for Utilities." *Journal AWWA* 98 (9): 81–84.

Gailmard, Sean, and John Patty. 2007. "Slackers and Zealots: Civil Service, Policy Discretion and Bureaucratic Expertise." *American Journal of Political Science* 51 (4): 873–89.

Gaur, Sanjay. 2007. "Policy Objectives in Designing Water Rates." *Journal AWWA* 99 (5): 112–16.

Gaus, John M. 1936. "The Responsibility of Public Administration." In *The Frontiers of Public Administration*, ed. John M. Gaus, Leonard D. White, and Marshall E. Dimock, 26–44. Chicago: University of Chicago Press.

Gerth, Jose. 2003. "Chief Robert White: New Leader Set to Take Reins." *Louisville Courier-Journal*, January 5, A01.

Giblin, Matthew J. 2006. "Structural Elaboration and Institutional Isomorphism: The Case of Crime Analysis Units." *Policing: An International Journal of Police Strategies and Management* 29 (4): 643–64.

Gowing, Marylin K. 2001. "Measurement of Individual Emotional Competence." In *The Emotionally Intelligent Workplace*, ed. Gary Cherniss and Daniel Goleman, 83–131. San Francisco, CA: Jossey-Bass.

Green, Roy E. 1989. *The Profession of Local Government Management: Management Expertise and the American Community*. New York: Praeger.

Greiner, Larry, Thomas Cummings, and Arvind Bhambri. 2003. "When New CEOs Succeed and Fail: 4-D Theory of Strategic Transformation." *Organizational Dynamics* 32 (1): 1–16.

Groves, Robert M., F. J. Fowler, Mick P. Couper, James M. Lepkowski, Eleanor Singer, and R. Tourangeau. 2004. *Survey Methodology*. New York: Wiley.

Grupp, Fred W., Jr. 1975. "Correlates of the Power Motive within the State Bureaucracy." Paper presented at Yale University, Conference on Psychology and Politics, New Haven, CT.

Hall, Julie L., Steven J. Stanton, and Oliver C. Schultheiss. 2010. "Biopsychological and Neural Processes of Implicit Motivation." In *Implicit Motives*, ed. Oliver Schultheiss and Joachim Brunstein, 279–307. New York: Oxford University Press.

Hasson, David S. 2002. "Water Utility Options for Low-Income Assistance Programs." *Journal AWWA* 94 (4): 128–38.

Hewitt, Julie A. 2000. "An Investigation into the Reasons Why Water Utilities Choose Particular Residential Rate Structures." In *The Political Economy of Water Pricing Reforms*, ed. Ariel Dinar, 259–277. New York: Oxford University Press.

Hirschman, Albert O. 1970. *Exit, Voice, and Loyalty*. Cambridge, MA: Harvard University Press.

Hoffbuhr, Jack. 2000. "Who Are You Going to Hire?" *Journal AWWA* 92 (12): 6.

Hogan, James B. 1976. *The Chief Administrative Officer: An Alternative to Council-Manager Government*. Tuscon: University of Arizona Press.

Holmstrom, Bengt. 1982. "Moral Hazard in Teams." *Bell Journal of Economics* 13 (2): 324–40.

Hood, Christopher. 1991. "A Public Management for All Seasons?" *Public Administration* 69 (1): 3–19.

Hougland, Steven M. 2004. *Exploring the Perceptions of Florida Police Executives: Understanding Accreditation*. Doctoral dissertation, University of Central Florida.

Houston, David J. 2000. "Public Service Motivation: A Multivariate Test." *Journal of Public Administration Research and Theory* 10 (4): 713–27.

Huber, John, and Charles Shipan. 2003. *Deliberate Discretion? Institutional Foundations of Bureaucratic Autonomy*. New York: Cambridge University Press.

Hughes, Adam. 2010. "Police Accreditation and Functional Preferences." Senior thesis, Colgate University.

Jennings, M. Kent. 1963. "Public Administrators and Community Decision Making." *Administrative Science Quarterly* 8 (1): 18–43.

Johari, Harish. 1980. *Leela: The Game of Self-Knowledge*. London: Routledge & Kegan Paul.

Jones-Correa, Michael. 2004. "Racial and Ethnic Diversity and the Politics of Education in Suburbia." Paper presented at the annual meeting of the American Political Science Association, Chicago.

Kaarbøe, Oddvar M., and Trond E. Olsen. 2003. "Career Concerns, Monetary Incentives, and Job Design." *Scandinavian Journal of Economics* 108 (2): 299–316.

Kaufman, Herbert. 2006 (1960). *The Forest Ranger: A Study in Administrative Behavior*. Washington, DC: Resources for the Future.

Kettl, Donald F. 2002. *The Transformation of Governance*. Baltimore: Johns Hopkins University Press.

———. 2009. "The 2008 John Gaus Lecture: Administrative Accountability and the Rule of Law." *PS: Political Science and Politics* 42 (1): 11–17.

King, Gary, Michael Tomz, and Jason Wittenburg. 2000. "Making the Most of Statistical Analyses: Improving Interpretation and Presentation." *American Journal of Political Science* 44 (2): 347–61.

Kingdon, John. 1984. *Agendas, Alternatives, and Public Policies*. Boston: Little, Brown.

Koontz, Tomas M. 2007. "Federal and State Public Forest Administration in the New Millennium: Revisiting Herbert Kaufman's *The Forest Ranger*." *Public Administration Review* 67 (1): 152–64.

Krislov, Samuel. 1974. *Representative Bureaucracy*. Englewood Cliffs, NJ: Prentice Hall.

Lagan-Fox, Janice, and Susanna Roth. 1995. "Achievement Motivation and Female Entrepreneurs." *Journal of Occupational and Organizational Psychology* 68 (3): 209–18.

Larson, Magali S. 1977. *The Rise of Professionalism*. Berkeley: University of California Press.

Lasswell, Harold. 1934. *Psychopathology and Politics*. Chicago: University of Chicago Press.

LeRoux, Kelly, and Sanjay K. Pandey. 2008. "City Managers, Career Incentives, and Service Delivery Decisions: The Effects of Managerial Ambition on Interlocal Cooperation Choices." Paper presented at the annual meeting of the American Political Science Association, Boston, MA.

Lin, Ann Chih. 2000. *Reform in the Making: The Implementation of Social Policy in Prison*. Princeton, NJ: Princeton University Press.

Lipsky, Michael. 1980. *Street-Level Bureaucracy: Dilemmas of the Individual in Public Service*. New York: Russell Sage Foundation.

Long, Norton. 1952. "Bureaucracy and Constitutionalism." *American Political Science Review* 46 (3): 808–18.

Loveridge, Ronald. 1971. *City Managers in Legislative Politics*. New York: Bobbs-Merrill.

Lubell, Mark, and Alan Fulton. 2008. "Local Policy Networks and Watershed Management." *Journal of Public Administration Research and Theory* 18 (4): 673–96.

Maestas, Cherie D., Sarah Fulton, L. Sandy Maisel, and Walter J. Stone. 2006. "When to Risk It? Institutions, Ambitions, and the Decision to Run for the U.S. House." *American Political Science Review* 100 (2): 195–208.

Manna, Paul. 2006. *School's In: Federalism and the National Education Agenda*. Washington, DC: Georgetown University Press.

March, James C., and James G. March. 1977. "Almost Random Careers: The Wisconsin School Superintendency, 1940–1972." *Administrative Science Quarterly* 22 (3): 377–409.

March, James G., and Johan P. Olson. 1983. "Organizing Political Life: What Administrative Reorganization Tells Us about Government." *American Political Science Review* 77 (2): 281–96.

Mastrofski, Stephen D. 1986. "Police Agency Accreditation: The Prospects of Reform." *American Journal of Police* 5 (2): 45–81.

Mayhew, David. 1974. *Congress: The Electoral Connection*. New Haven, CT: Yale University Press.

McCabe, Barbara Coyle, Richard C. Feiock, James C. Clingermayer, and Christopher Stream. 2008. "Turnover among City Managers: The Role of Political and Economic Change." *Public Administration Review* 68 (2): 380–86.

McCabe, Kimberly A., and Robin G. Fajardo. 2001. "Law Enforcement Accreditation: A National Comparison of Accredited vs. Nonaccredited Agencies." *Journal of Criminal Justice* 29 (2): 127–31.

McCain, Katie. 2005. "Opening General Session Address." Delivered at the American Water Works Association Annual Conference and Exposition, San Francisco, CA (June).

McClelland, David C. 1961. *The Achieving Society*. New York: Free Press.

———. 1975. *Power: The Inner Experience*. New York: Irvington.

———. 1998. "Identifying Competencies with Behavioral-Event Interviews." *Psychological Science* 9 (5): 331–39.

McClelland, David C., and Richard Boyatzis. 1982. "The Leadership Motive Pattern and Long-Term Success in Management." *Journal of Applied Psychology* 67 (9): 737–43.

McClelland, David C., Richard Koestner, and Joel Weinberger. 1989. "How Do Self-Attributed and Implicit Motives Differ?" *Psychological Review* 96 (4): 690–702.

McCubbins, Mathew, and Thomas Schwartz. 1984. "Police Patrols vs. Fire Alarms." *American Journal of Political Science* 28 (1): 165–79.

Meier, Kenneth J., and John Bohte. 2001. "Structure and Discretion: Missing Links in Representative Bureaucracy." *Journal of Public Administration and Research and Theory* 11 (4): 455–70.

Meier, Kenneth J., and Laurence J. O'Toole Jr. 2002. "Public Management and Organizational Performance: The Effect of Managerial Quality." *Journal of Policy Analysis and Management* 21 (4): 629–43.

———. 2006. *Bureaucracy in a Democratic State: A Governance Perspective.* Baltimore: Johns Hopkins University Press.

Meier, Kenneth J., and Joseph Stewart Jr. 1992. "The Impact of Representative Bureaucracies: Educational Systems and Public Policies." *American Review of Public Administration* 22 (3): 157–71.

Michelson, Ari M. J., Thomas McGuckin, and Donna M. Stumpf. 1998. *Effectiveness of Residential Water Conservation Price and Nonprice Programs.* Denver, CO: AWWA Research Foundation.

Mill, John Stuart. [1848] 1909. *Principles of Political Economy.* Reprint. London: Longman, Greens.

Miller, Gary J. 2000. "Above Politics: Credible Commitment and Efficiency in the Design of Public Agencies." *Journal of Public Administration Research and Theory* 10 (2): 289–327.

———. 2005. "The Political Evolution of Principal-Agent Models." *Annual Review of Political Science* 8 (1): 203–25.

Miner, Dan. 2010. "Utica's Next Police Chief: Mark Williams." *Utica Observer-Dispatch,* February 2, 1A.

Mintrom, Michael. 2000. *Policy Entrepreneurs and School Choice.* Washington, DC: Georgetown University Press.

Mintrom, Michael, and Phillipa Norman. 2009. "Policy Entrepreneurship and Policy Change." *Policy Studies Journal* 37 (4): 649–67.

Mintrom, Michael, and Sandra Vergari. 1998. "Policy Networks and Innovation Diffusion: The Case of State Education Reform." *Journal of Politics* 60 (1): 126–48.

Moe, Terry M. 1982. "Regulatory Performance and Presidential Administration." *American Journal of Political Science* 26 (1): 197–224.

———. 1984. "The New Economics of Organization." *American Journal of Political Science* 28 (4): 739–77.

Monroe, Kristen Renwick, William Chiu, Adam Martin, and Bridgette Portman. 2009. "What Is Political Psychology?" *Perspectives on Politics* 7 (4): 859–82.

Mosher, Frederick. 1968. *Democracy and the Public Service.* New York: Oxford University Press.

Moynihan, Donald P., and Sanjay K. Pandey. 2007. "The Role of Organizations in Fostering Public Service Motivation." *Public Administration Review* 67 (1): 40–53.

Mullin, Megan. 2008. "The Conditional Effect of Specialized Governance on Public Policy." *American Journal of Political Science* 52 (1): 125–41.

Nalbandian, John. 1991. *Professionalism in Local Government*. San Francisco, CA: Jossey-Bass.

National Association of Realtors (NAR). 2005. "Code of Ethics and Standards of Practice of the National Association of Realtors." Form no. 166–288. Chicago: National Association of Realtors.

Niskanen, William. 1971. *Bureaucracy and Representative Government*. Chicago: Aldine-Atherton.

North, Douglass C. 1990. *Institutions, Institutional Change, and Economic Performance*. New York: Cambridge University Press.

O'Leary, Rosemary. 2005. *The Ethics of Dissent: Managing Guerrilla Government*. Washington, DC: CQ Press.

Olson, Mancur. 1965. *The Logic of Collective Action*. Cambridge, MA: Harvard University Press.

Perry, James L. 1997. "Antecedents of Public Service Motivation." *Journal of Public Administration Research and Theory* 7 (2): 181–97.

Perry, James L., and Lois Recascino Wise. 1990. "The Motivational Basis of Public Service." *Public Administration Review* 50 (2): 367–73.

Polanyi, Karl. 1957. *The Great Transformation*. Boston: Beacon Press.

Posner, Paul L. 1998. *The Politics of Unfunded Mandates: Whither Federalism?* Washington, DC: Georgetown University Press.

Postel, Sandra. 1999. *Pillar of Sand*. New York: W. W. Norton.

Prendergast, Canice. 2007. "The Motivation and Bias of Bureaucrats." *American Economic Review* 97 (1): 180–96.

Quinn, Robert E. 1996. *Deep Change: Discovering the Leader Within*. San Francisco, CA: Jossey-Bass.

Rabe, Barry G. 2004. *Statehouse and Greenhouse*. Washington, DC: Brookings Institution Press.

Roberts, Patrick. 2005. "The Master of Disaster as Bureaucratic Entrepreneur." *PS, Political Science and Politics* 38 (2): 331.

Rosenthal, Donald B., and Robert L. Crain. 1968. "Structure and Values in Local Political Systems: The Case of Fluoridation Decisions." In *City Politics and Public Policy*, ed. James Q. Wilson, 217–42. New York: John Wiley & Sons.

Rozas, Angela, and Mickey Ciokajlo. 2007. "Louisville Chief May Be in Race for City Top Cop." *Chicago Tribune*, November 14, Metro 3.

Sagie, Abraham, and Dov Elizur. 1999. "Achievement Motive and Entrepreneurial Orientation: A Structural Analysis." *Journal of Organizational Behavior* 20 (3): 357–87.

Salvato, Albert. 2005. "In Louisville, a Measured Police Response." *New York Times*, September 27, A12.

Schall, Ellen. 1997a. "Public Sector Succession: A Strategic Approach to Sustaining Innovation." *Public Administration Review* 57 (1): 4–10.

———. 1997b. "Notes from a Reflective Practitioner of Innovation." In *Innovation in American Government: Challenges, Opportunities, and Dilemmas*, ed. Alan A. Altshuler and Robert D. Behn, 360–77. Washington, DC: Brookings Institution Press.

Schlesinger, Joseph. 1966. *Ambition and Politics: Political Careers in the United States*. Chicago: Rand McNally.

Schneider, Mark, Paul Teske, and Michael Mintrom. 1995. *Public Entrepreneurs*. Princeton, NJ: Princeton University Press.

Scholz, John T., Ramiro Berardo, and Brad Kile. 2008. "Do Networks Solve Collective Action Problems? Credibility, Search, and Collaboration." *Journal of Politics* 70 (2): 393–406.

Schultheiss, Oliver C., Kenneth L. Campbell, and David C. McClelland. 1999. "Implicit Power Motivation Moderates Men's Testosterone Responses to Imagined and Real Dominance Success." *Hormones and Behavior* 36: 234–41.

Schultheiss, Oliver C., Michelle M. Wirth, and Steven J. Stanton. 2004. "Effects of Affiliation and Power Motivation Arousal on Salivary Progesterone and Testosterone." *Hormones and Behavior* 46: 592–99.

Schumpeter, Joseph A. 1989. *Essays on Entrepreneurs, Business Cycles, and the Evolution of Capitalism*. Piscataway, NJ: Transaction.

Sepkowitz, Kent. 2009. "Paging Dr. Feelgood: The Joys and Perils of Giving Celebrities What They Want." *Slate*, July 7, www.slate.com/id/2222395/.

Sheehan, Kim B., and Sally J. McMillan. 1999. "Response Variation in E-Mail Surveys: An Exploration." *Journal of Advertising Research* 39 (4): 45–54.

Simon, Herbert A. 1985. "Human Nature in Politics: The Dialogue of Psychology with Political Science." *American Political Science Review* 79 (2): 293–304.

———. 1997. *Administrative Behavior*. 4th ed. New York: Simon & Schuster.

Snider, Don M. 2003. "Jointness, Defense Transformation, and the Need for a New Joint Warfare Profession." *Parameters* 33 (3): 17–30.

Spencer, Lyle M. 2001. "The Economic Value of Emotional Intelligence Competencies and EIC-based HR Programs." In *The Emotionally Intelligent Workplace*, ed. Gary Cherniss and Daniel Goleman, 45–82. San Francisco, CA: Jossey-Bass.

Spencer, Lyle M., and Signe M. Spencer. 1993. *Competence at Work: Models for Superior Performance*. New York: Wiley & Sons.

Staats, Elmer B. 1988. "Public Service and the Public Interest." *Public Administration Review* 48 (4): 601–5.

Staufenberger, Richard A. 1977. "The Professionalization of Police: Efforts and Obstacles." *Public Administration Review* 37 (6): 678–85.

Stewart, Wayne H., and Philip L. Roth. 2007. "A Meta-analysis of Achievement Motivation Differences between Entrepreneurs and Managers." *Journal of Small Business Management* 45 (4): 401–21.

Sykes, Gary W. 1994. "Accreditation and Community Policing: Passing Fads or Basic Reforms?" *Journal of Contemporary Criminal Justice* 10 (1): 1–16.

Teodoro, Manuel P. 2005. "Measuring Fairness: Assessing the Equity of Municipal Water Rates." *Journal AWWA* 97 (4): 111–24.

Thacker, Stephen B., Denise Koo, and Judy Delany. 2008. "Career Paths to Public Health: Programs at the Centers for Disease Control and Prevention." *American Journal of Preventive Medicine* 35 (3): 279–83.

Tilson, Hugh H., and Kristine M. Gebbie. 2001. "Public Health Physicians: An Endangered Species." *American Journal of Preventive Medicine* 21 (3): 233–40.

Timmins, Christopher. 2002. "Does the Median Voter Consume Too Much Water? Analyzing the Redistributive Role of Residential Water Bills." *National Tax Journal* 55 (4): 687–702.

Tipple, Terence J., and J. Douglas Wellman. 1991. "Herbert Kaufman's Forest Ranger Thirty Years Later: From Simplicity and Homogeneity to Complexity and Diversity." *Public Administration Review* 51 (5): 421–28.

Tiwari, Banarasi D., Madan M. Godbole, Naibedya Chattopadhyay, Anita Mandal, and Ambrish Mithal. 1996. "Learning Disabilities and Poor Motivation to Achieve Due to Prolonged Iodine Deficiency." *American Journal of Clinical Nutrition* 63 (5): 782–86.

Traugott, Michael W., Robert M. Groves, and James M. Lepkowski. 1987. "Using Dual Frame Designs to Reduce Nonresponse in Telephone Surveys." *Public Opinion Quarterly* 51 (4): 522–39.

U.S. Census Bureau. 2002. *2002 Census of Governments*, vol. 1, no. 1: *Government Organization*. Washington, DC: Government Printing Office.

U.S. Department of Justice, Bureau of Justice Statistics. 2003. *Census of State and Local Law Enforcement Agencies (CSLLEA)*. 3rd ICPSR ed. Ann Arbor, MI: Inter-University Consortium for Political and Social Research.

Van Riper, Paul P. 1983. "The American Administrative State: Wilson and the Founders—An Unorthodox View." *Public Administration Review* 43 (6): 477–90.

Wainer, Herbert A., and Irwin M. Rubin. 1969. "Motivation of Research and Development Entrepreneurs: Determinants of Company Success." *Journal of Applied Psychology* 53 (3): 178–84.

Walker, Jack. 1969. "The Diffusion of Innovations among the American States." *American Political Science Review* 63 (3): 880–99.

Waste, Robert. 1989. *The Ecology of City Policymaking*. New York: Oxford University Press.

Weber, Max. 1978. "Bureaucracy." In *Economy and Society*, ed. Guenther Roth and Claus Wittich, 956–1005. Berkeley: University of California Press.

Weingast, Barry R. 2002. "Rational-Choice Institutionalism." In *Political Science: State of the Discipine*, ed. Ira Katznelson and Helen V. Milner, 660–692. New York: W. W. Norton.

Wilder, Laura Ingalls. 2004. *These Happy Golden Years*. New York: HarperCollins.

Wilensky, Harold. 1964. "The Professionalization of Everyone?" *American Journal of Sociology* 70 (2): 137–58.

Willmott, Cort J., and Johannes J. Feddema. 1992. "A More Rational Climatic Moisture Index." *Professional Geographer* 44 (1): 84–87.

Wilson, James Q. 1968. "Dilemmas of Police Administration." *Public Administration Review* 28 (5): 407–17.

———. 1989. *Bureaucracy: What Government Agencies Do and Why They Do It.* New York: Basic Books.

Wilson, Timothy. 2002. *Strangers to Ourselves: Discovering the Adaptive Unconscious.* Cambridge, MA: Belknap Press.

Wilson, Woodrow. 1887. "The Study of Administration." *Political Science Quarterly* 2 (2): 197–220.

Winter, David G. 1973. *The Power Motive.* New York: Free Press.

———. 1978. "Navy Leadership and Management Competencies: Convergence among Interviews, Test Scores, and Supervisors' Ratings." Unpublished paper, Wesleyan University and McBer.

———. 1980. "Measuring the Motives of Southern Africa Political Leaders at a Distance." *Political Psychology* 2 (2): 75–85.

———. 1987. "Leader Appeal, Leader Performance, and the Motive Profiles of Leaders and Followers: A Study of American Presidents and Elections." *Journal of Personality and Social Psychology* 52 (1): 196–202.

———. 1991. "Measuring Personality at a Distance: Development of an Integrated System for Scoring Motives in Running Text." In *Perspectives in Personality*, ed. A. J. Stewart, J. M. Healy Jr., and D. Ozer, 59–89. London: Jessica Kingsley Publishers.

———. 1994. *Manual for Scoring Motive Imagery in Running Text*, Version 4.2. University of Michigan Department of Psychology.

———. 1996. *Personality: Analysis and Interpretation of Lives.* Boston, MA: McGraw-Hill.

———. 2002a. "The Motivational Dimensions of Leadership: Power, Achievement, and Affiliation." In *Multiple Intelligences and Leadership*, ed. R. E. Riggio, S. E. Murphy, and F. J. Pirozzolo, 119–38. Mahwah, NJ: Erlbaum.

———. 2002b. "Motivation and Political Leadership." In *Political Leadership for the New Century: Personality and Behavior among American Leaders*, ed. L. O. Valenty and O. Feldman, 27–47. New York: Praeger.

———. 2003. "Measuring the Motives of Political Actors at a Distance." In *The Psychological Assessment of Political Leaders*, ed. J. W. Post, ed., 153–77. Ann Arbor: University of Michigan Press.

Wirt, Frederick. 1985. "The Dependent City? External Influences upon Local Control." *Journal of Politics* 47 (1): 83–112.

Wood, B. Dan, and Richard W. Waterman. 1991. "The Dynamics of Political Control of the Bureaucracy." *American Political Science Review* 85 (3): 801–28.

Wright, Bradley E. 2001. "Public Sector Work Motivation: A Review of the Current

Literature and a Revised Conceptual Model." *Journal of Public Administration Research and Theory* 11 (4): 559–86.

Young, Robert A. 1991. "Budget Size and Bureaucratic Careers." In *The Budget-Maximizing Bureaucrat: Appraisals and Evidence*, ed. Andre Blais and Stephanie Dion, ed., 33–58. Pittsburgh, PA: University of Pittsburgh Press.

Index

Page numbers in *italics* indicate tables.